GHOSTED

CREATED BY
JOSHUA WILLIAMSON

GHOSTED

JOSHUA WILLIAMSON
WRITER

DAVIDE GIANFELICE
ARTIST

MIROSLAV MRVA
COLORIST

RUS WOOTON
LETTERER

SEAN MACKIEWICZ
EDITOR

COVERS BY
MATTEO SCALERA

IMAGE COMICS, INC.
Robert Kirkman – Chief Operating Officer
Erik Larsen – Chief Financial Officer
Todd McFarlane – President
Marc Silvestri – Chief Executive Officer
Jim Valentino – Vice-President

Eric Stephenson – Publisher
Ron Richards – Director of Business Development
Jennifer de Guzman – Director of Trade Book Sales
Kat Salazar – Director of PR & Marketing
Jeremy Sullivan – Director of Digital Sales
Emilio Bautista – Sales Assistant
Branwyn Bigglestone – Senior Accounts Manager
Emily Miller – Accounts Manager
Jessica Ambriz – Administrative Assistant
Tyler Shainline – Events Coordinator
David Brothers – Content Manager
Jonathan Chan – Production Manager
Drew Gill – Art Director
Meredith Wallace – Print Manager
Monica Garcia – Senior Production Artist
Jenna Savage – Production Artist
Addison Duke – Production Artist
Tricia Ramos – Production Assistant
IMAGECOMICS.COM

For SKYBOUND ENTERTAINMENT

Robert Kirkman - CEO
Sean Mackiewicz - Editorial Director
Shawn Kirkham - Director of Business Development
Brian Huntington - Online Editorial Director
June Alian - Publicity Director
Helen Leigh - Assistant Editor
Rachel Skidmore - Office Manager
Lizzy Iverson - Administrative Assistant
Dan Petersen - Operations Manager
Nick Palmer - Operations Coordinator

International inquiries: foreign@skybound.com
Licensing inquiries: contact@skybound.com

WWW.SKYBOUND.COM

GHOSTED VOL. 2: BOOKS OF THE DEAD TP. ISBN: 978-1-63215-046-2. First Printing. Published by Image Comics, Inc. Office of publication: 2001 Center Street, 6th Floor, Berkeley, CA 94704.

CHAPTER ONE

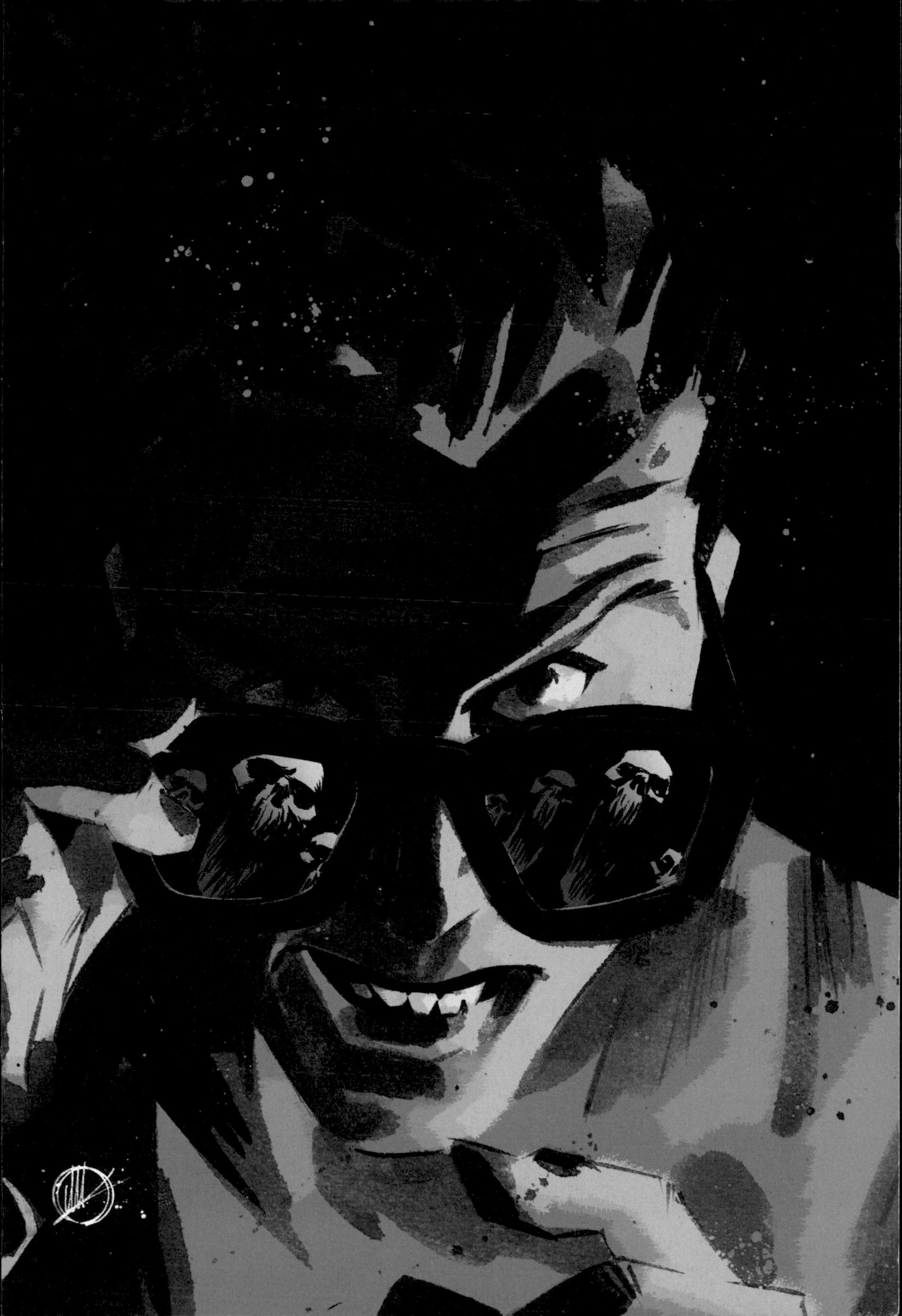

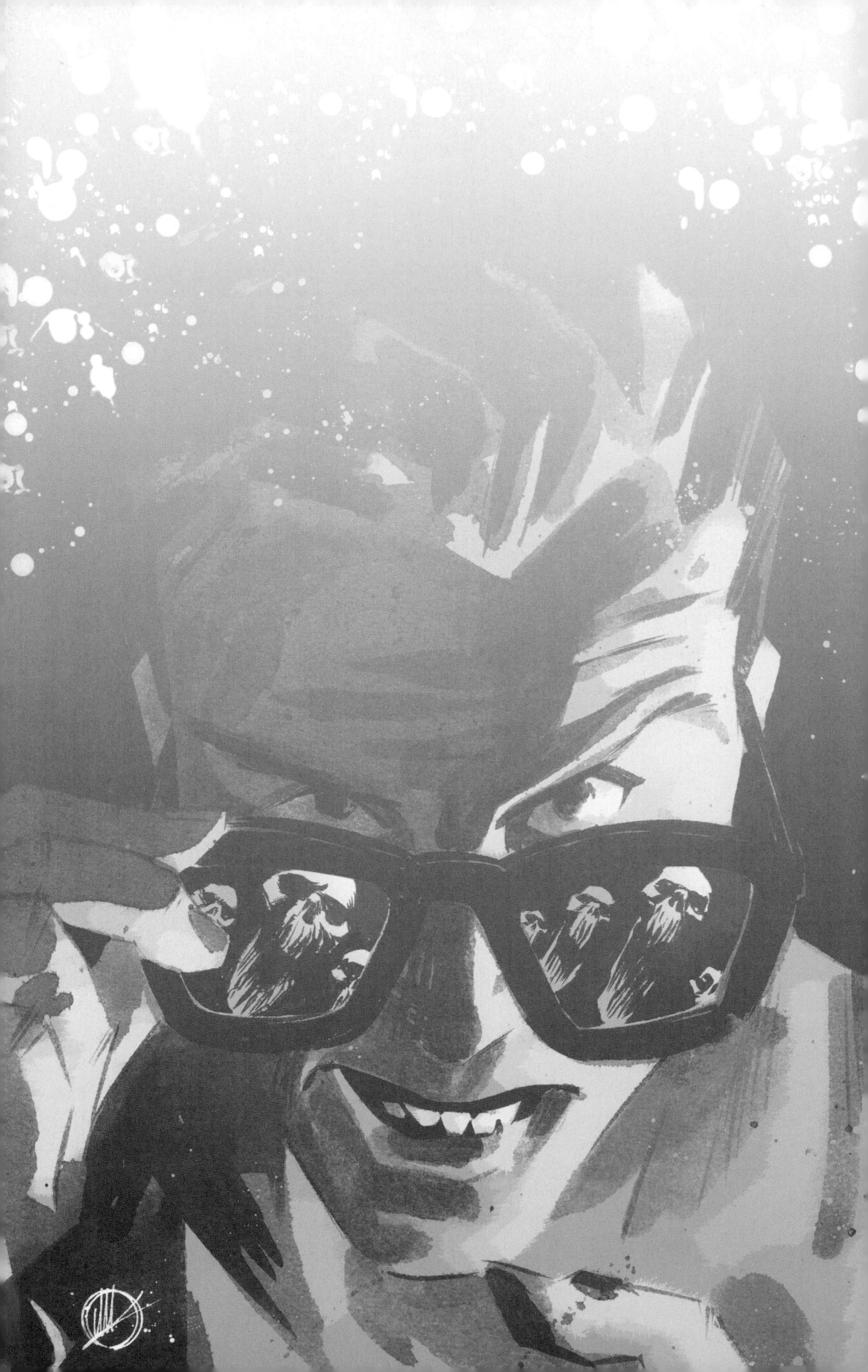

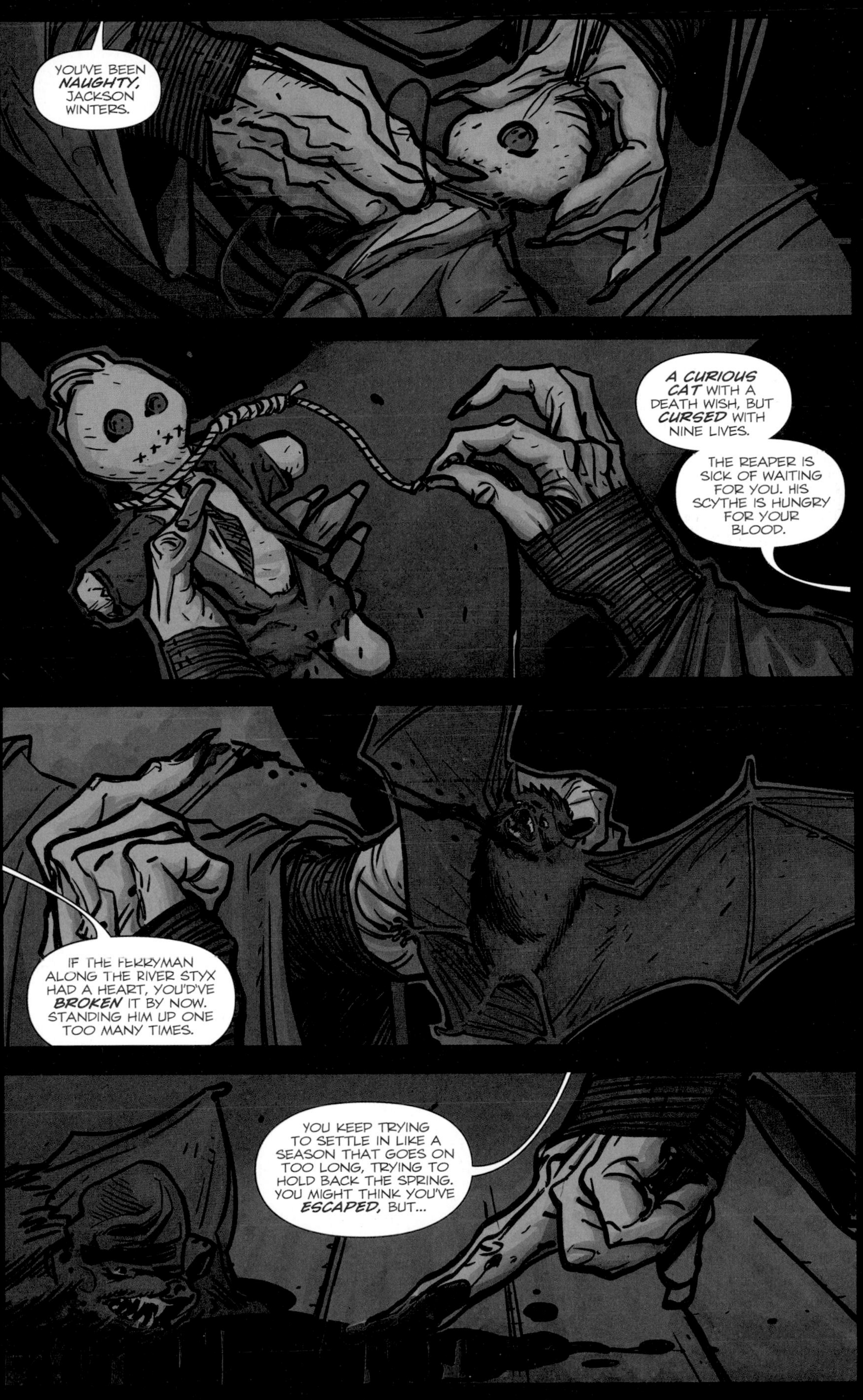
YOU'VE BEEN NAUGHTY, JACKSON WINTERS.
A CURIOUS CAT WITH A DEATH WISH, BUT CURSED WITH NINE LIVES.
THE REAPER IS SICK OF WAITING FOR YOU. HIS SCYTHE IS HUNGRY FOR YOUR BLOOD.
IF THE FERRYMAN ALONG THE RIVER STYX HAD A HEART, YOU'D'VE BROKEN IT BY NOW. STANDING HIM UP ONE TOO MANY TIMES.
YOU KEEP TRYING TO SETTLE IN LIKE A SEASON THAT GOES ON TOO LONG, TRYING TO HOLD BACK THE SPRING. YOU MIGHT THINK YOU'VE ESCAPED, BUT...

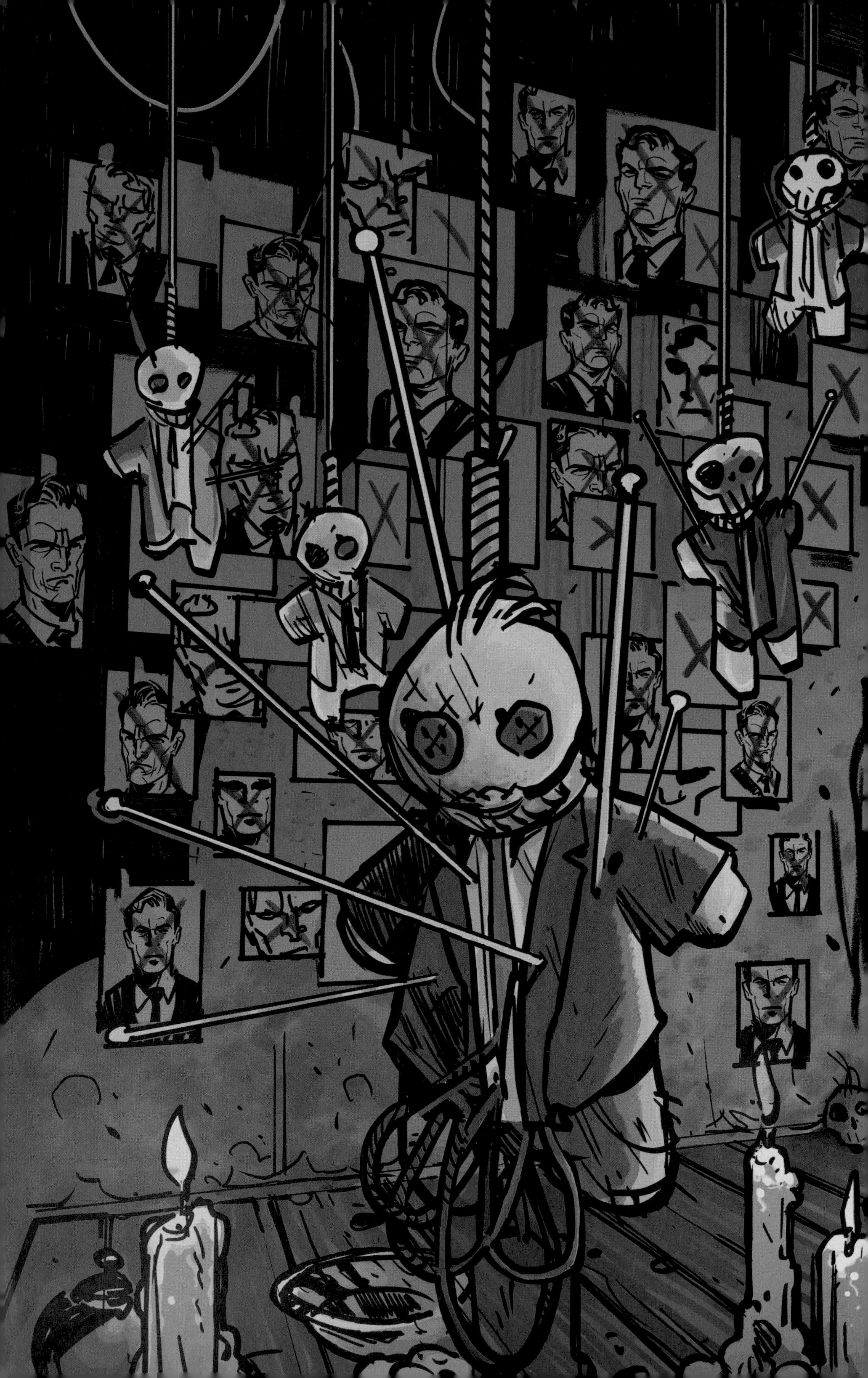

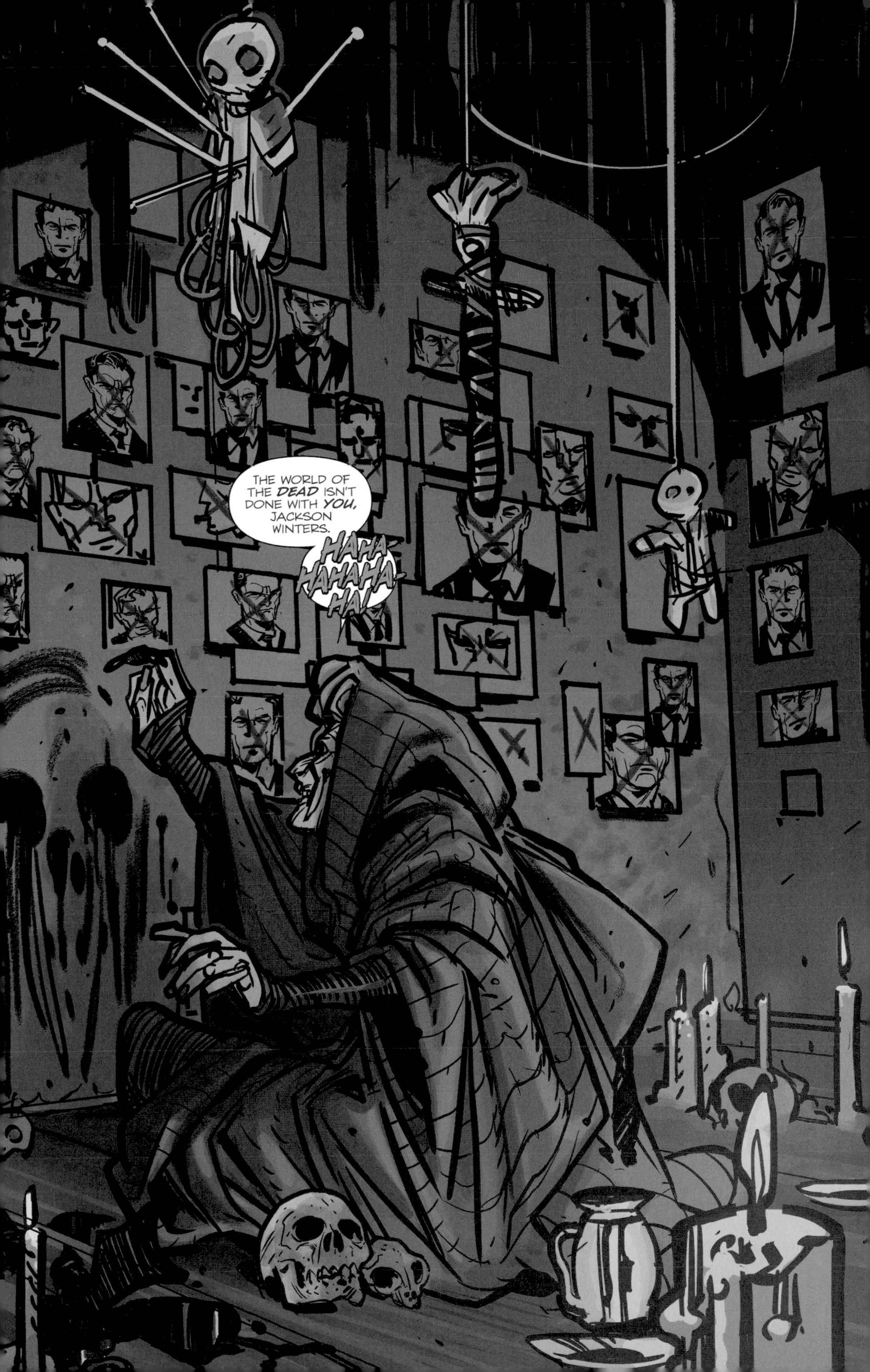
THE WORLD OF THE *DEAD* ISN'T DONE WITH *YOU*, JACKSON WINTERS.
HAHA HAHAHA-HA!

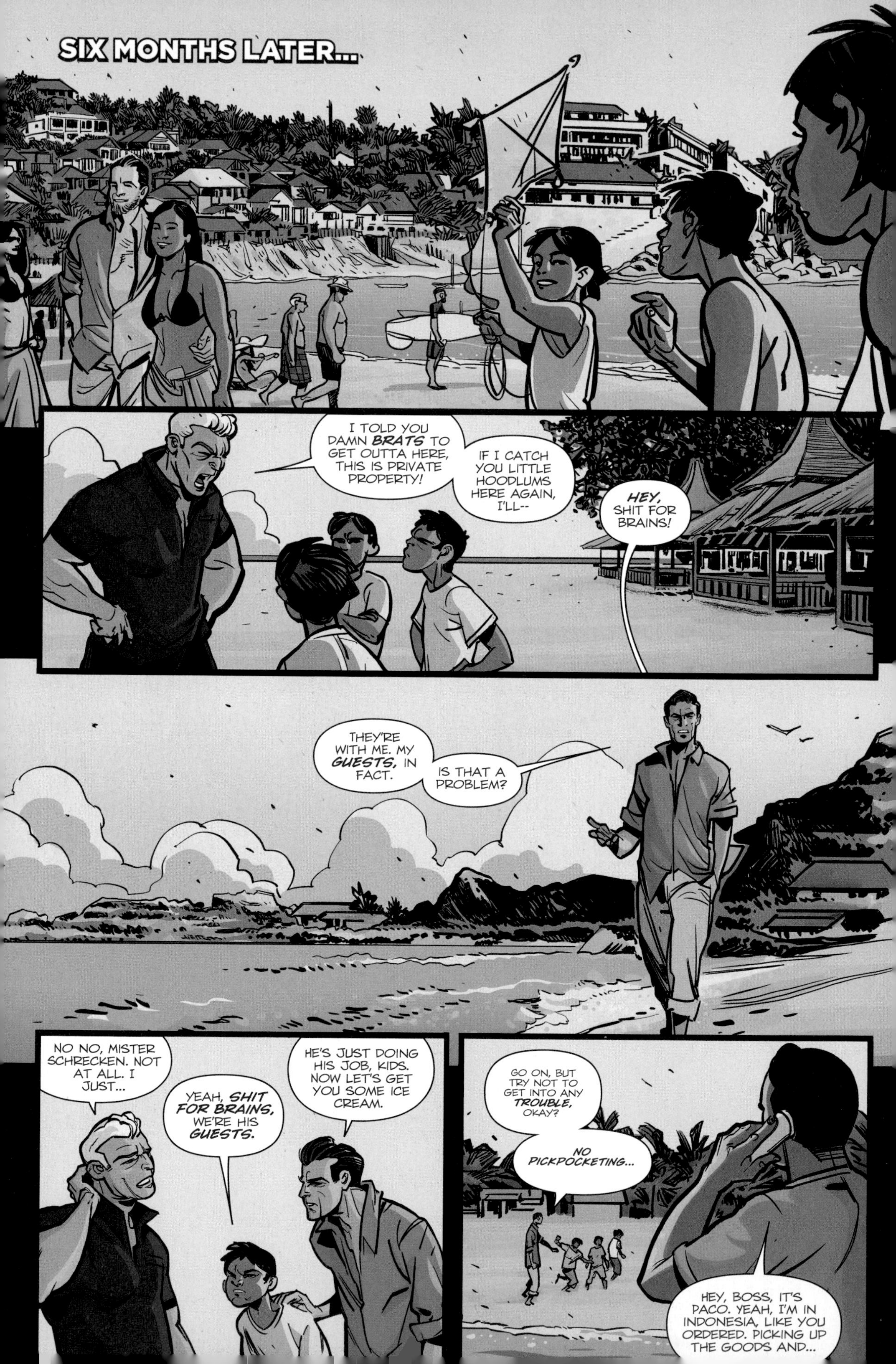
SIX MONTHS LATER...
I TOLD YOU DAMN BRATS TO GET OUTTA HERE, THIS IS PRIVATE PROPERTY!
IF I CATCH YOU LITTLE HOODLUMS HERE AGAIN, I'LL--
HEY, SHIT FOR BRAINS!
THEY'RE WITH ME. MY GUESTS, IN FACT.
IS THAT A PROBLEM?
NO NO, MISTER SCHRECKEN. NOT AT ALL. I JUST...
YEAH, SHIT FOR BRAINS, WE'RE HIS GUESTS.
HE'S JUST DOING HIS JOB, KIDS. NOW LET'S GET YOU SOME ICE CREAM.
GO ON, BUT TRY NOT TO GET INTO ANY TROUBLE, OKAY?
NO PICKPOCKETING...
HEY, BOSS, IT'S PACO. YEAH, I'M IN INDONESIA, LIKE YOU ORDERED. PICKING UP THE GOODS AND...

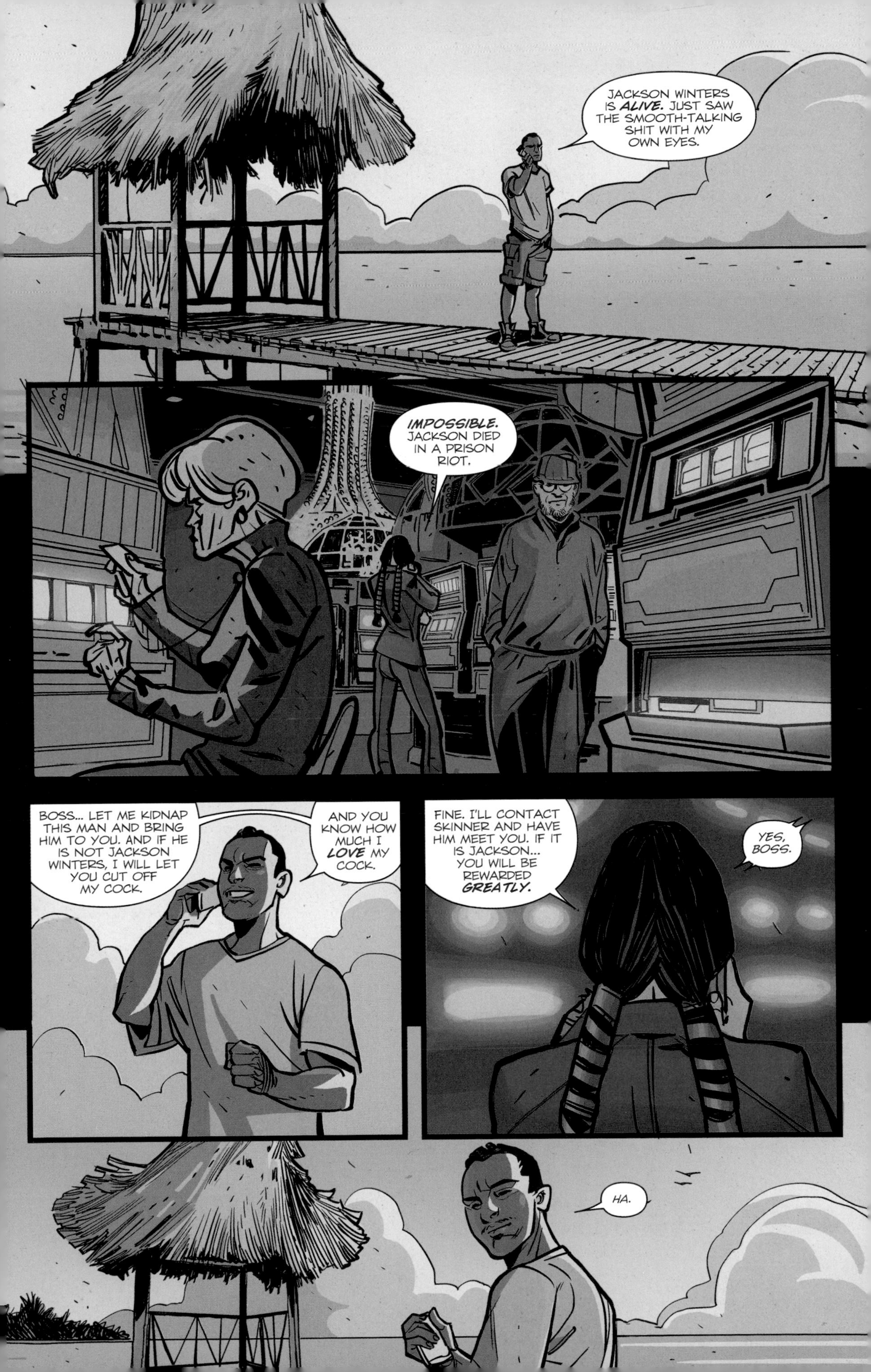
JACKSON WINTERS IS ALIVE. JUST SAW THE SMOOTH-TALKING SHIT WITH MY OWN EYES.
IMPOSSIBLE. JACKSON DIED IN A PRISON RIOT.
BOSS... LET ME KIDNAP THIS MAN AND BRING HIM TO YOU. AND IF HE IS NOT JACKSON WINTERS, I WILL LET YOU CUT OFF MY COCK.
AND YOU KNOW HOW MUCH I LOVE MY COCK.
FINE. I'LL CONTACT SKINNER AND HAVE HIM MEET YOU. IF IT IS JACKSON... YOU WILL BE REWARDED GREATLY.
YES, BOSS.
HA.

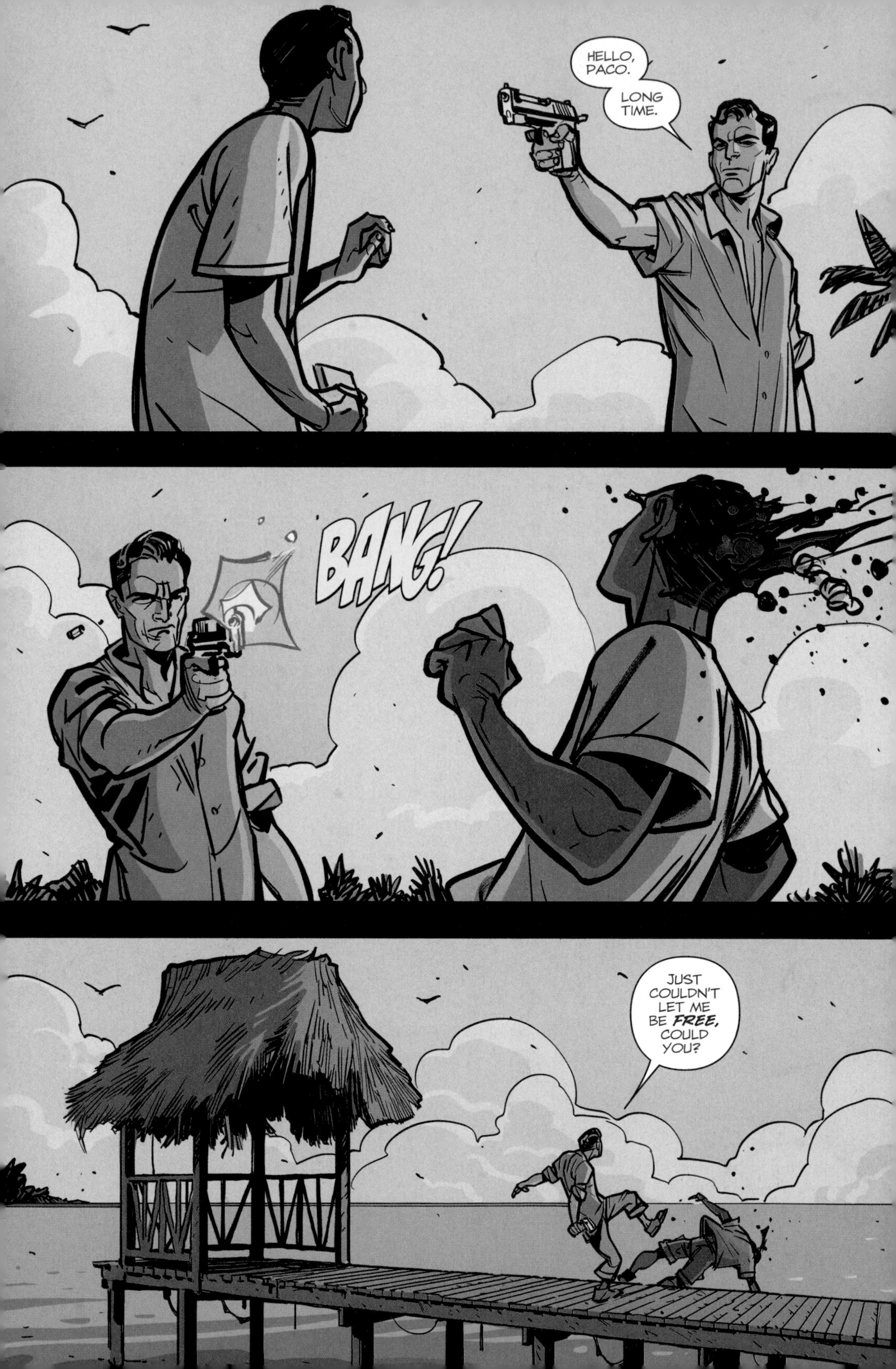
HELLO, PACO.
LONG TIME.
BANG!
JUST COULDN'T LET ME BE FREE, COULD YOU?

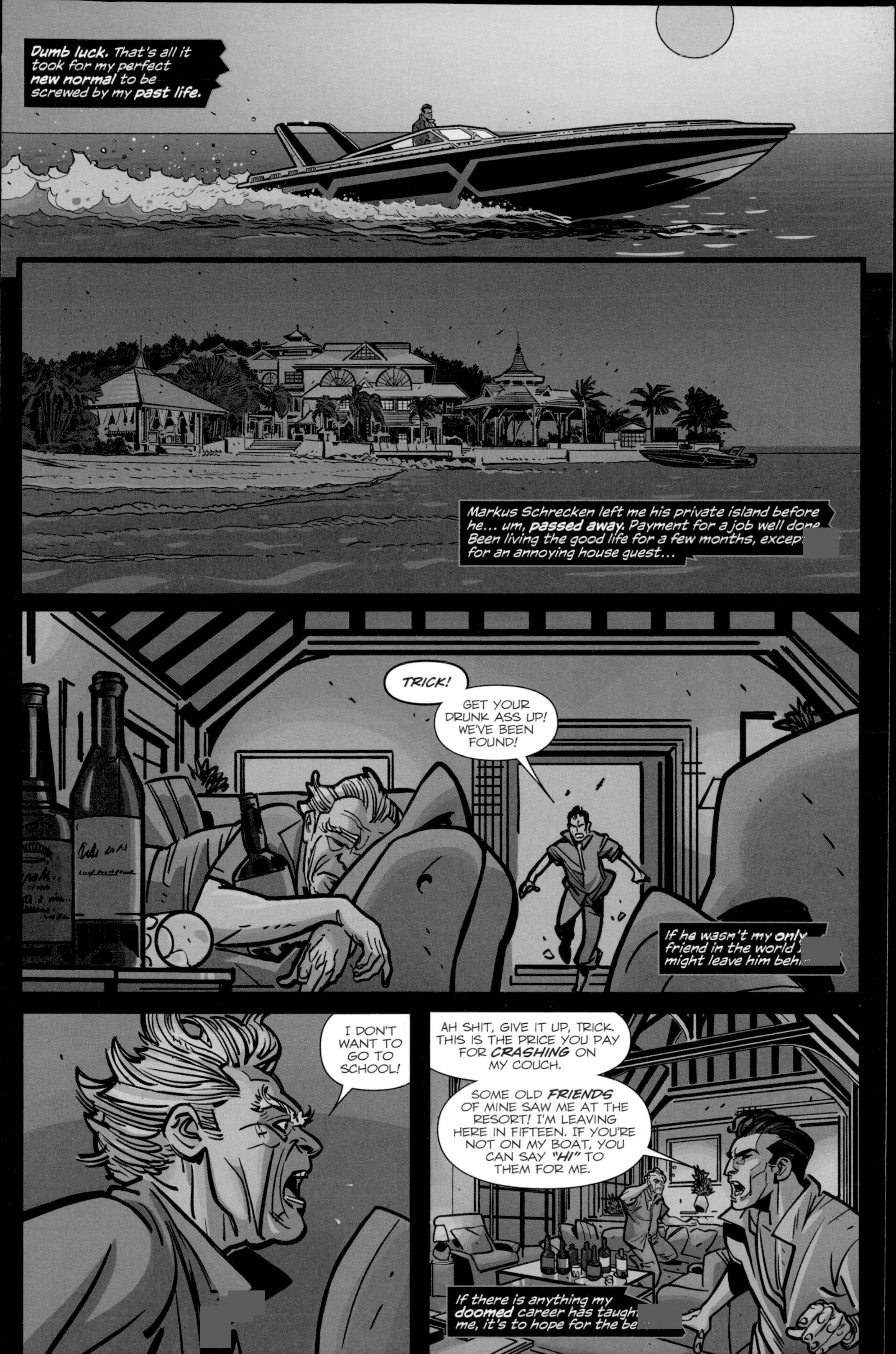

Dumb luck. That's all it took for my perfect new normal to be screwed by my past life.
Markus Schrecken left me his private island before he... um, passed away. Payment for a job well done. Been living the good life for a few months, excep
for an annoying house guest...
TRICK!
GET YOUR DRUNK ASS UP! WE'VE BEEN FOUND!
If he wasn't my only friend in the world
might leave him beh
I DON'T WANT TO GO TO SCHOOL!
AH SHIT, GIVE IT UP, TRICK. THIS IS THE PRICE YOU PAY FOR CRASHING ON MY COUCH.
SOME OLD FRIENDS OF MINE SAW ME AT THE RESORT! I'M LEAVING HERE IN FIFTEEN. IF YOU'RE NOT ON MY BOAT, YOU CAN SAY "HI" TO THEM FOR ME.
If there is anything my doomed career has taugh
me, it's to hope for the be

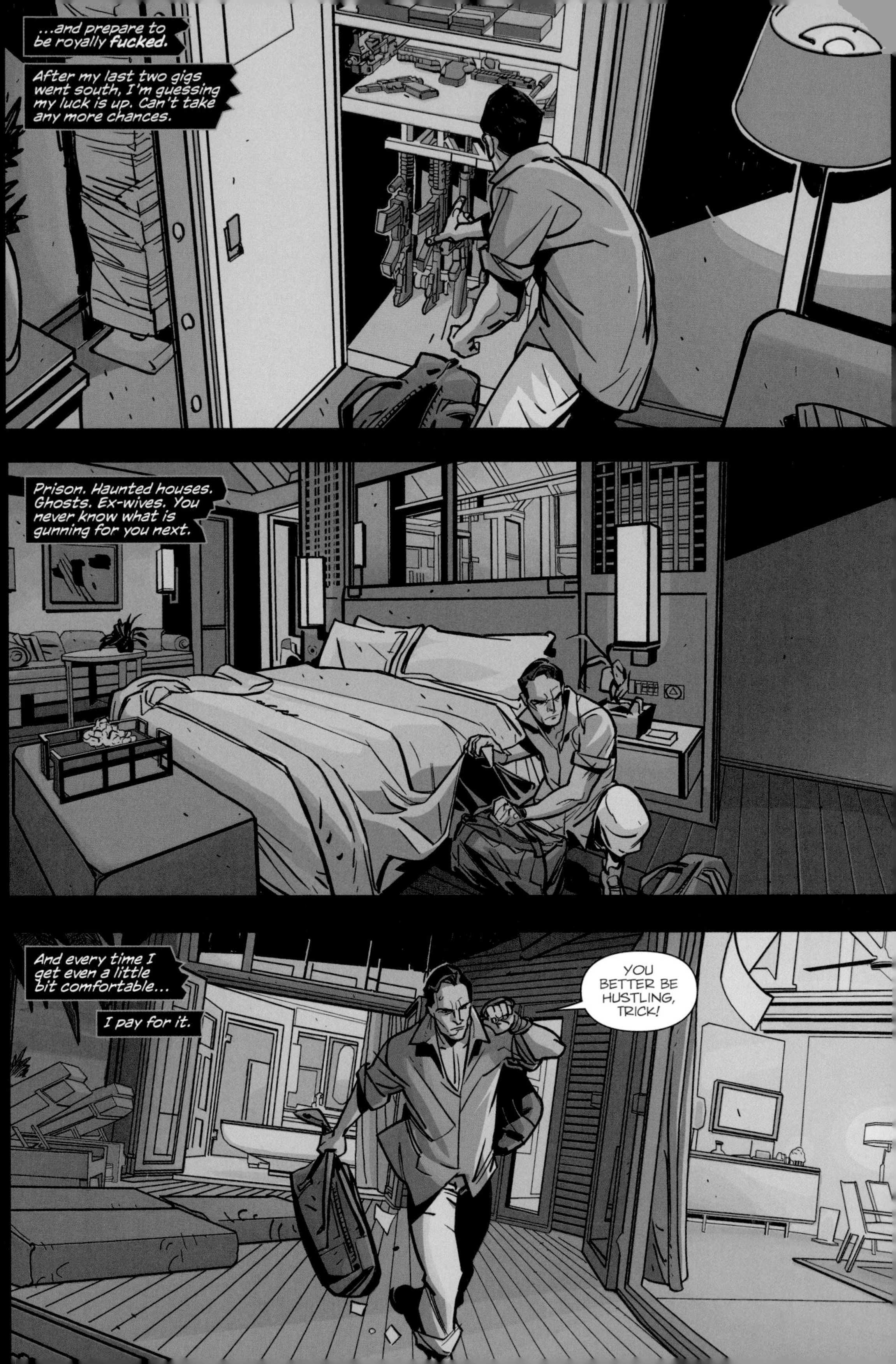
...and prepare to be royally **fucked.**
After my last two gigs went south, I'm guessing my luck is up. Can't take any more chances.
Prison. Haunted houses. Ghosts. Ex-wives. You never know what is gunning for you next.
And every time I get even a little bit comfortable...
I pay for it.
YOU BETTER BE HUSTLING, TRICK!

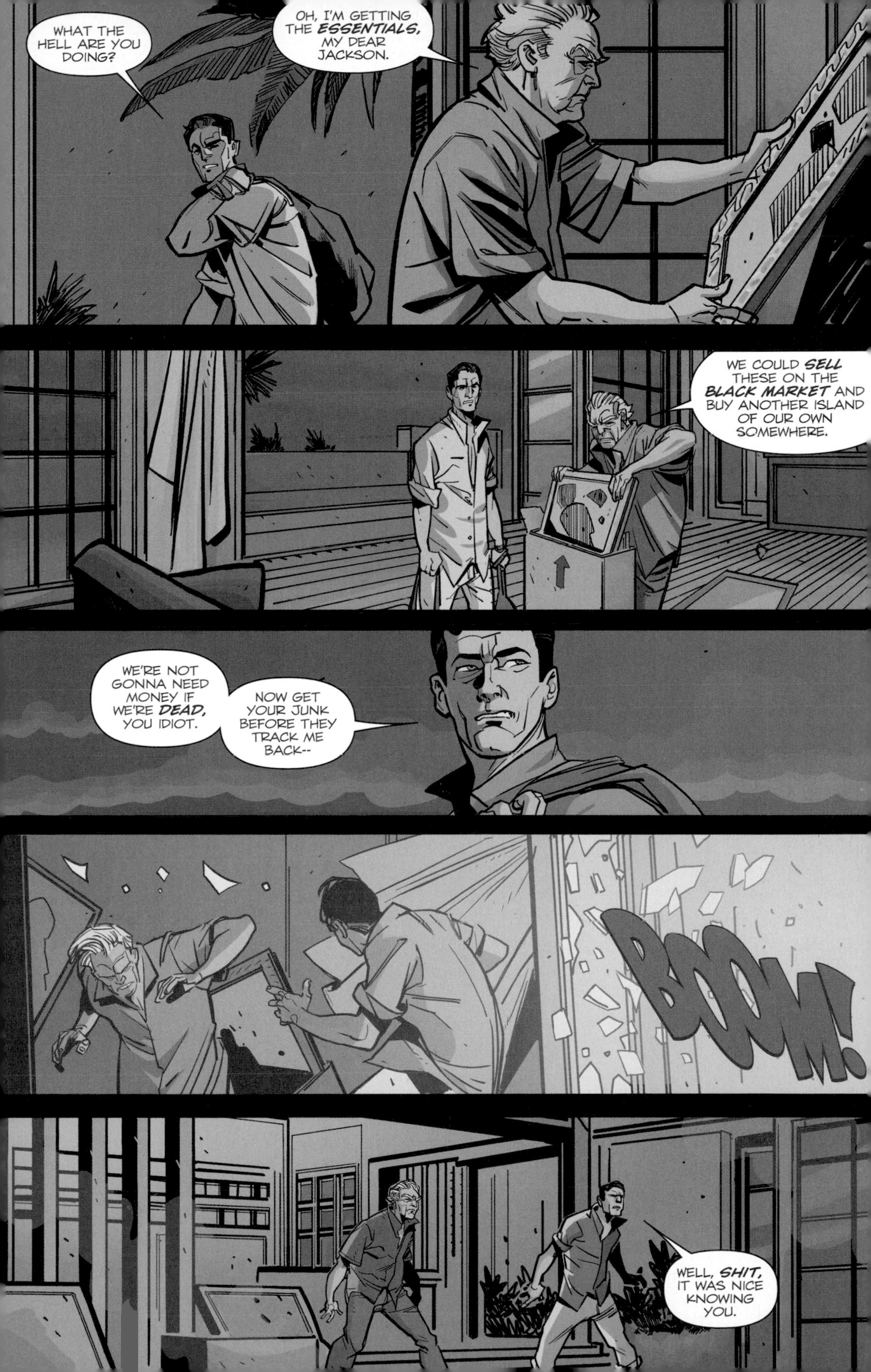
WHAT THE HELL ARE YOU DOING?
OH, I'M GETTING THE ESSENTIALS, MY DEAR JACKSON.
WE COULD SELL THESE ON THE BLACK MARKET AND BUY ANOTHER ISLAND OF OUR OWN SOMEWHERE.
WE'RE NOT GONNA NEED MONEY IF WE'RE DEAD, YOU IDIOT.
NOW GET YOUR JUNK BEFORE THEY TRACK ME BACK--
BOOM!
WELL, SHIT, IT WAS NICE KNOWING YOU.

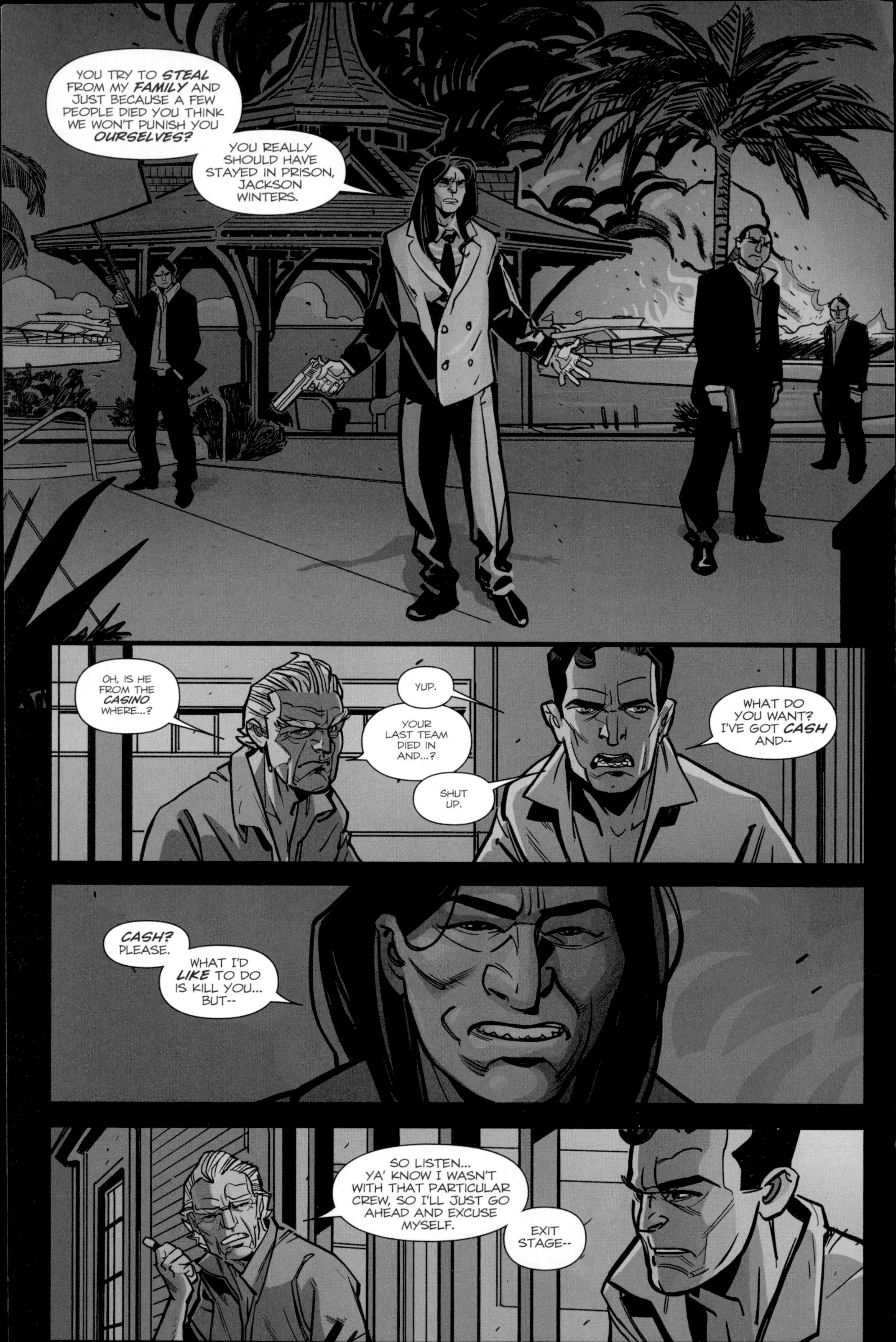
YOU TRY TO STEAL FROM MY FAMILY AND JUST BECAUSE A FEW PEOPLE DIED YOU THINK WE WON'T PUNISH YOU OURSELVES?
YOU REALLY SHOULD HAVE STAYED IN PRISON, JACKSON WINTERS.
OH, IS HE FROM THE CASINO WHERE...?
YUP.
YOUR LAST TEAM DIED IN AND...?
WHAT DO YOU WANT? I'VE GOT CASH AND--
SHUT UP.
CASH? PLEASE.
WHAT I'D LIKE TO DO IS KILL YOU... BUT--
SO LISTEN... YA' KNOW I WASN'T WITH THAT PARTICULAR CREW, SO I'LL JUST GO AHEAD AND EXCUSE MYSELF.
EXIT STAGE--

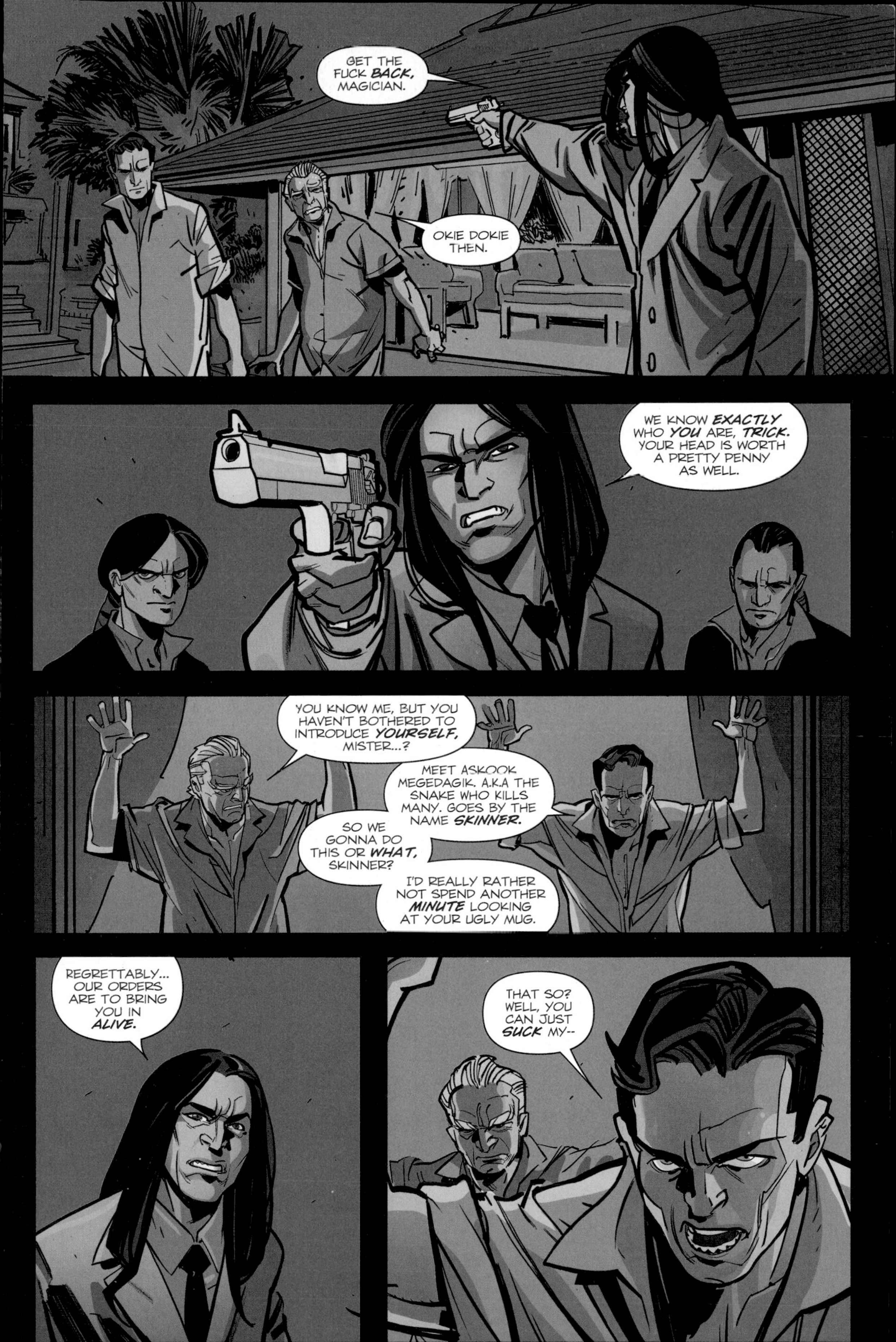
GET THE FUCK BACK, MAGICIAN.
OKIE DOKIE THEN.
WE KNOW EXACTLY WHO YOU ARE, TRICK. YOUR HEAD IS WORTH A PRETTY PENNY AS WELL.
YOU KNOW ME, BUT YOU HAVEN'T BOTHERED TO INTRODUCE YOURSELF, MISTER...?
MEET ASKOOK MEGEDAGIK. A.K.A THE SNAKE WHO KILLS MANY. GOES BY THE NAME SKINNER.
SO WE GONNA DO THIS OR WHAT, SKINNER?
I'D REALLY RATHER NOT SPEND ANOTHER MINUTE LOOKING AT YOUR UGLY MUG.
REGRETTABLY... OUR ORDERS ARE TO BRING YOU IN ALIVE.
THAT SO? WELL, YOU CAN JUST SUCK MY--

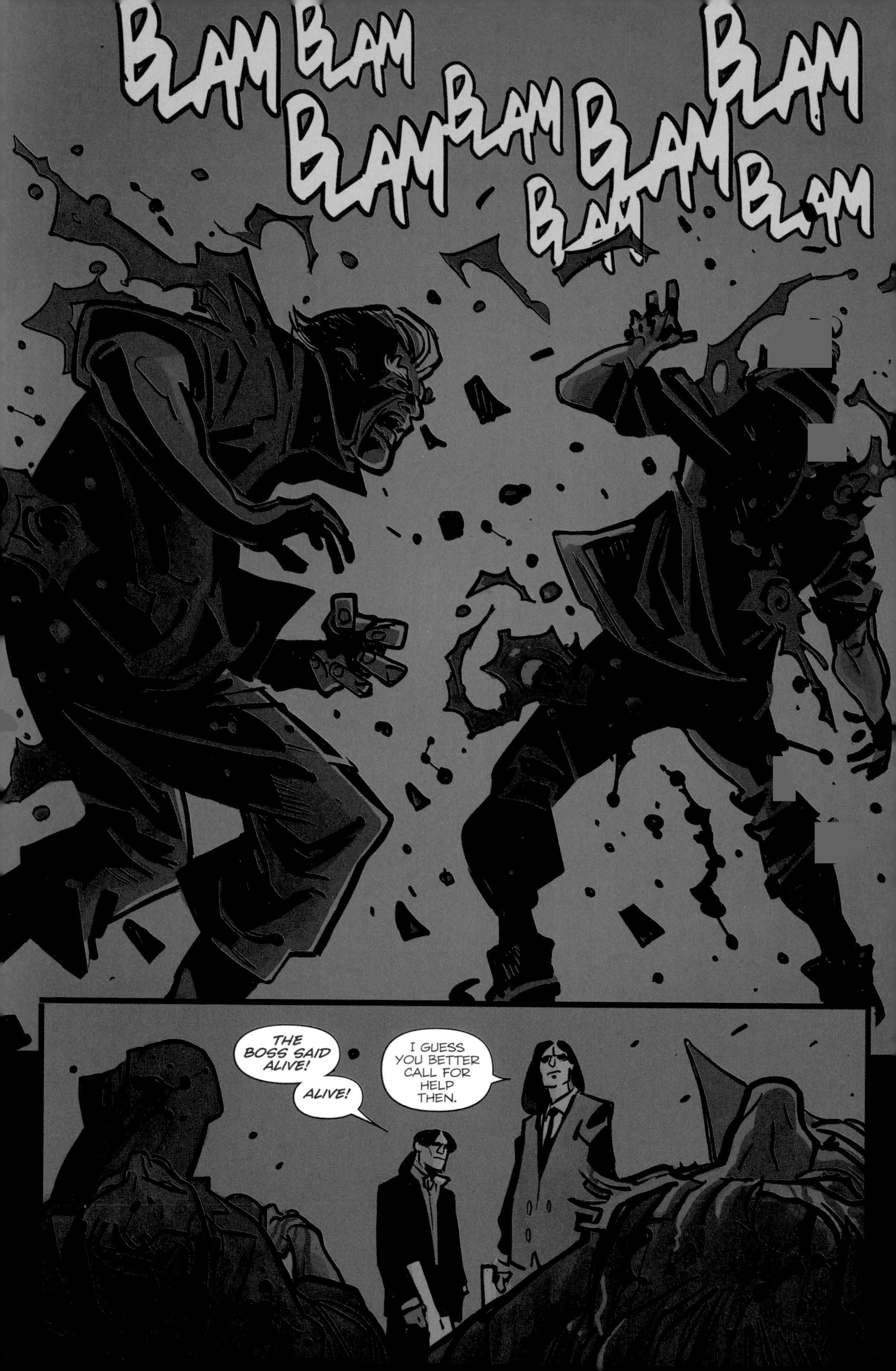
BLAM BLAM
BLAM
BLAM BLAM BLAM
BLAM BLAM
THE BOSS SAID ALIVE!
ALIVE!
I GUESS YOU BETTER CALL FOR HELP THEN.

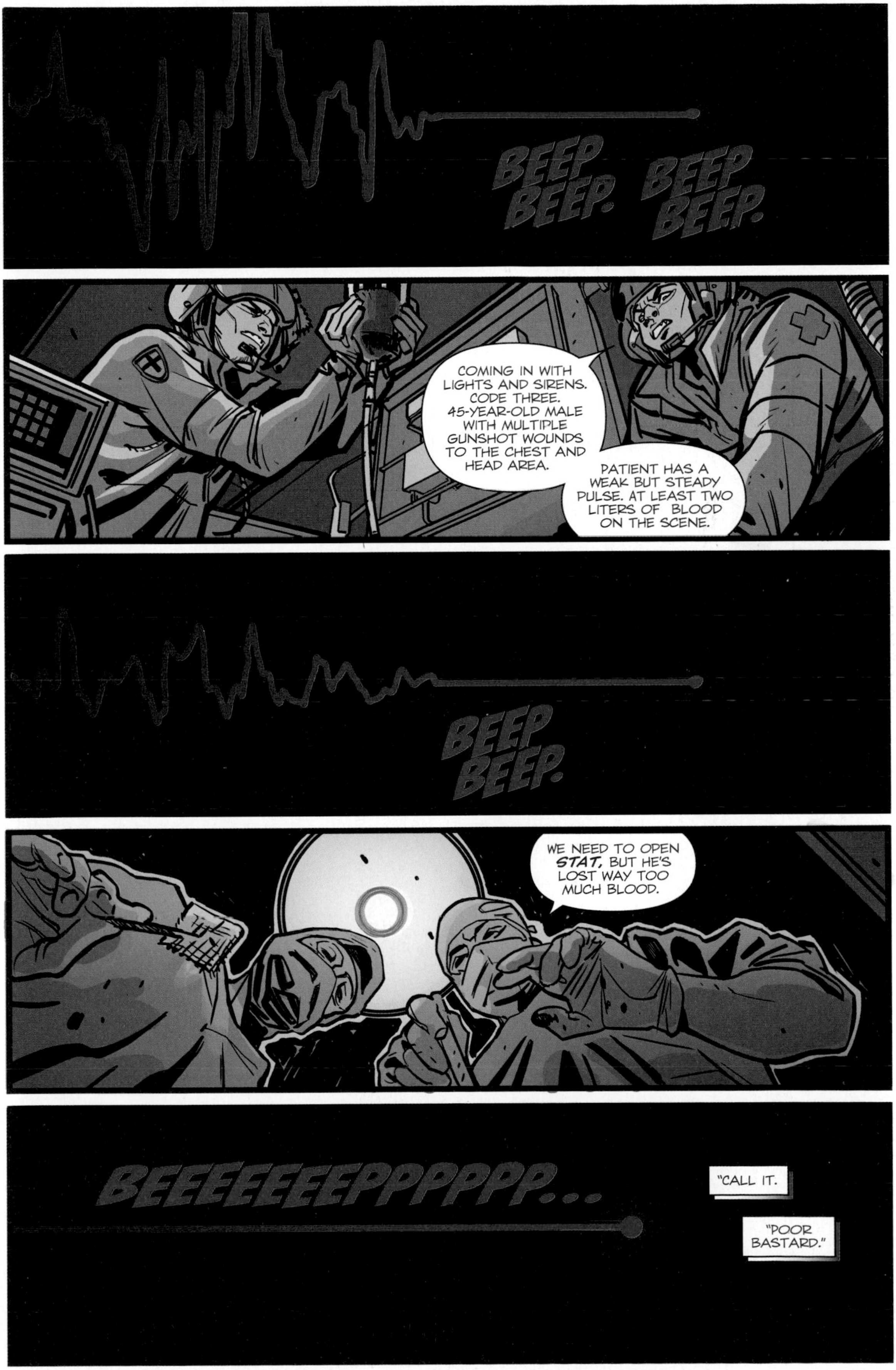
BEEP BEEP. BEEP BEEP.
COMING IN WITH LIGHTS AND SIRENS. CODE THREE. 45-YEAR-OLD MALE WITH MULTIPLE GUNSHOT WOUNDS TO THE CHEST AND HEAD AREA.
PATIENT HAS A WEAK BUT STEADY PULSE. AT LEAST TWO LITERS OF BLOOD ON THE SCENE.
BEEP BEEP.
WE NEED TO OPEN STAT, BUT HE'S LOST WAY TOO MUCH BLOOD.
BEEEEEEEEPPPPPP...
"CALL IT.
"POOR BASTARD."

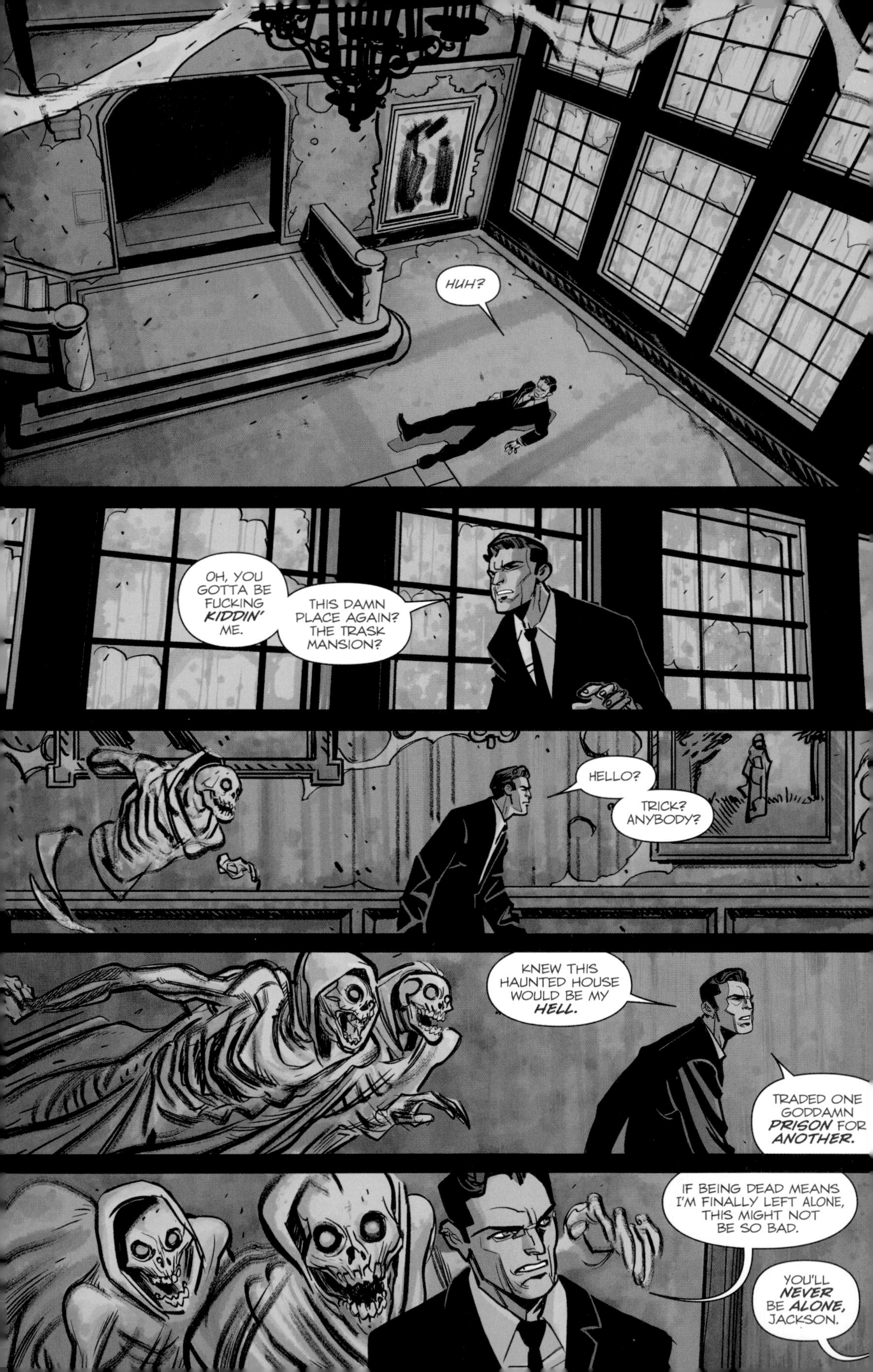
HUH?
OH, YOU GOTTA BE FUCKING *KIDDIN'* ME.
THIS DAMN PLACE AGAIN? THE TRASK MANSION?
HELLO?
TRICK? ANYBODY?
KNEW THIS HAUNTED HOUSE WOULD BE MY *HELL.*
TRADED ONE GODDAMN *PRISON* FOR *ANOTHER.*
IF BEING DEAD MEANS I'M FINALLY LEFT ALONE, THIS MIGHT NOT BE SO BAD.
YOU'LL *NEVER* BE *ALONE,* JACKSON.

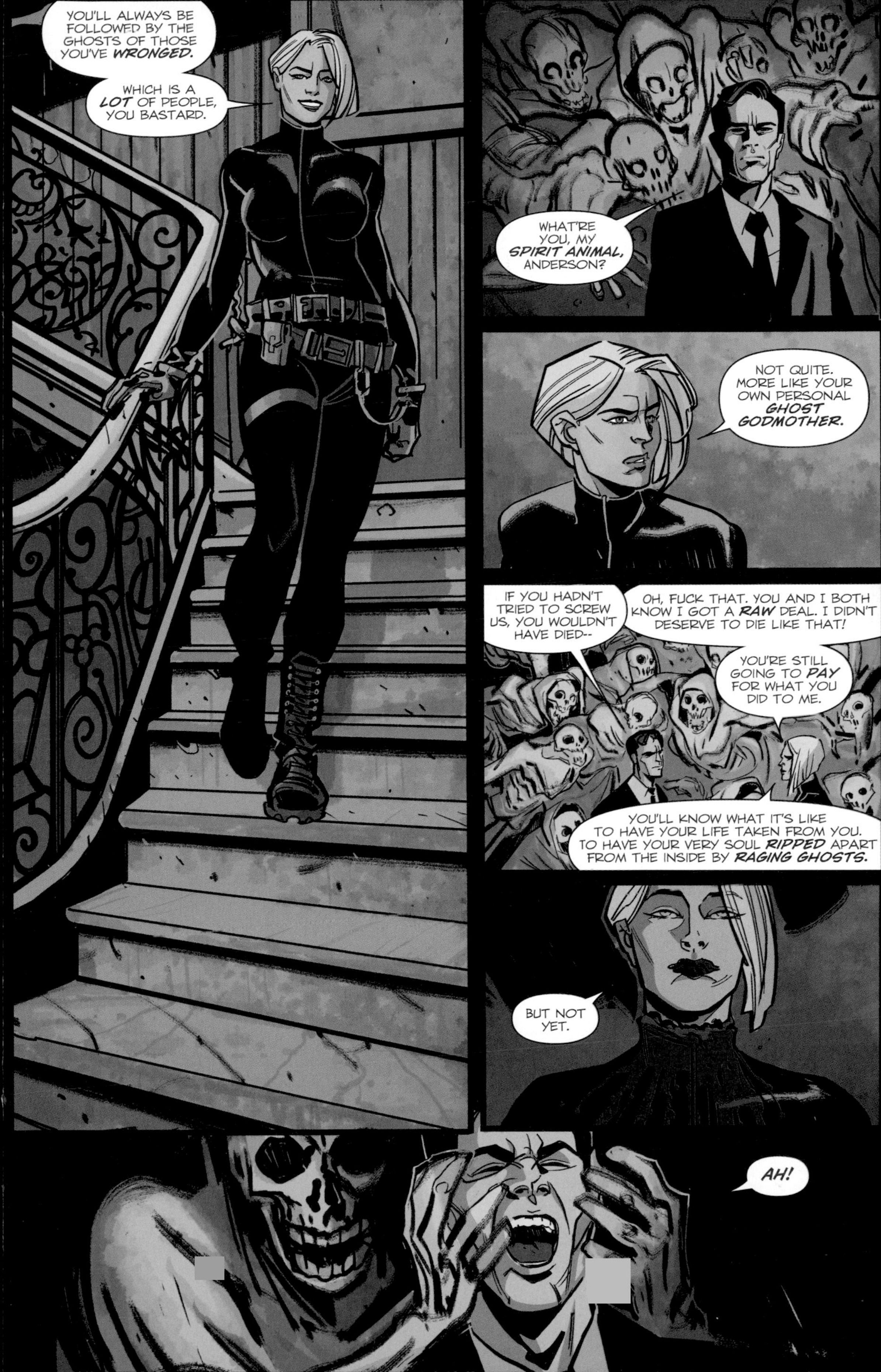
YOU'LL ALWAYS BE FOLLOWED BY THE GHOSTS OF THOSE YOU'VE WRONGED.
WHICH IS A LOT OF PEOPLE, YOU BASTARD.
WHAT'RE YOU, MY SPIRIT ANIMAL, ANDERSON?
NOT QUITE. MORE LIKE YOUR OWN PERSONAL GHOST GODMOTHER.
IF YOU HADN'T TRIED TO SCREW US, YOU WOULDN'T HAVE DIED--
OH, FUCK THAT. YOU AND I BOTH KNOW I GOT A RAW DEAL. I DIDN'T DESERVE TO DIE LIKE THAT!
YOU'RE STILL GOING TO PAY FOR WHAT YOU DID TO ME.
YOU'LL KNOW WHAT IT'S LIKE TO HAVE YOUR LIFE TAKEN FROM YOU. TO HAVE YOUR VERY SOUL RIPPED APART FROM THE INSIDE BY RAGING GHOSTS.
BUT NOT YET.
AH!

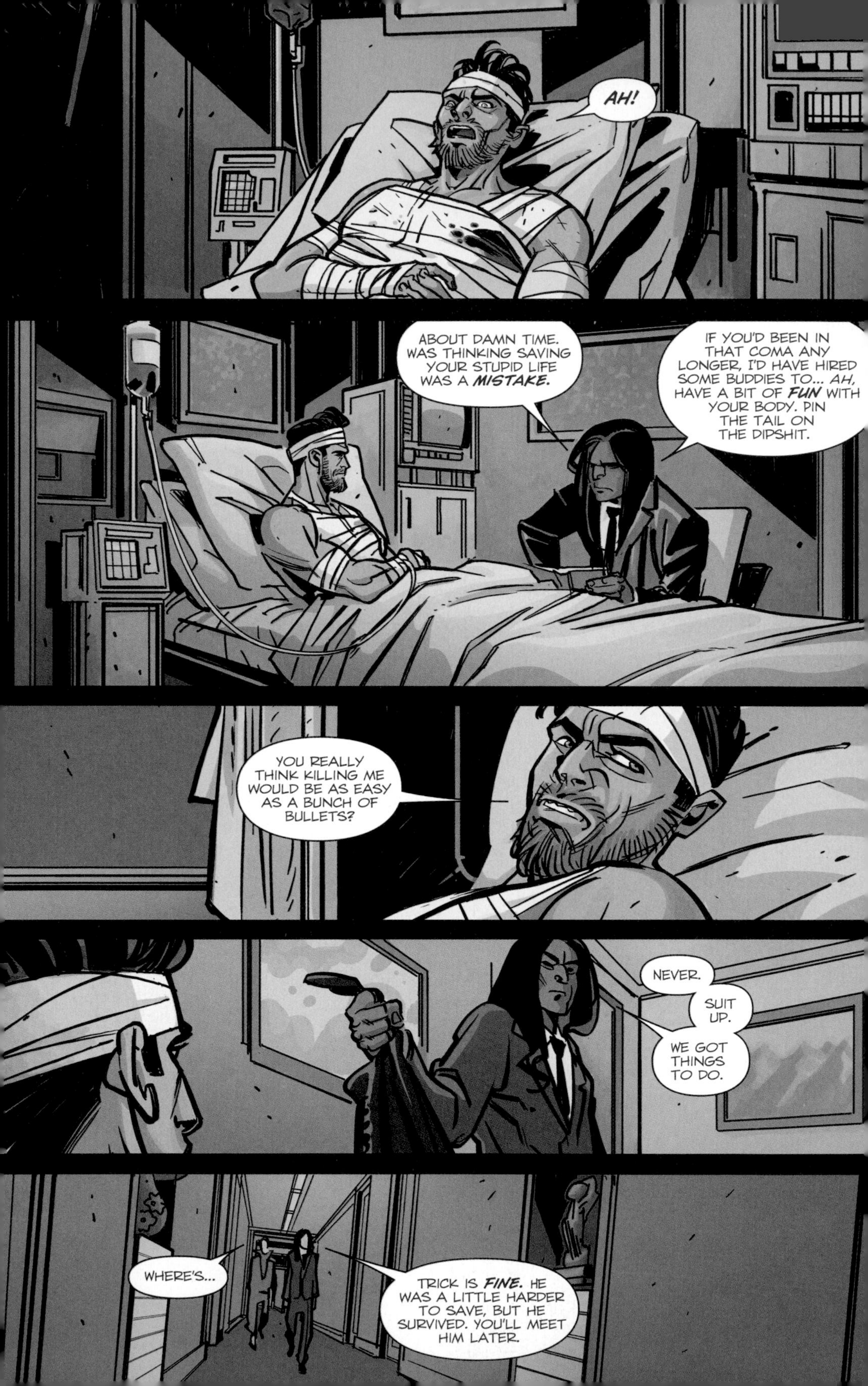
AH!
ABOUT DAMN TIME. WAS THINKING SAVING YOUR STUPID LIFE WAS A MISTAKE.
IF YOU'D BEEN IN THAT COMA ANY LONGER, I'D HAVE HIRED SOME BUDDIES TO... AH, HAVE A BIT OF FUN WITH YOUR BODY. PIN THE TAIL ON THE DIPSHIT.
YOU REALLY THINK KILLING ME WOULD BE AS EASY AS A BUNCH OF BULLETS?
NEVER.
SUIT UP.
WE GOT THINGS TO DO.
WHERE'S...
TRICK IS FINE. HE WAS A LITTLE HARDER TO SAVE, BUT HE SURVIVED. YOU'LL MEET HIM LATER.

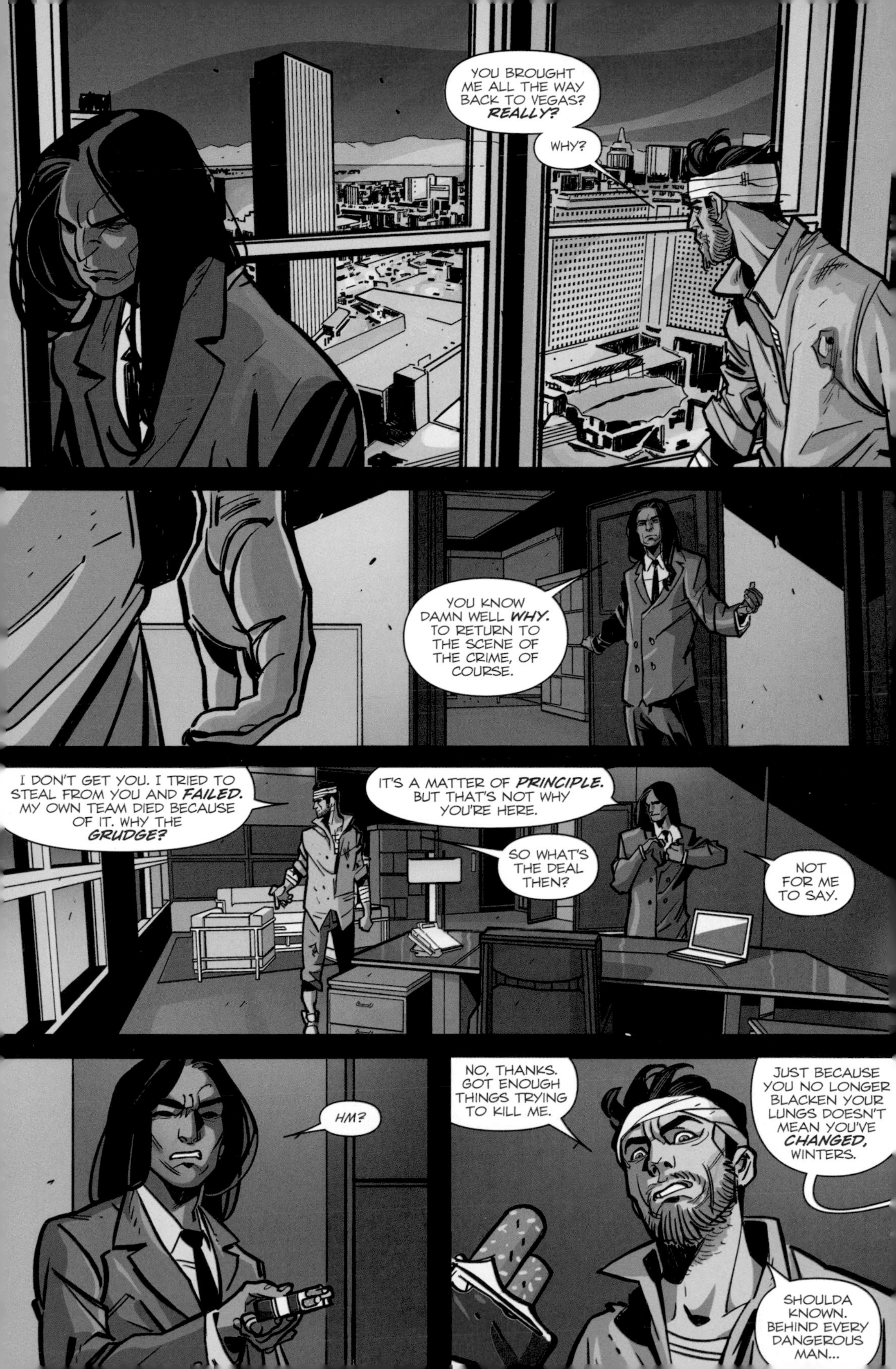
YOU BROUGHT ME ALL THE WAY BACK TO VEGAS? **REALLY?**
WHY?
YOU KNOW DAMN WELL **WHY.** TO RETURN TO THE SCENE OF THE CRIME, OF COURSE.
I DON'T GET YOU. I TRIED TO STEAL FROM YOU AND **FAILED.** MY OWN TEAM DIED BECAUSE OF IT. WHY THE **GRUDGE?**
IT'S A MATTER OF **PRINCIPLE.** BUT THAT'S NOT WHY YOU'RE HERE.
SO WHAT'S THE DEAL THEN?
NOT FOR ME TO SAY.
HM?
NO, THANKS. GOT ENOUGH THINGS TRYING TO KILL ME.
JUST BECAUSE YOU NO LONGER BLACKEN YOUR LUNGS DOESN'T MEAN YOU'VE **CHANGED,** WINTERS.
SHOULDA KNOWN. BEHIND EVERY DANGEROUS MAN...

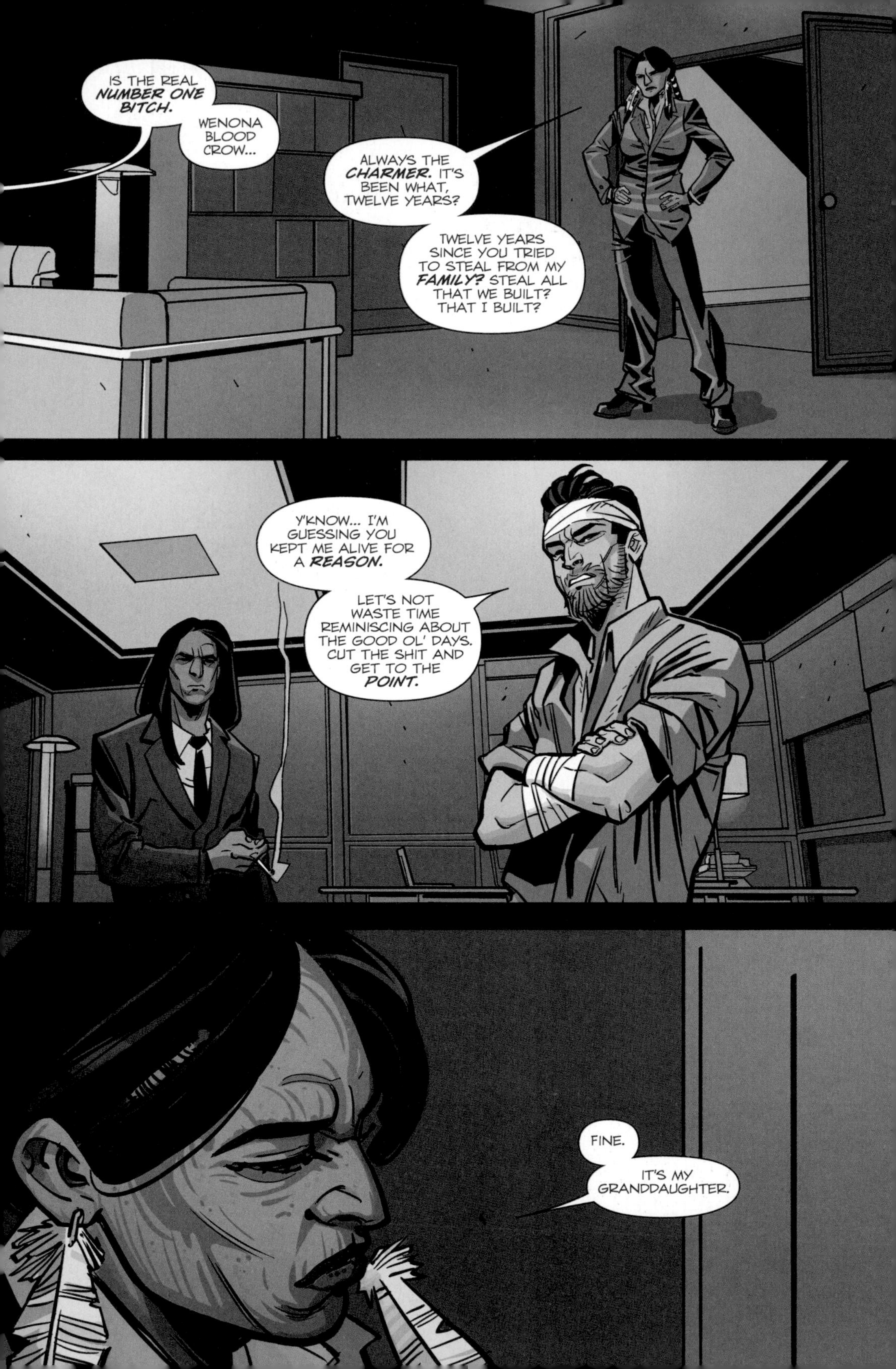
IS THE REAL NUMBER ONE BITCH.
WENONA BLOOD CROW...
ALWAYS THE CHARMER. IT'S BEEN WHAT, TWELVE YEARS?
TWELVE YEARS SINCE YOU TRIED TO STEAL FROM MY FAMILY? STEAL ALL THAT WE BUILT? THAT I BUILT?
Y'KNOW... I'M GUESSING YOU KEPT ME ALIVE FOR A REASON.
LET'S NOT WASTE TIME REMINISCING ABOUT THE GOOD OL' DAYS. CUT THE SHIT AND GET TO THE POINT.
FINE.
IT'S MY GRANDDAUGHTER.

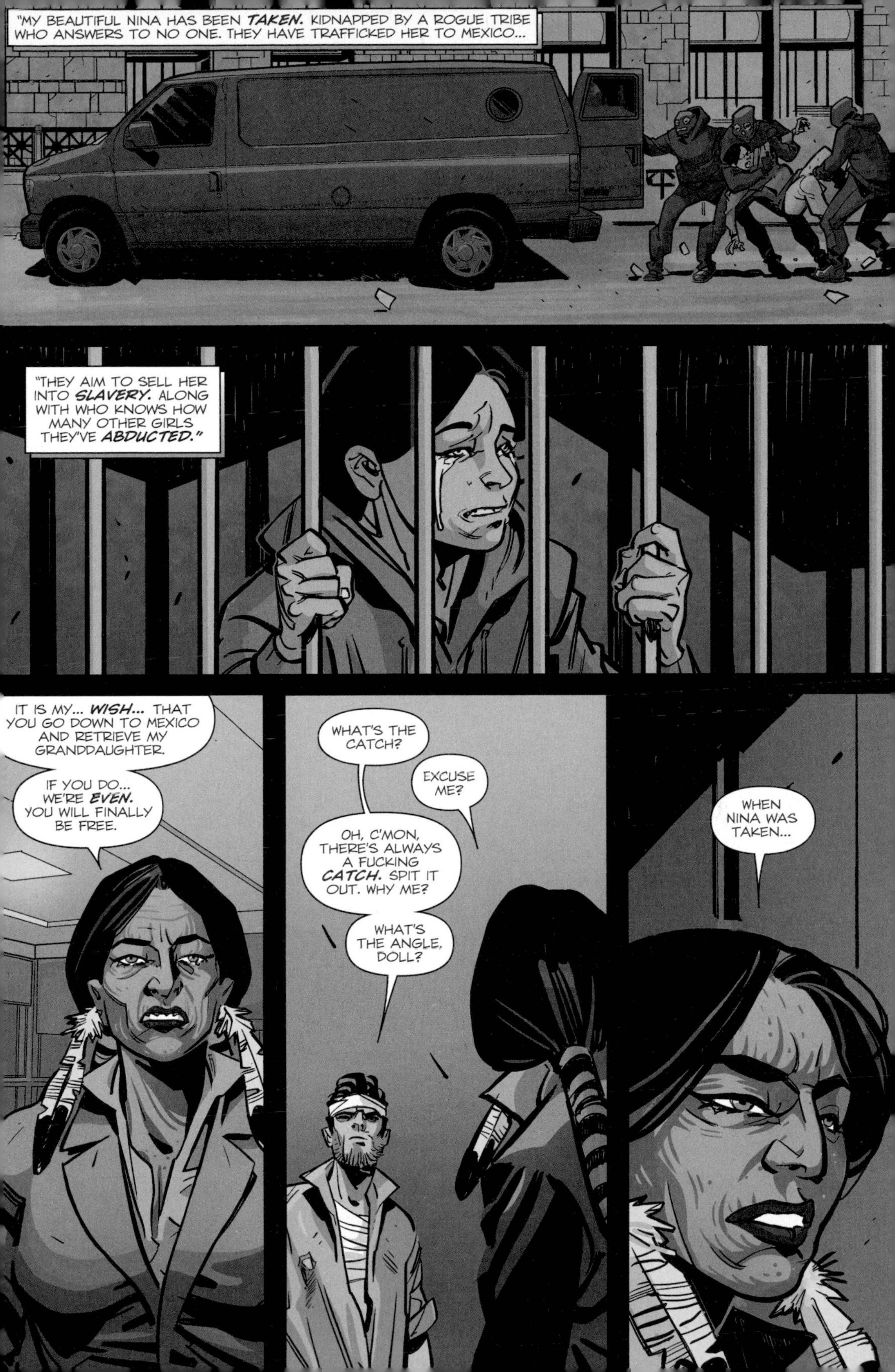
"MY BEAUTIFUL NINA HAS BEEN TAKEN. KIDNAPPED BY A ROGUE TRIBE WHO ANSWERS TO NO ONE. THEY HAVE TRAFFICKED HER TO MEXICO...
"THEY AIM TO SELL HER INTO SLAVERY. ALONG WITH WHO KNOWS HOW MANY OTHER GIRLS THEY'VE ABDUCTED."
IT IS MY... WISH... THAT YOU GO DOWN TO MEXICO AND RETRIEVE MY GRANDDAUGHTER.
IF YOU DO... WE'RE EVEN. YOU WILL FINALLY BE FREE.
WHAT'S THE CATCH?
EXCUSE ME?
OH, C'MON, THERE'S ALWAYS A FUCKING CATCH. SPIT IT OUT. WHY ME?
WHAT'S THE ANGLE, DOLL?
WHEN NINA WAS TAKEN...

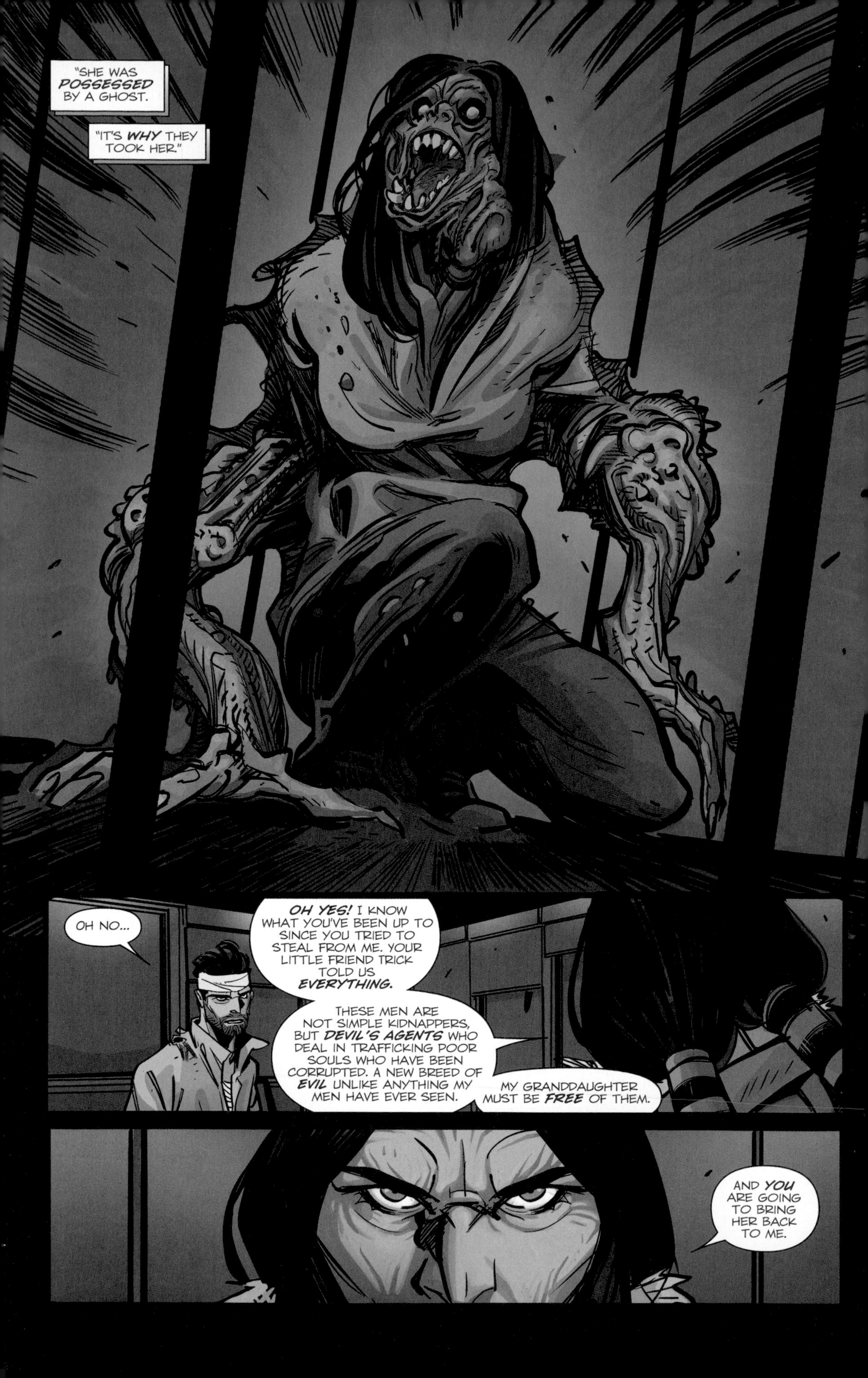
"SHE WAS POSSESSED BY A GHOST.
"IT'S WHY THEY TOOK HER."
OH NO...
OH YES! I KNOW WHAT YOU'VE BEEN UP TO SINCE YOU TRIED TO STEAL FROM ME. YOUR LITTLE FRIEND TRICK TOLD US EVERYTHING.
THESE MEN ARE NOT SIMPLE KIDNAPPERS, BUT DEVIL'S AGENTS WHO DEAL IN TRAFFICKING POOR SOULS WHO HAVE BEEN CORRUPTED. A NEW BREED OF EVIL UNLIKE ANYTHING MY MEN HAVE EVER SEEN.
MY GRANDDAUGHTER MUST BE FREE OF THEM.
AND YOU ARE GOING TO BRING HER BACK TO ME.

CHAPTER TWO

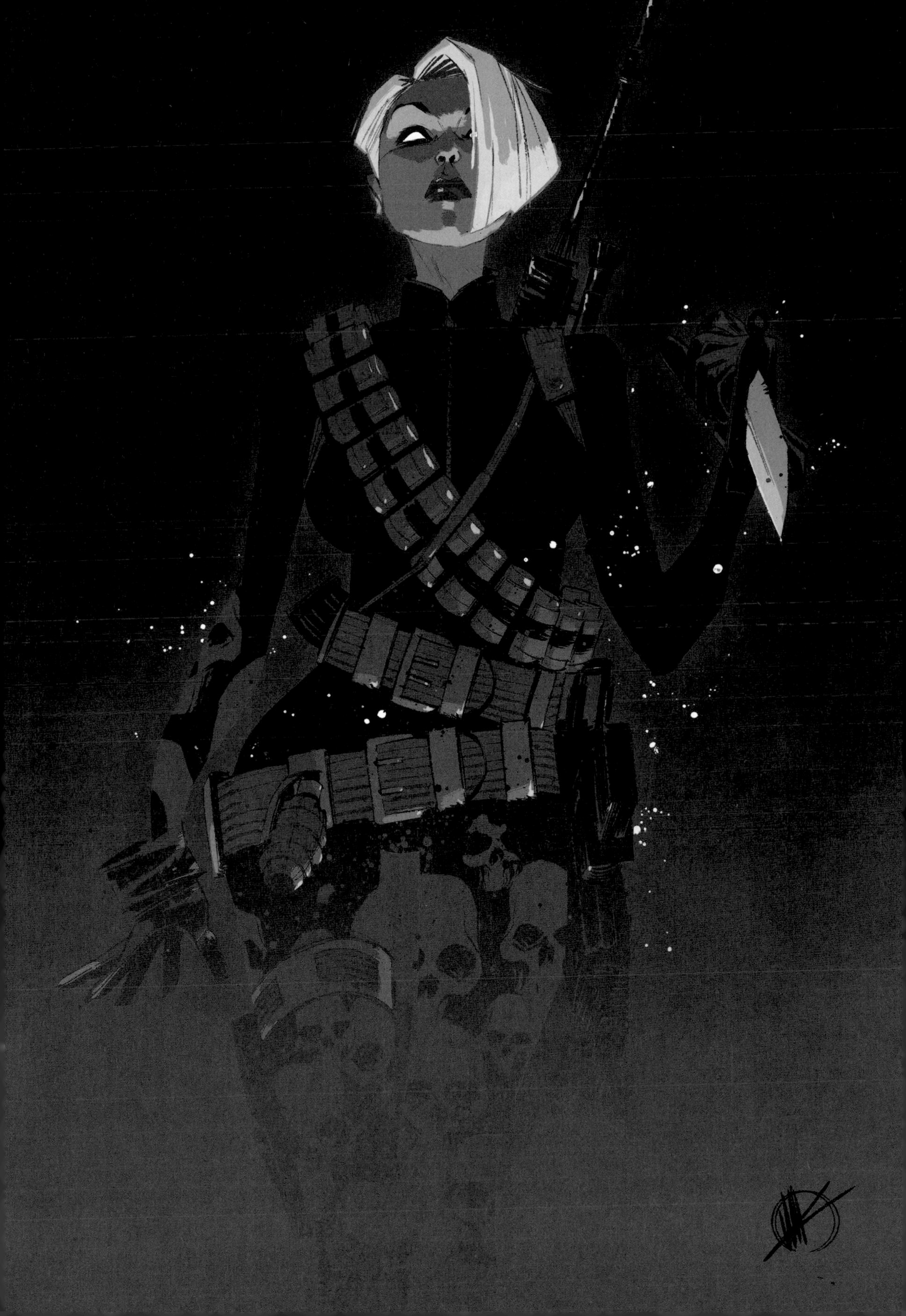

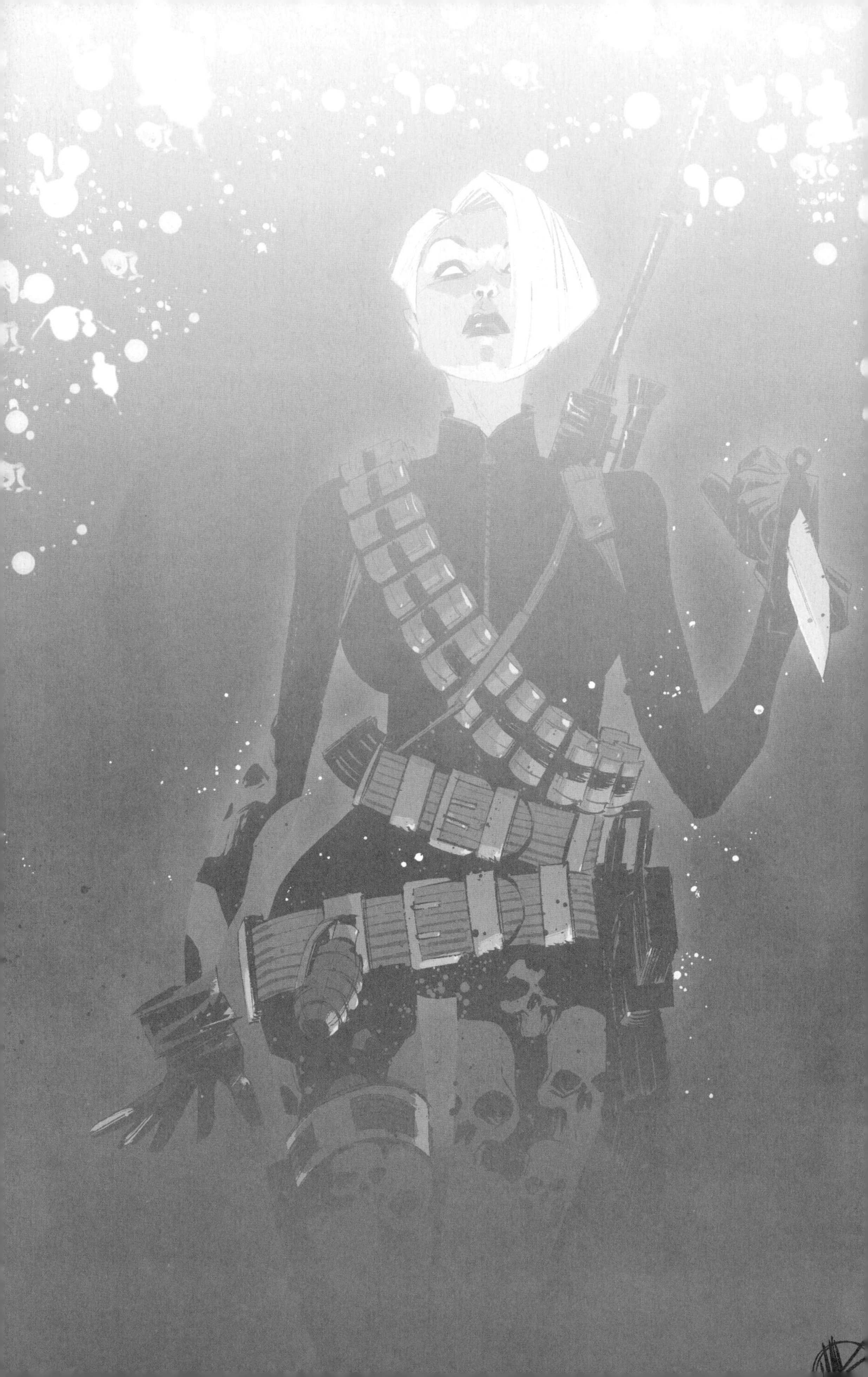

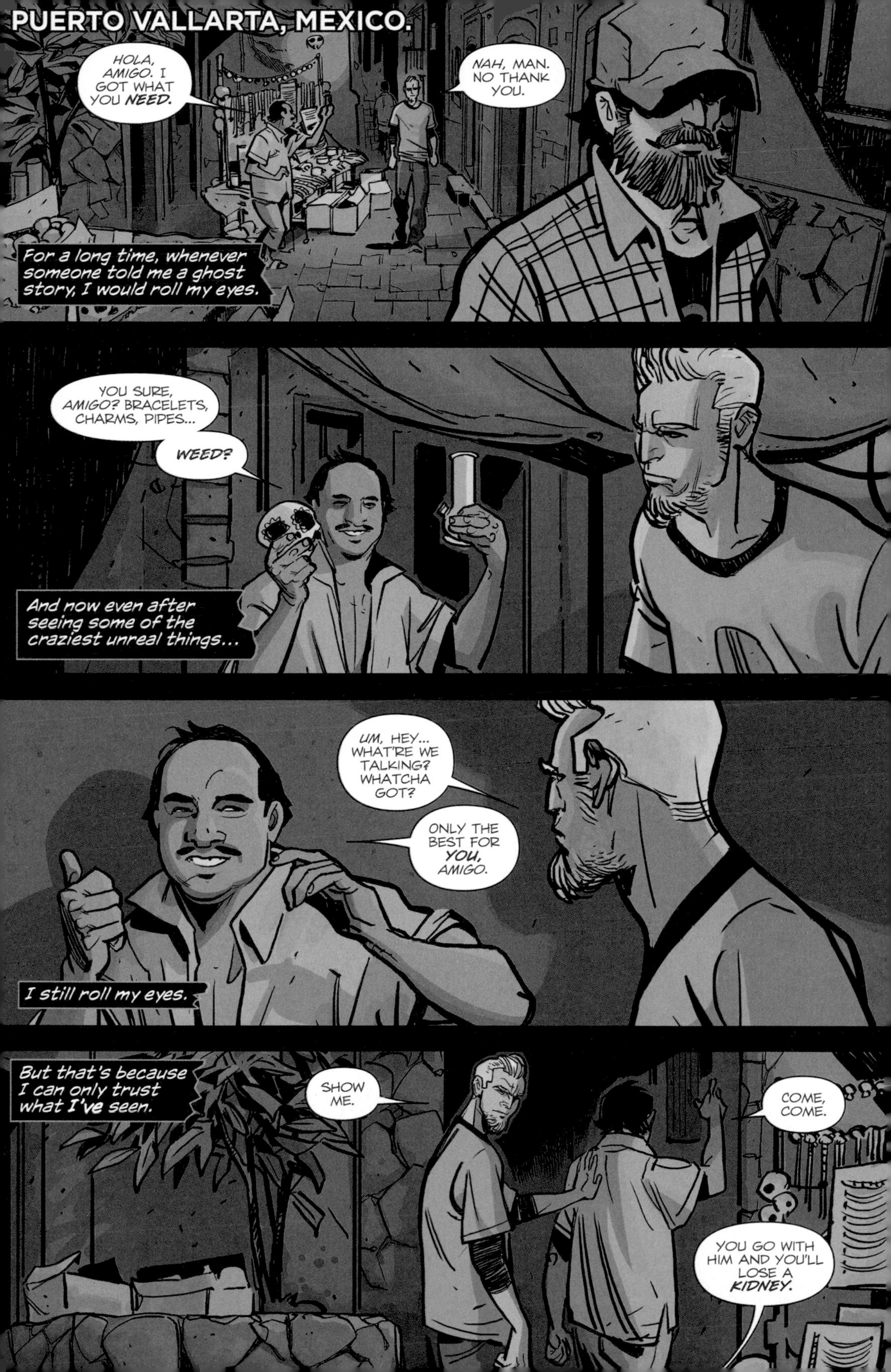
PUERTO VALLARTA, MEXICO.
HOLA, AMIGO. I GOT WHAT YOU NEED.
NAH, MAN. NO THANK YOU.
For a long time, whenever someone told me a ghost story, I would roll my eyes.
YOU SURE, AMIGO? BRACELETS, CHARMS, PIPES...
WEED?
And now even after seeing some of the craziest unreal things...
UM, HEY... WHAT'RE WE TALKING? WHATCHA GOT?
ONLY THE BEST FOR YOU, AMIGO.
I still roll my eyes.
But that's because I can only trust what I've seen.
SHOW ME.
COME, COME.
YOU GO WITH HIM AND YOU'LL LOSE A KIDNEY.

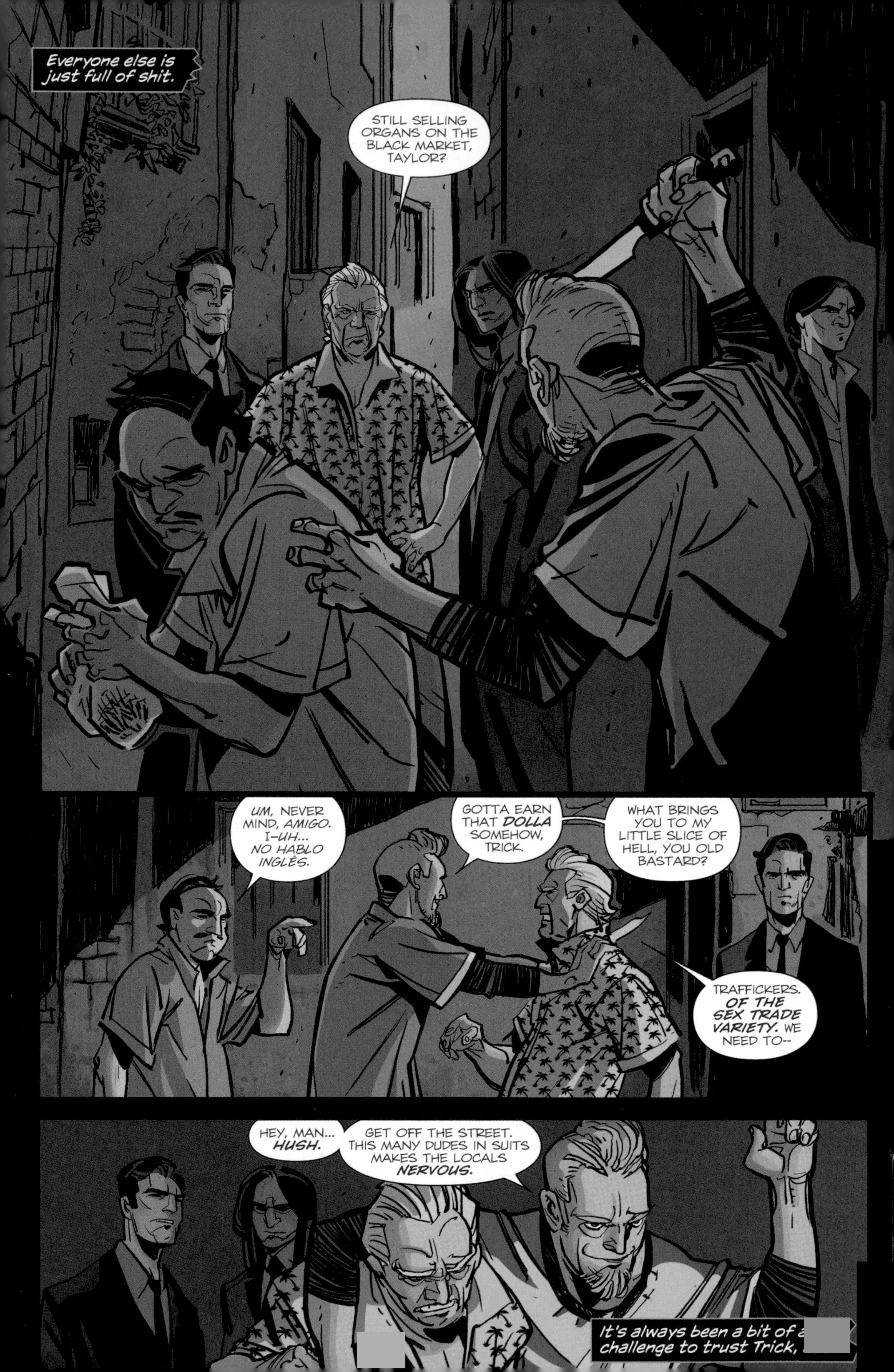
Everyone else is just full of shit.
STILL SELLING ORGANS ON THE BLACK MARKET, TAYLOR?
UM, NEVER MIND, AMIGO. I-UH... NO HABLO INGLÉS.
GOTTA EARN THAT DOLLA SOMEHOW, TRICK.
WHAT BRINGS YOU TO MY LITTLE SLICE OF HELL, YOU OLD BASTARD?
TRAFFICKERS. OF THE SEX TRADE VARIETY. WE NEED TO--
HEY, MAN... HUSH.
GET OFF THE STREET. THIS MANY DUDES IN SUITS MAKES THE LOCALS NERVOUS.
It's always been a bit of a
challenge to trust Trick,

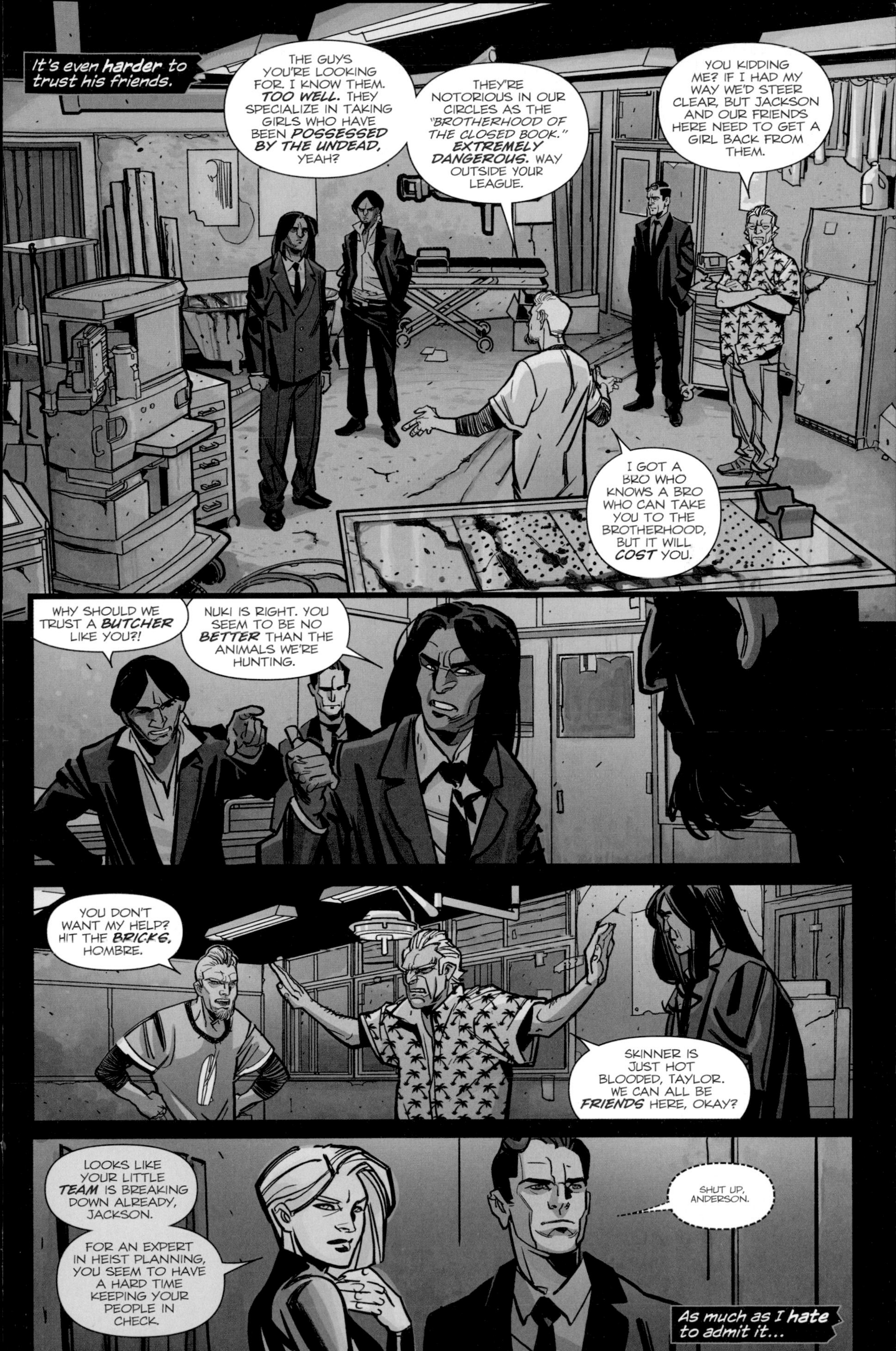
It's even harder to trust his friends.
THE GUYS YOU'RE LOOKING FOR. I KNOW THEM. TOO WELL. THEY SPECIALIZE IN TAKING GIRLS WHO HAVE BEEN POSSESSED BY THE UNDEAD, YEAH?
THEY'RE NOTORIOUS IN OUR CIRCLES AS THE "BROTHERHOOD OF THE CLOSED BOOK." EXTREMELY DANGEROUS. WAY OUTSIDE YOUR LEAGUE.
YOU KIDDING ME? IF I HAD MY WAY WE'D STEER CLEAR, BUT JACKSON AND OUR FRIENDS HERE NEED TO GET A GIRL BACK FROM THEM.
I GOT A BRO WHO KNOWS A BRO WHO CAN TAKE YOU TO THE BROTHERHOOD, BUT IT WILL COST YOU.
WHY SHOULD WE TRUST A BUTCHER LIKE YOU?!
NUKI IS RIGHT. YOU SEEM TO BE NO BETTER THAN THE ANIMALS WE'RE HUNTING.
YOU DON'T WANT MY HELP? HIT THE BRICKS, HOMBRE.
SKINNER IS JUST HOT BLOODED, TAYLOR. WE CAN ALL BE FRIENDS HERE, OKAY?
LOOKS LIKE YOUR LITTLE TEAM IS BREAKING DOWN ALREADY, JACKSON.
FOR AN EXPERT IN HEIST PLANNING, YOU SEEM TO HAVE A HARD TIME KEEPING YOUR PEOPLE IN CHECK.
SHUT UP, ANDERSON.
As much as I hate to admit it...

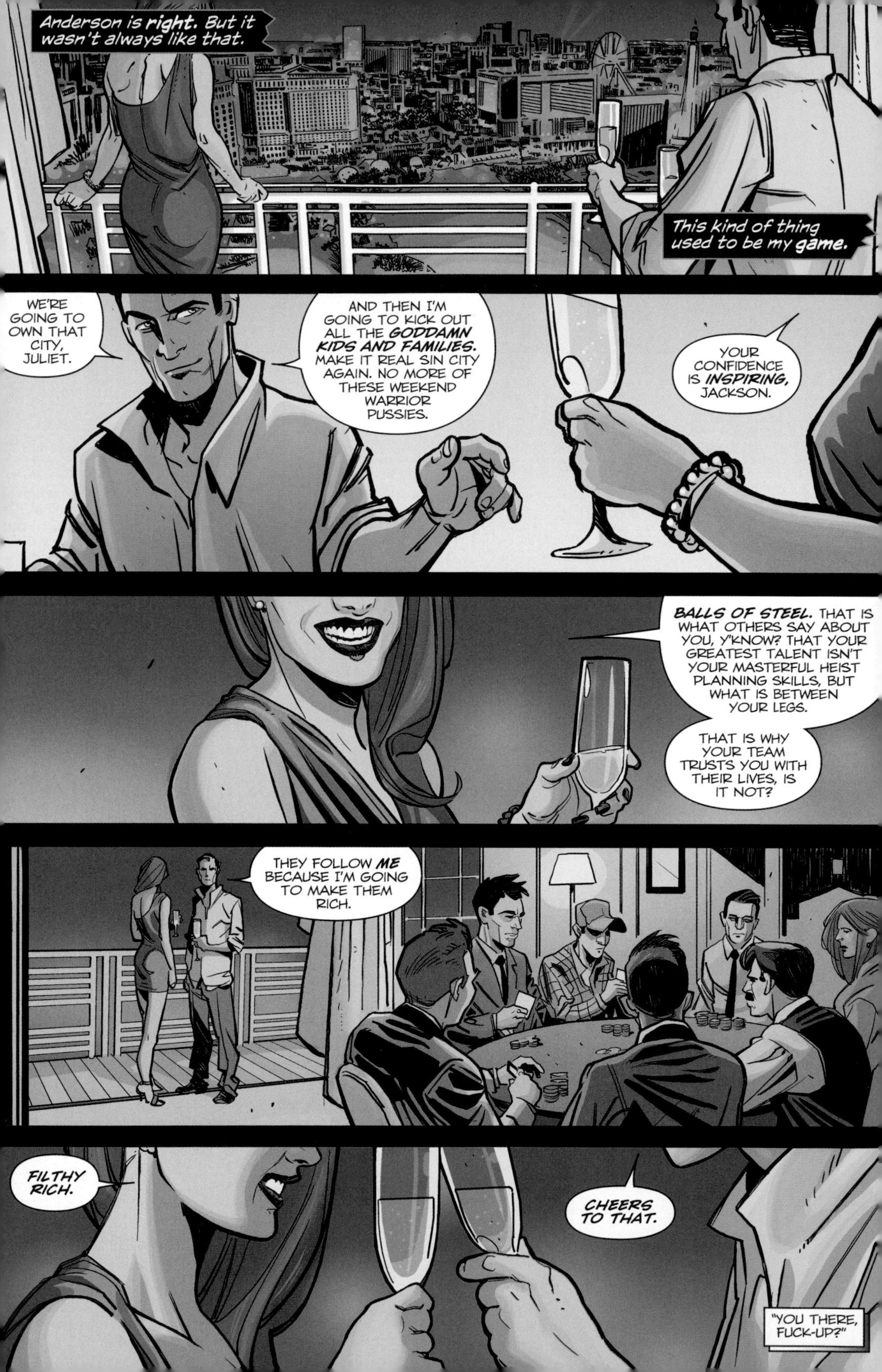
Anderson is **right.** But it wasn't always like that.
This kind of thing used to be my **game.**
WE'RE GOING TO OWN THAT CITY, JULIET.
AND THEN I'M GOING TO KICK OUT ALL THE ***GODDAMN KIDS AND FAMILIES.*** MAKE IT REAL SIN CITY AGAIN. NO MORE OF THESE WEEKEND WARRIOR PUSSIES.
YOUR CONFIDENCE IS ***INSPIRING,*** JACKSON.
BALLS OF STEEL. THAT IS WHAT OTHERS SAY ABOUT YOU, Y'KNOW? THAT YOUR GREATEST TALENT ISN'T YOUR MASTERFUL HEIST PLANNING SKILLS, BUT WHAT IS BETWEEN YOUR LEGS.
THAT IS WHY YOUR TEAM TRUSTS YOU WITH THEIR LIVES, IS IT NOT?
THEY FOLLOW ***ME*** BECAUSE I'M GOING TO MAKE THEM RICH.
FILTHY RICH.
CHEERS TO THAT.
"YOU THERE, FUCK-UP?"

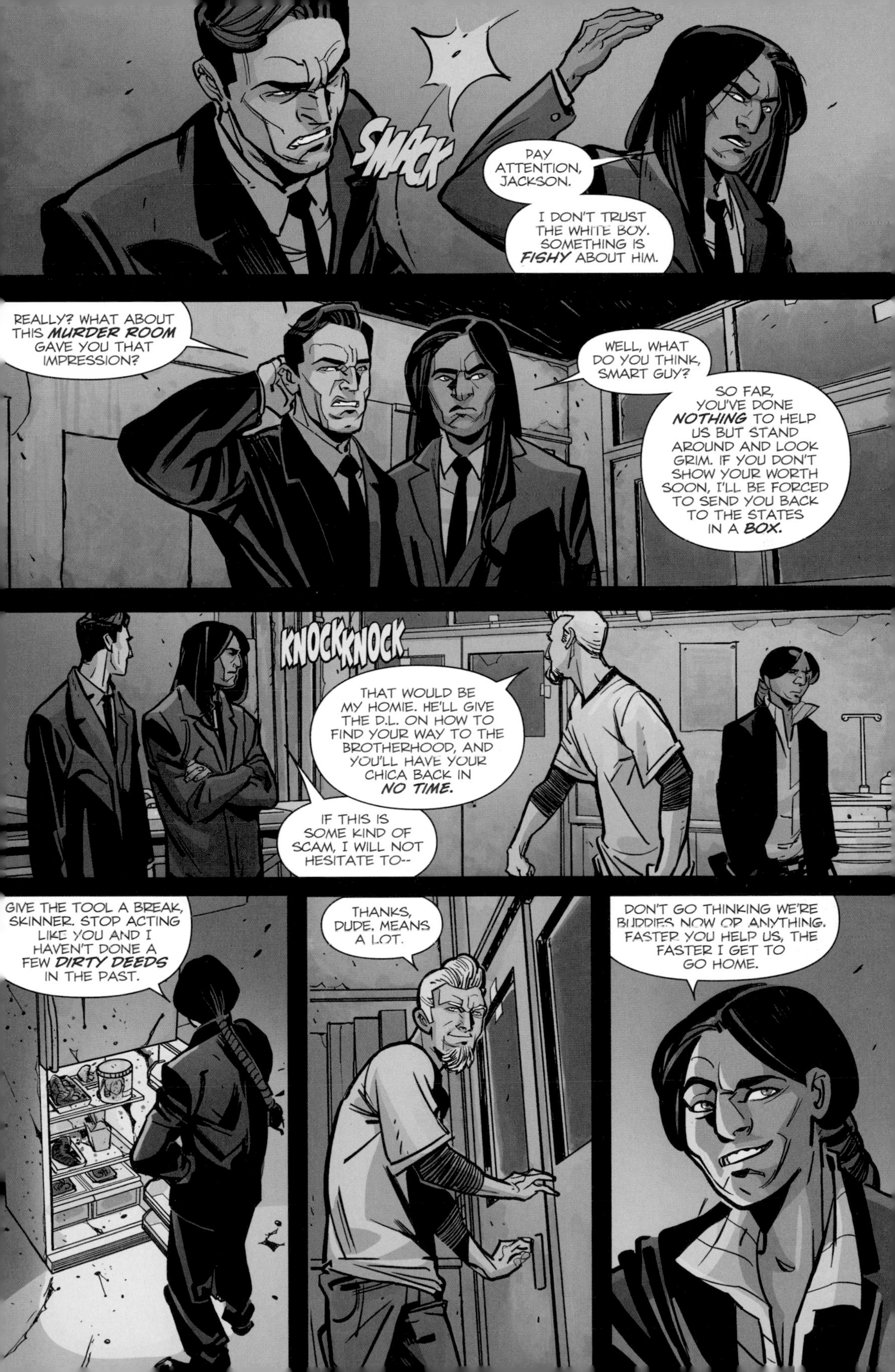
SMACK
PAY ATTENTION, JACKSON.
I DON'T TRUST THE WHITE BOY. SOMETHING IS FISHY ABOUT HIM.
REALLY? WHAT ABOUT THIS MURDER ROOM GAVE YOU THAT IMPRESSION?
WELL, WHAT DO YOU THINK, SMART GUY?
SO FAR, YOU'VE DONE NOTHING TO HELP US BUT STAND AROUND AND LOOK GRIM. IF YOU DON'T SHOW YOUR WORTH SOON, I'LL BE FORCED TO SEND YOU BACK TO THE STATES IN A BOX.
KNOCK KNOCK
THAT WOULD BE MY HOMIE. HE'LL GIVE THE D.L. ON HOW TO FIND YOUR WAY TO THE BROTHERHOOD, AND YOU'LL HAVE YOUR CHICA BACK IN NO TIME.
IF THIS IS SOME KIND OF SCAM, I WILL NOT HESITATE TO--
GIVE THE TOOL A BREAK, SKINNER. STOP ACTING LIKE YOU AND I HAVEN'T DONE A FEW DIRTY DEEDS IN THE PAST.
THANKS, DUDE. MEANS A LOT.
DON'T GO THINKING WE'RE BUDDIES NOW OR ANYTHING. FASTER YOU HELP US, THE FASTER I GET TO GO HOME.

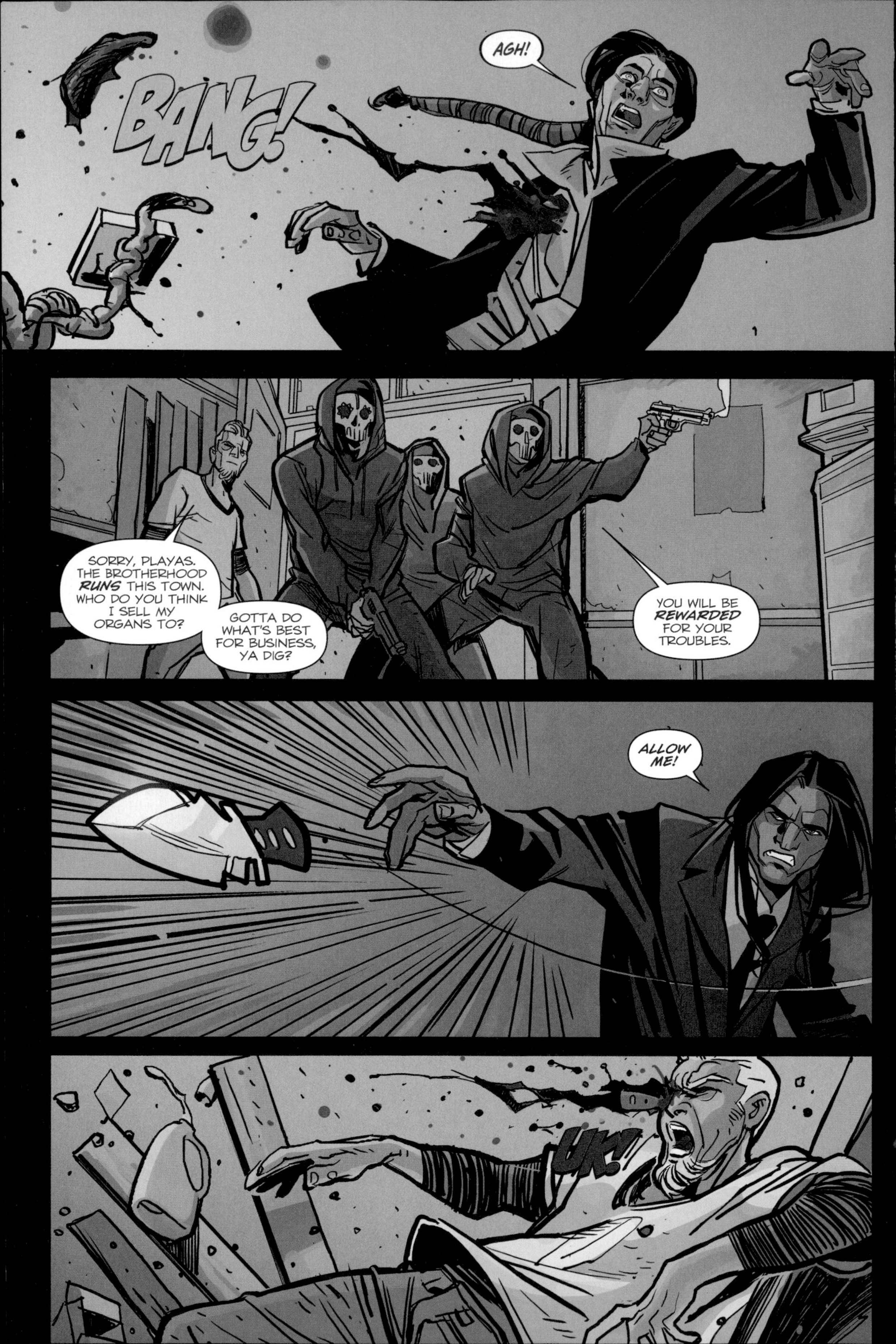
BANG!
AGH!
SORRY, PLAYAS. THE BROTHERHOOD RUNS THIS TOWN. WHO DO YOU THINK I SELL MY ORGANS TO?
GOTTA DO WHAT'S BEST FOR BUSINESS, YA DIG?
YOU WILL BE REWARDED FOR YOUR TROUBLES.
ALLOW ME!
UK!

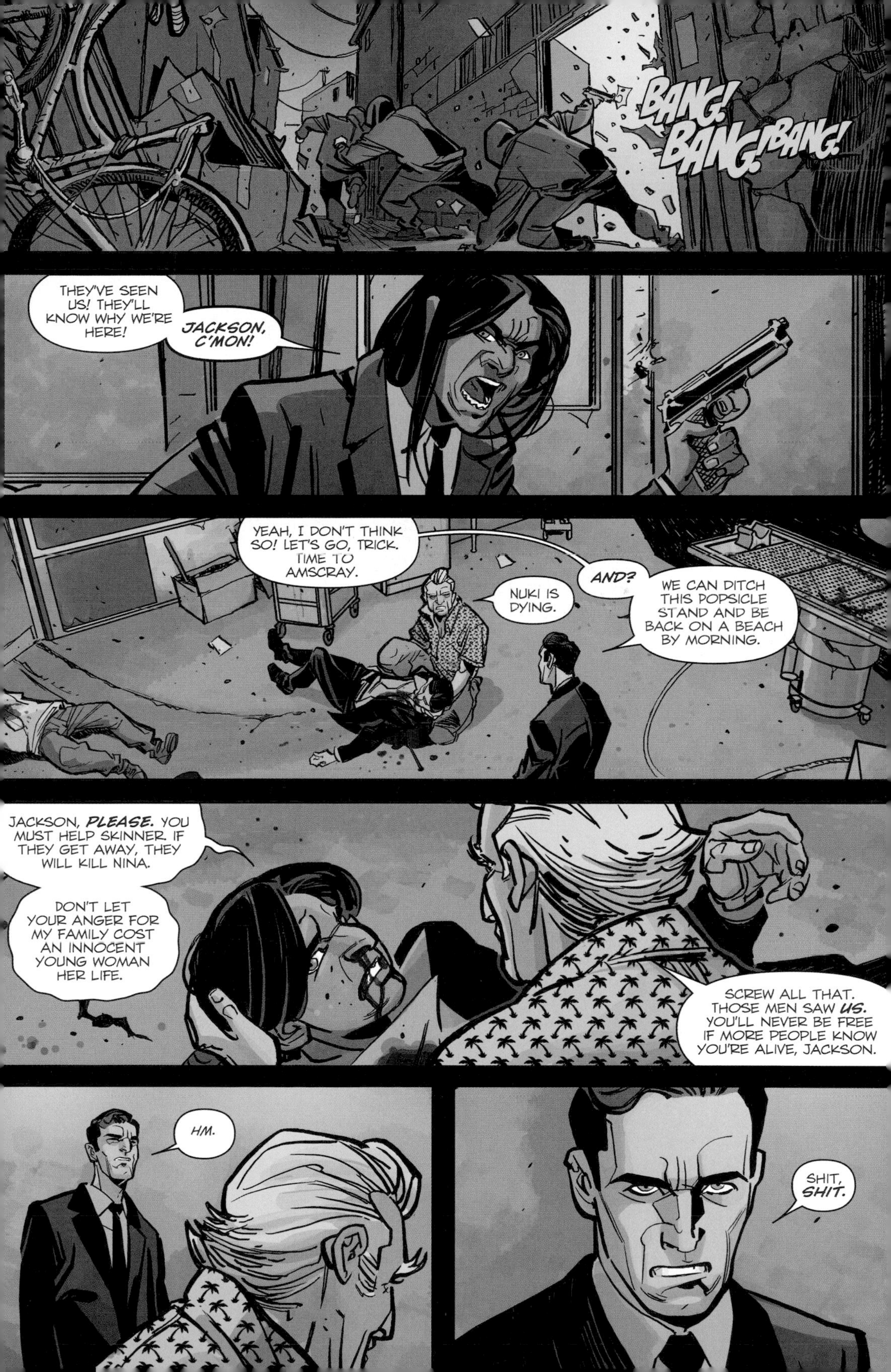
BANG! BANG! BANG!
THEY'VE SEEN US! THEY'LL KNOW WHY WE'RE HERE!
JACKSON, C'MON!
YEAH, I DON'T THINK SO! LET'S GO, TRICK. TIME TO AMSCRAY.
NUKI IS DYING.
AND?
WE CAN DITCH THIS POPSICLE STAND AND BE BACK ON A BEACH BY MORNING.
JACKSON, PLEASE. YOU MUST HELP SKINNER. IF THEY GET AWAY, THEY WILL KILL NINA.
DON'T LET YOUR ANGER FOR MY FAMILY COST AN INNOCENT YOUNG WOMAN HER LIFE.
SCREW ALL THAT. THOSE MEN SAW US. YOU'LL NEVER BE FREE IF MORE PEOPLE KNOW YOU'RE ALIVE, JACKSON.
HM.
SHIT, SHIT.

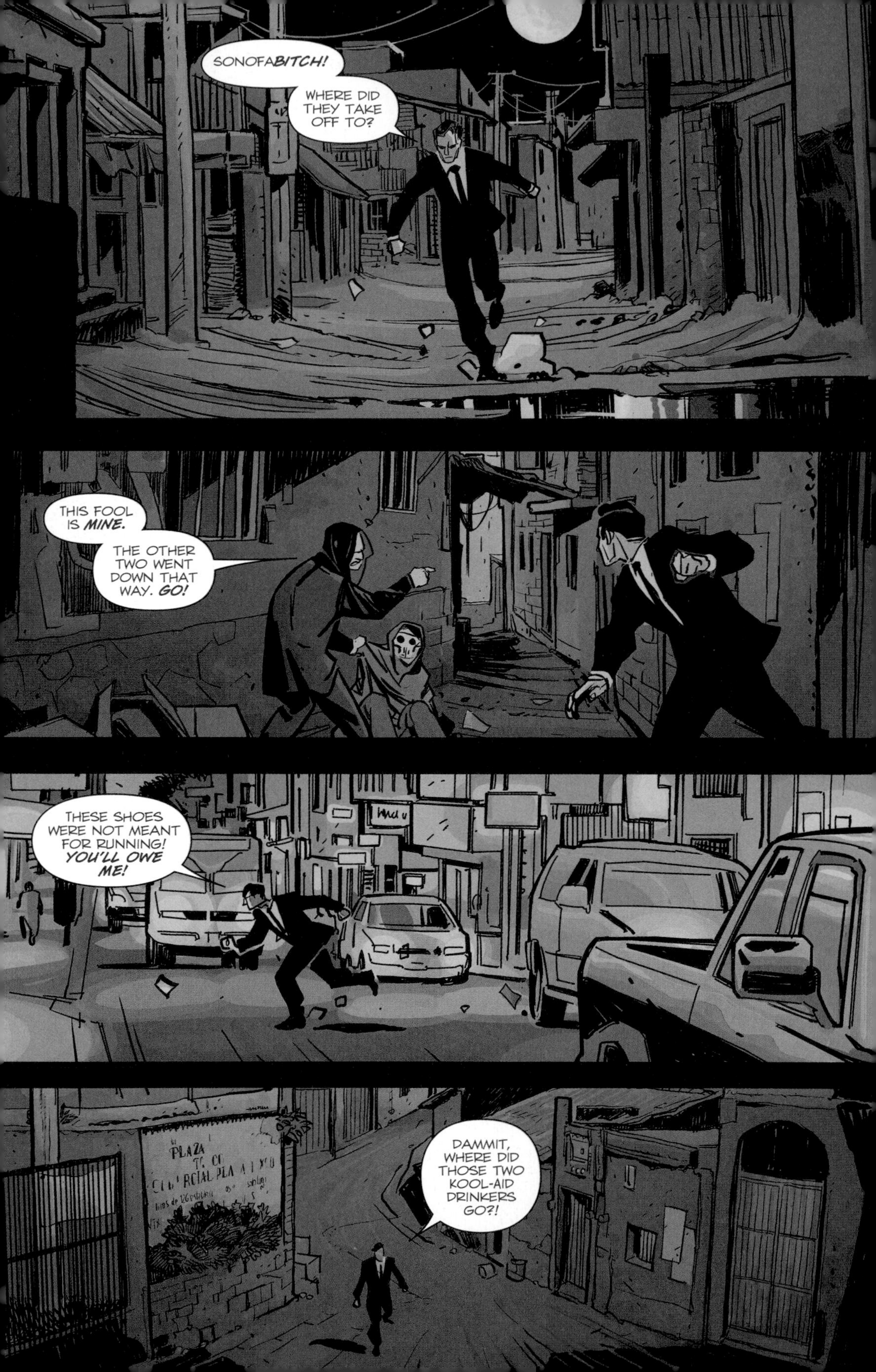
SONOFA**BITCH!**
WHERE DID THEY TAKE OFF TO?
THIS FOOL IS ***MINE.***
THE OTHER TWO WENT DOWN THAT WAY. ***GO!***
THESE SHOES WERE NOT MEANT FOR RUNNING! ***YOU'LL OWE ME!***
PLAZA
DAMMIT, WHERE DID THOSE TWO KOOL-AID DRINKERS GO?!

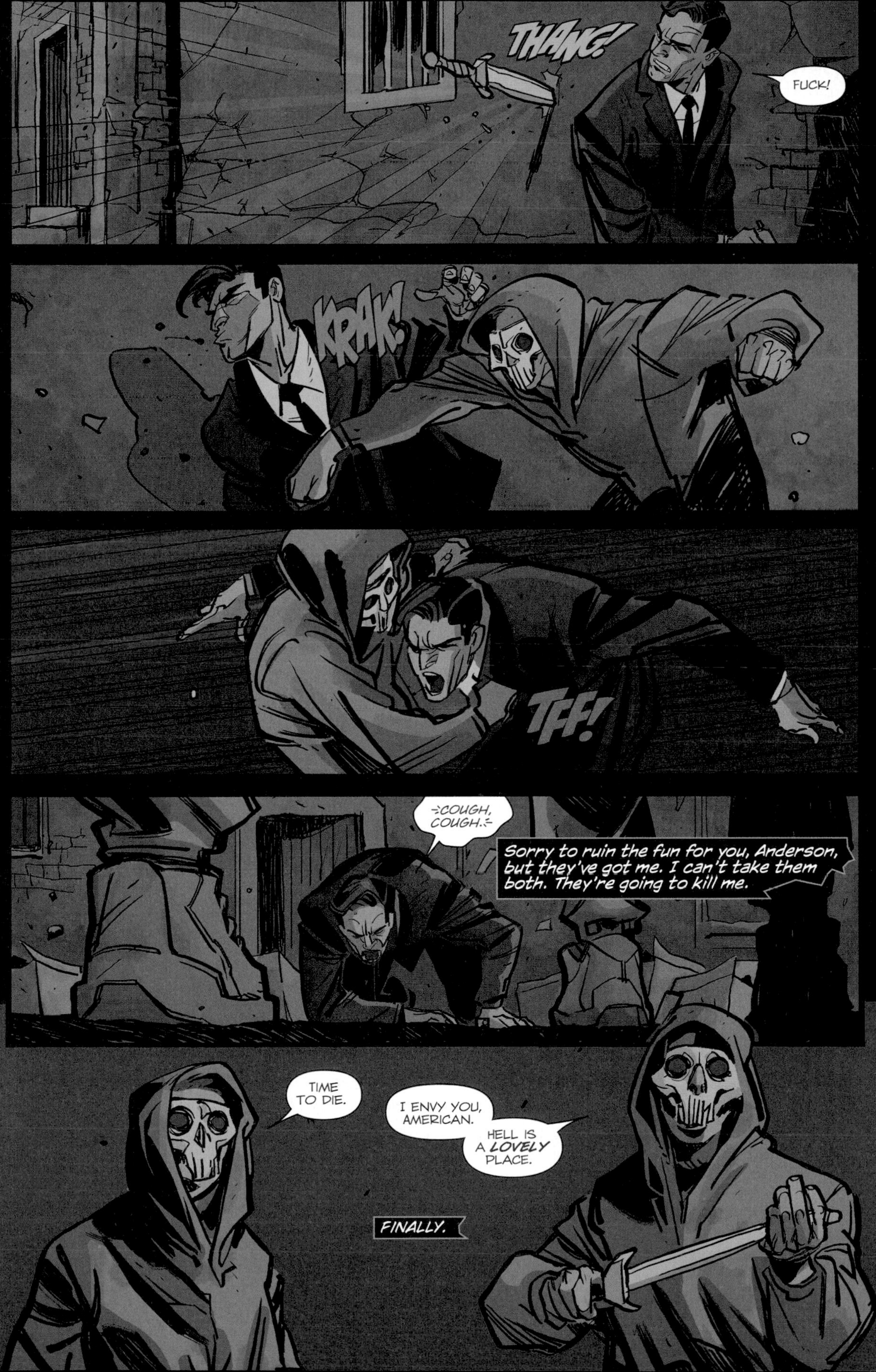
THANG!
FUCK!
KRAK!
TFF!
-COUGH, COUGH.-
Sorry to ruin the fun for you, Anderson, but they've got me. I can't take them both. They're going to kill me.
TIME TO DIE.
I ENVY YOU, AMERICAN.
HELL IS A LOVELY PLACE.
FINALLY.

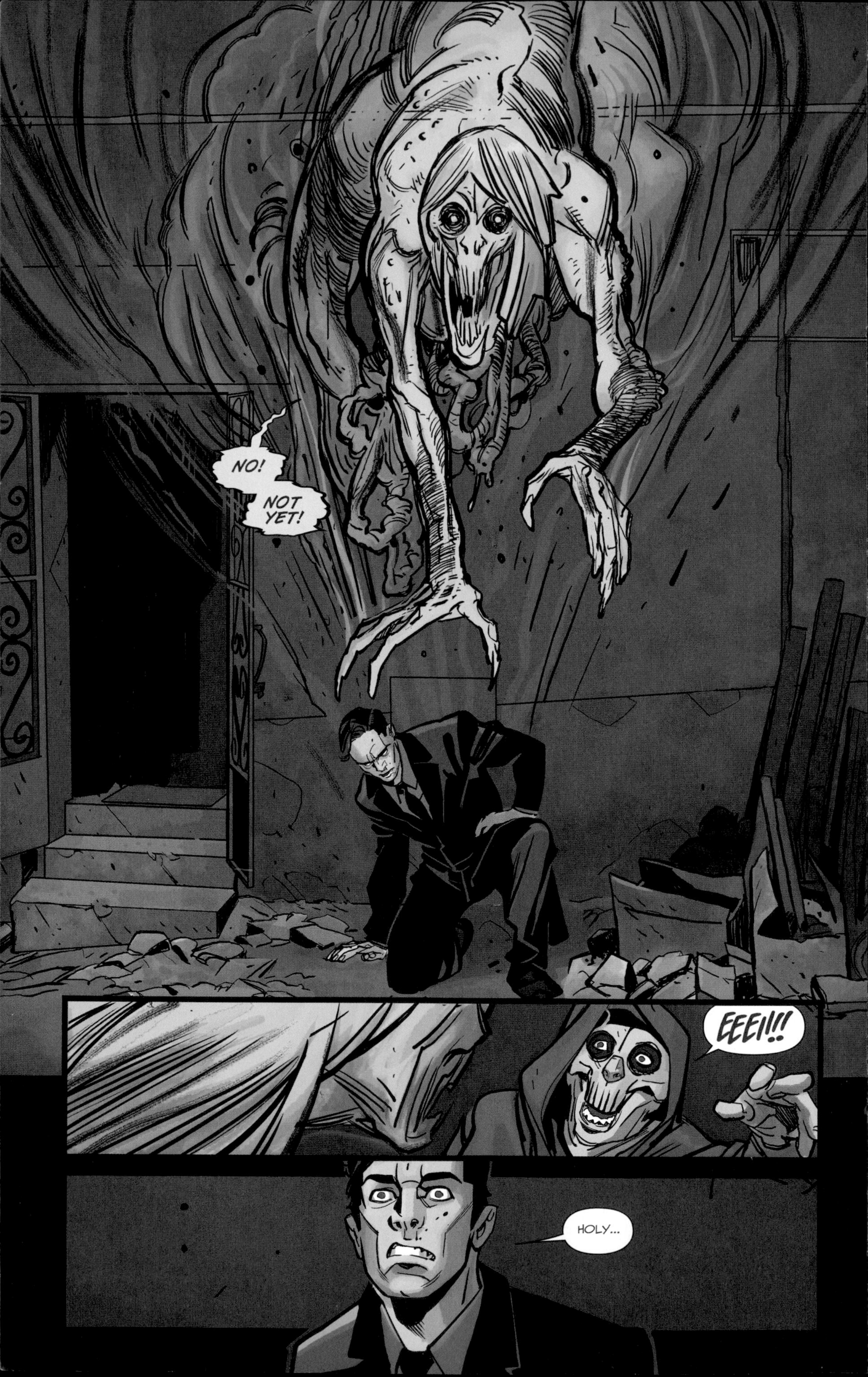
NO!
NOT YET!
EEEI!!!
HOLY...

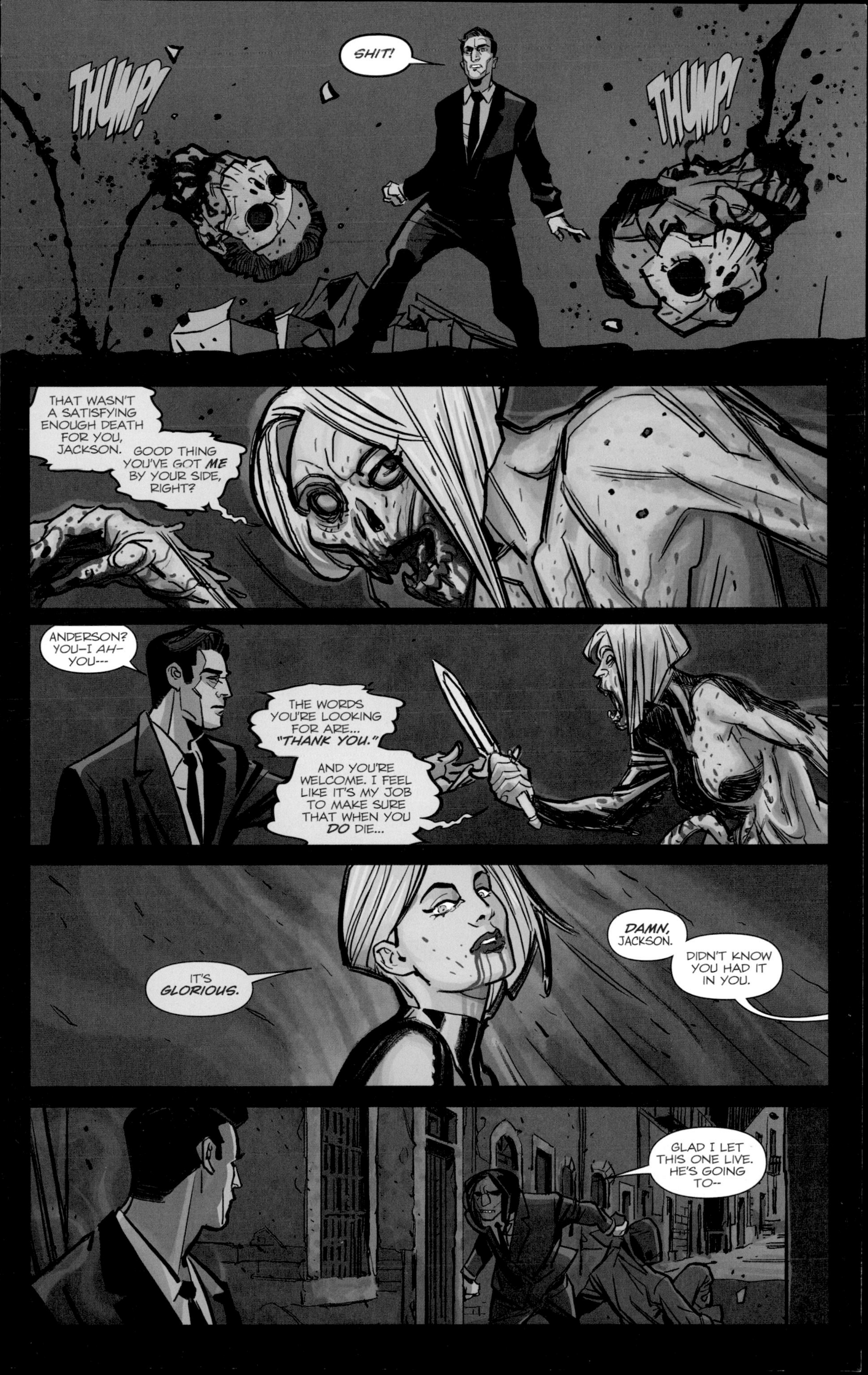
SHIT!
THUMP!
THUMP!
THAT WASN'T A SATISFYING ENOUGH DEATH FOR YOU, JACKSON.
GOOD THING YOU'VE GOT ME BY YOUR SIDE, RIGHT?
ANDERSON? YOU--I AH-YOU---
THE WORDS YOU'RE LOOKING FOR ARE... "THANK YOU."
AND YOU'RE WELCOME. I FEEL LIKE IT'S MY JOB TO MAKE SURE THAT WHEN YOU DO DIE...
IT'S GLORIOUS.
DAMN, JACKSON.
DIDN'T KNOW YOU HAD IT IN YOU.
GLAD I LET THIS ONE LIVE. HE'S GOING TO--

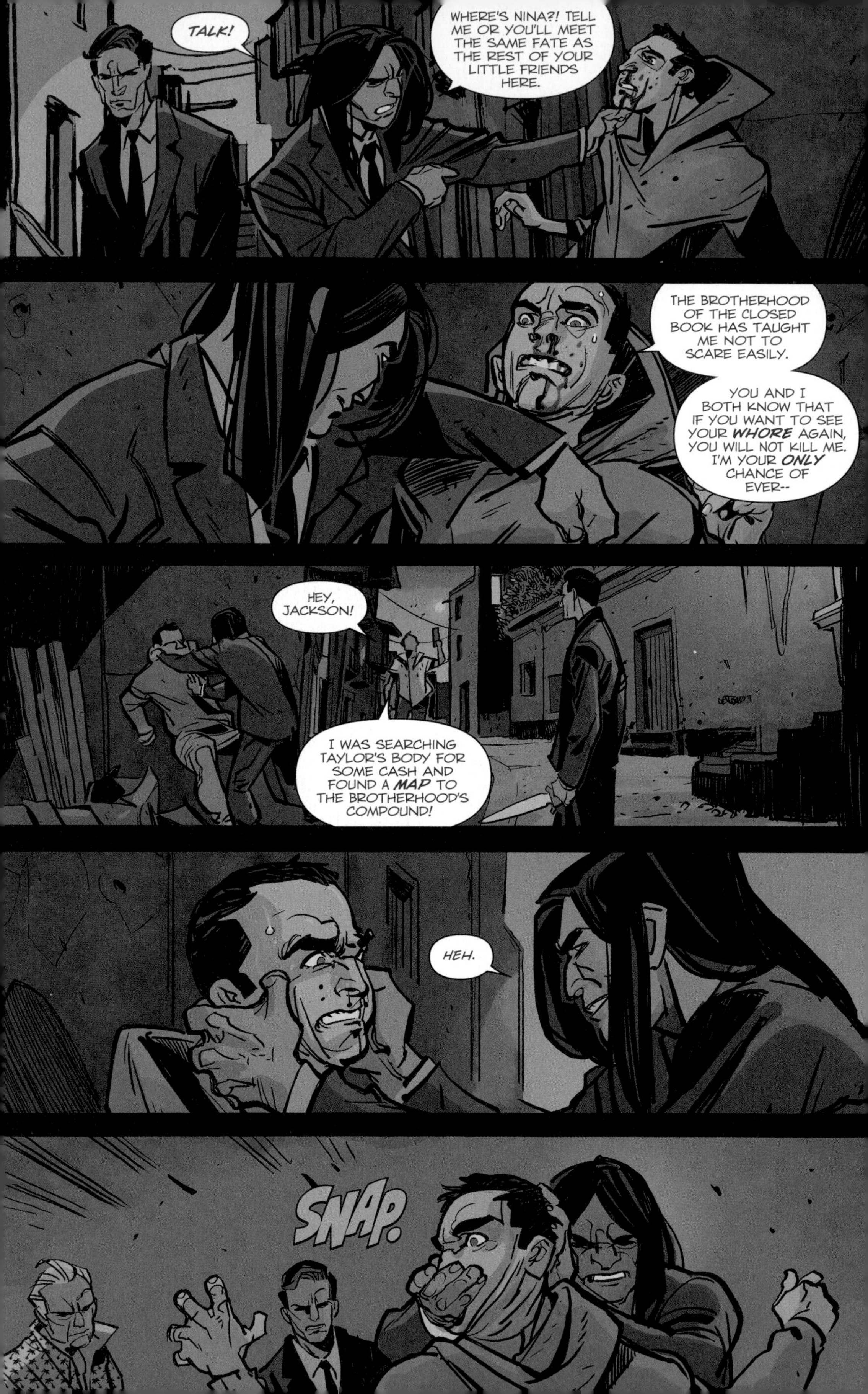
TALK!
WHERE'S NINA?! TELL ME OR YOU'LL MEET THE SAME FATE AS THE REST OF YOUR LITTLE FRIENDS HERE.
THE BROTHERHOOD OF THE CLOSED BOOK HAS TAUGHT ME NOT TO SCARE EASILY.
YOU AND I BOTH KNOW THAT IF YOU WANT TO SEE YOUR WHORE AGAIN, YOU WILL NOT KILL ME. I'M YOUR ONLY CHANCE OF EVER--
HEY, JACKSON!
I WAS SEARCHING TAYLOR'S BODY FOR SOME CASH AND FOUND A MAP TO THE BROTHERHOOD'S COMPOUND!
HEH.
SNAP.

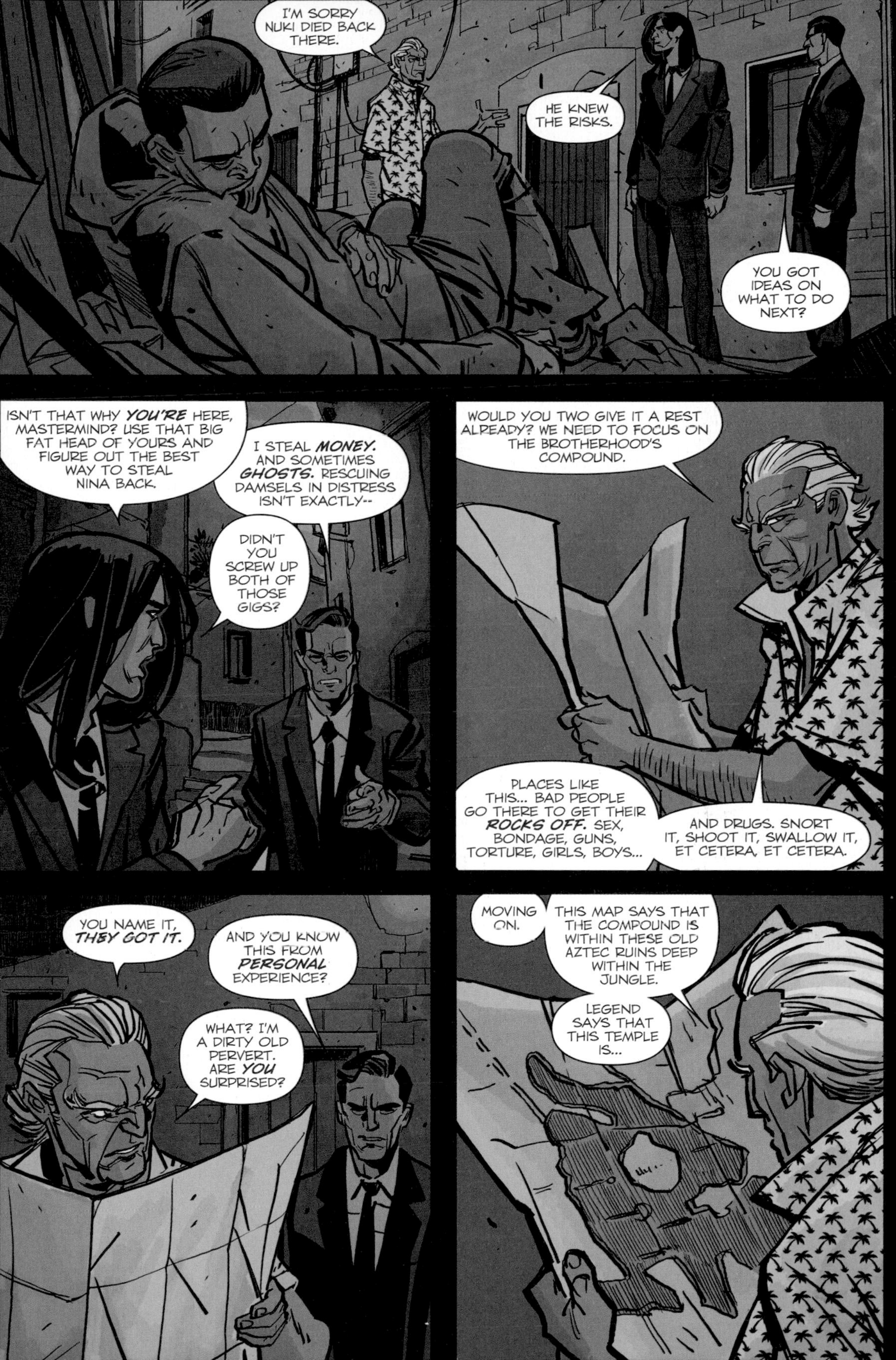

I'M SORRY NUKI DIED BACK THERE.
HE KNEW THE RISKS.
YOU GOT IDEAS ON WHAT TO DO NEXT?
ISN'T THAT WHY *YOU'RE* HERE, MASTERMIND? USE THAT BIG FAT HEAD OF YOURS AND FIGURE OUT THE BEST WAY TO STEAL NINA BACK.
I STEAL ***MONEY.*** AND SOMETIMES ***GHOSTS.*** RESCUING DAMSELS IN DISTRESS ISN'T EXACTLY--
DIDN'T YOU SCREW UP BOTH OF THOSE GIGS?
WOULD YOU TWO GIVE IT A REST ALREADY? WE NEED TO FOCUS ON THE BROTHERHOOD'S COMPOUND.
PLACES LIKE THIS... BAD PEOPLE GO THERE TO GET THEIR ***ROCKS OFF.*** SEX, BONDAGE, GUNS, TORTURE, GIRLS, BOYS...
AND DRUGS. SNORT IT, SHOOT IT, SWALLOW IT, ET CETERA, ET CETERA.
YOU NAME IT, ***THEY GOT IT.***
AND YOU KNOW THIS FROM ***PERSONAL*** EXPERIENCE?
WHAT? I'M A DIRTY OLD PERVERT. ARE ***YOU*** SURPRISED?
MOVING ON.
THIS MAP SAYS THAT THE COMPOUND IS WITHIN THESE OLD AZTEC RUINS DEEP WITHIN THE JUNGLE.
LEGEND SAYS THAT THIS TEMPLE IS...

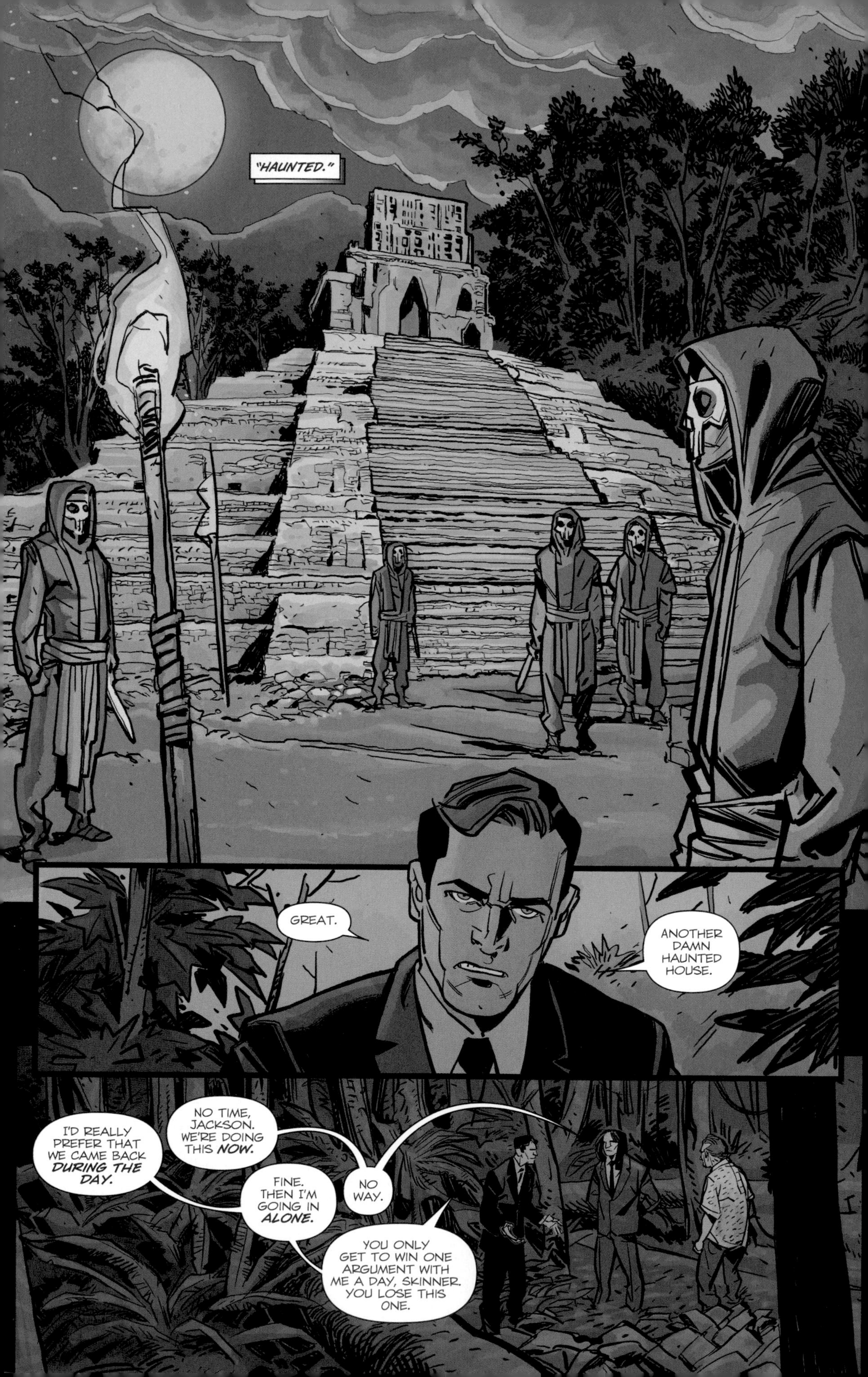
"HAUNTED."
GREAT.
ANOTHER DAMN HAUNTED HOUSE.
I'D REALLY PREFER THAT WE CAME BACK DURING THE DAY.
NO TIME, JACKSON. WE'RE DOING THIS NOW.
FINE. THEN I'M GOING IN ALONE.
NO WAY.
YOU ONLY GET TO WIN ONE ARGUMENT WITH ME A DAY, SKINNER. YOU LOSE THIS ONE.

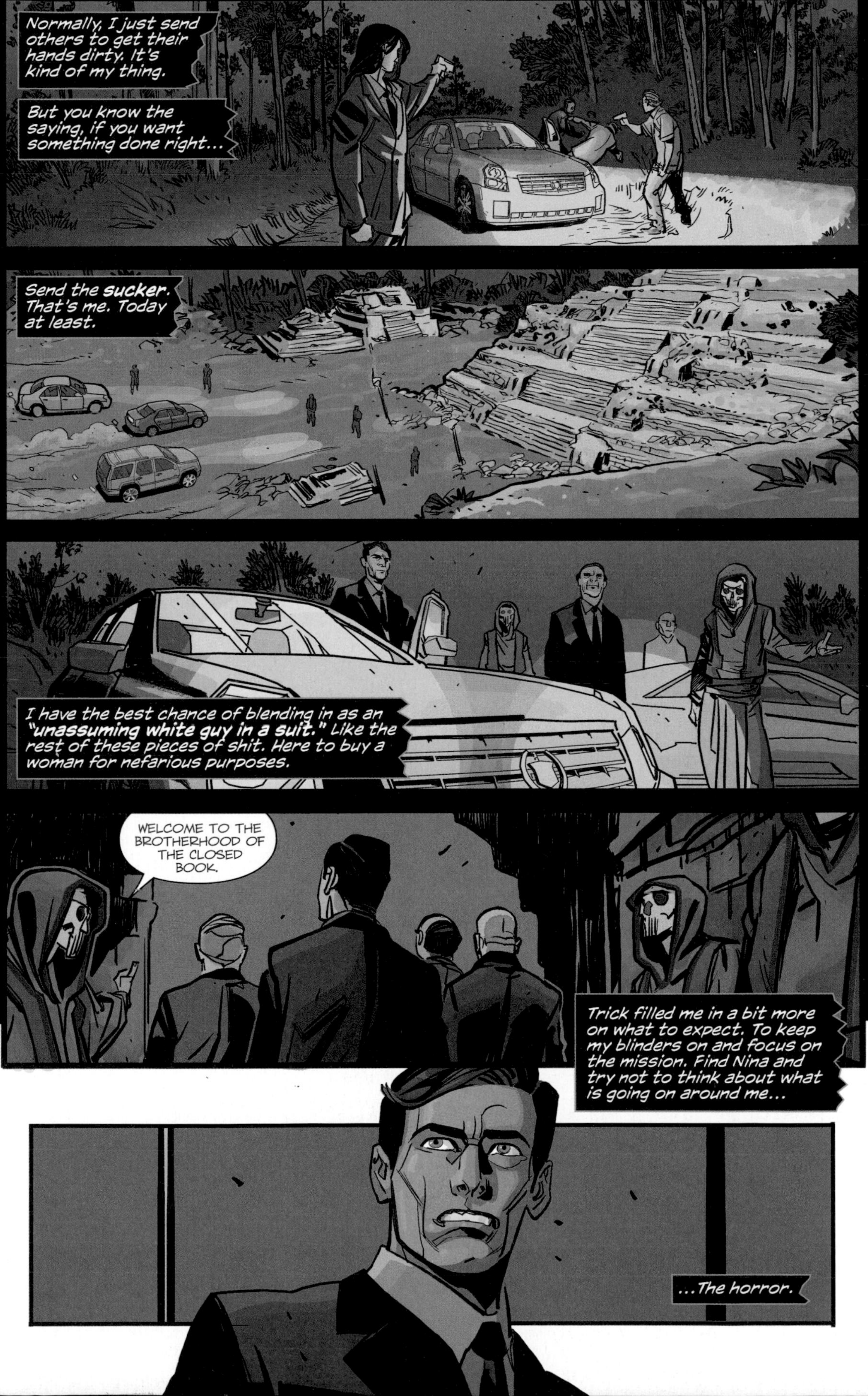
Normally, I just send others to get their hands dirty. It's kind of my thing.
But you know the saying, if you want something done right...
Send the **sucker**. That's me. Today at least.
I have the best chance of blending in as an **"unassuming white guy in a suit."** Like the rest of these pieces of shit. Here to buy a woman for nefarious purposes.
WELCOME TO THE BROTHERHOOD OF THE CLOSED BOOK.
Trick filled me in a bit more on what to expect. To keep my blinders on and focus on the mission. Find Nina and try not to think about what is going on around me...
...The horror.

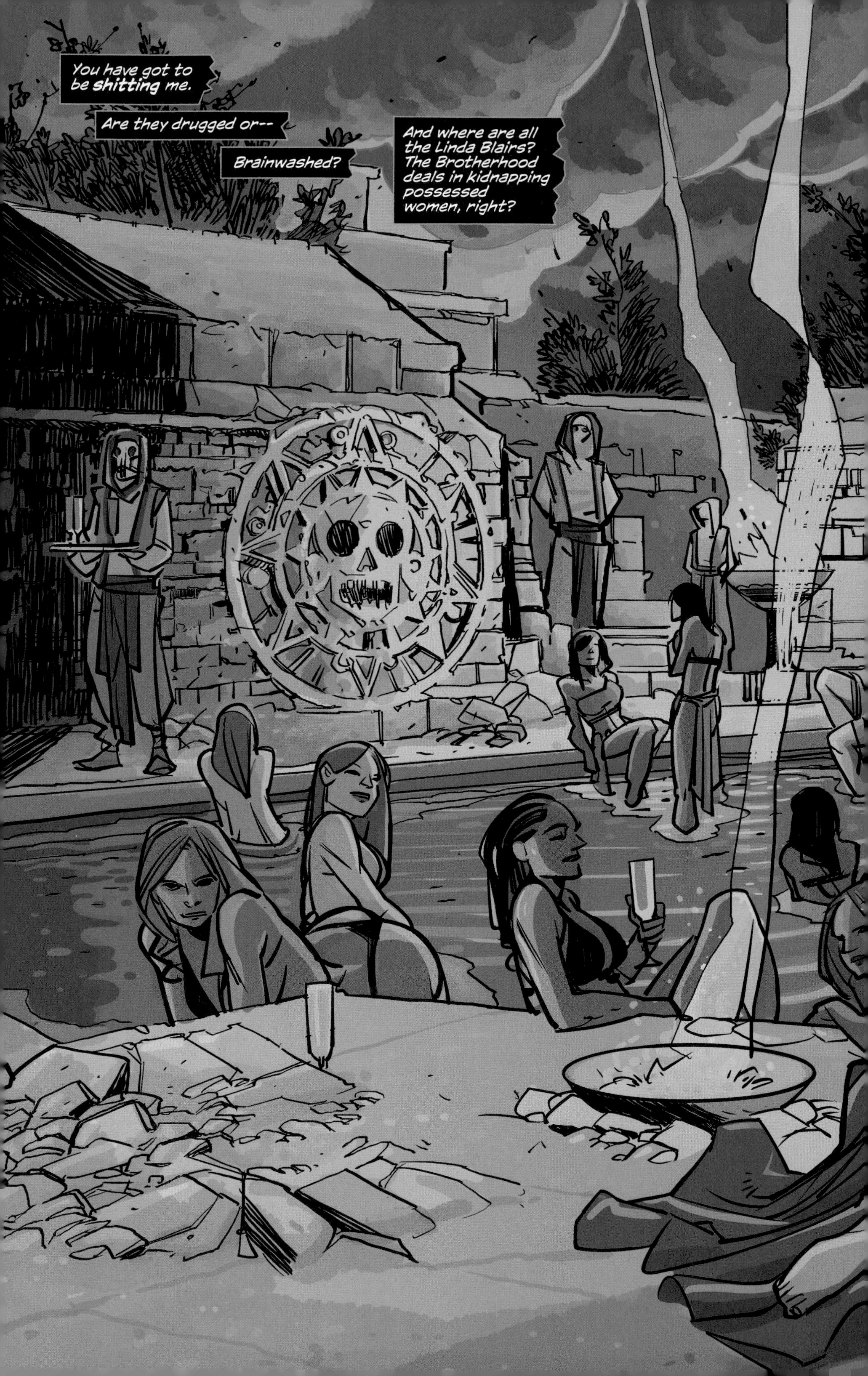
You have got to be **shitting** me.
Are they drugged or--
Brainwashed?
And where are all the Linda Blairs? The Brotherhood deals in kidnapping possessed women, right?

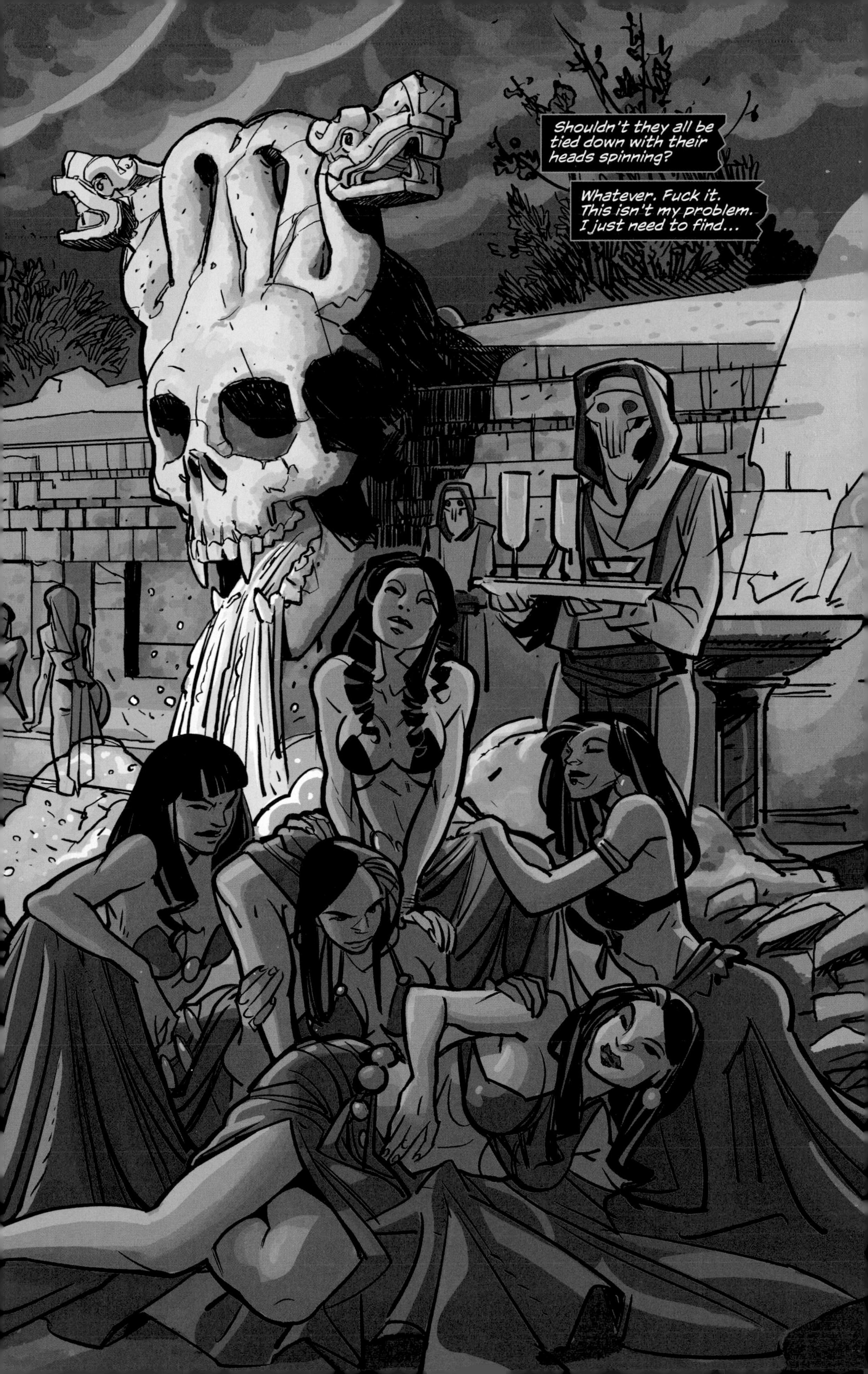
Shouldn't they all be tied down with their heads spinning?
Whatever. Fuck it. This isn't my problem. I just need to find...

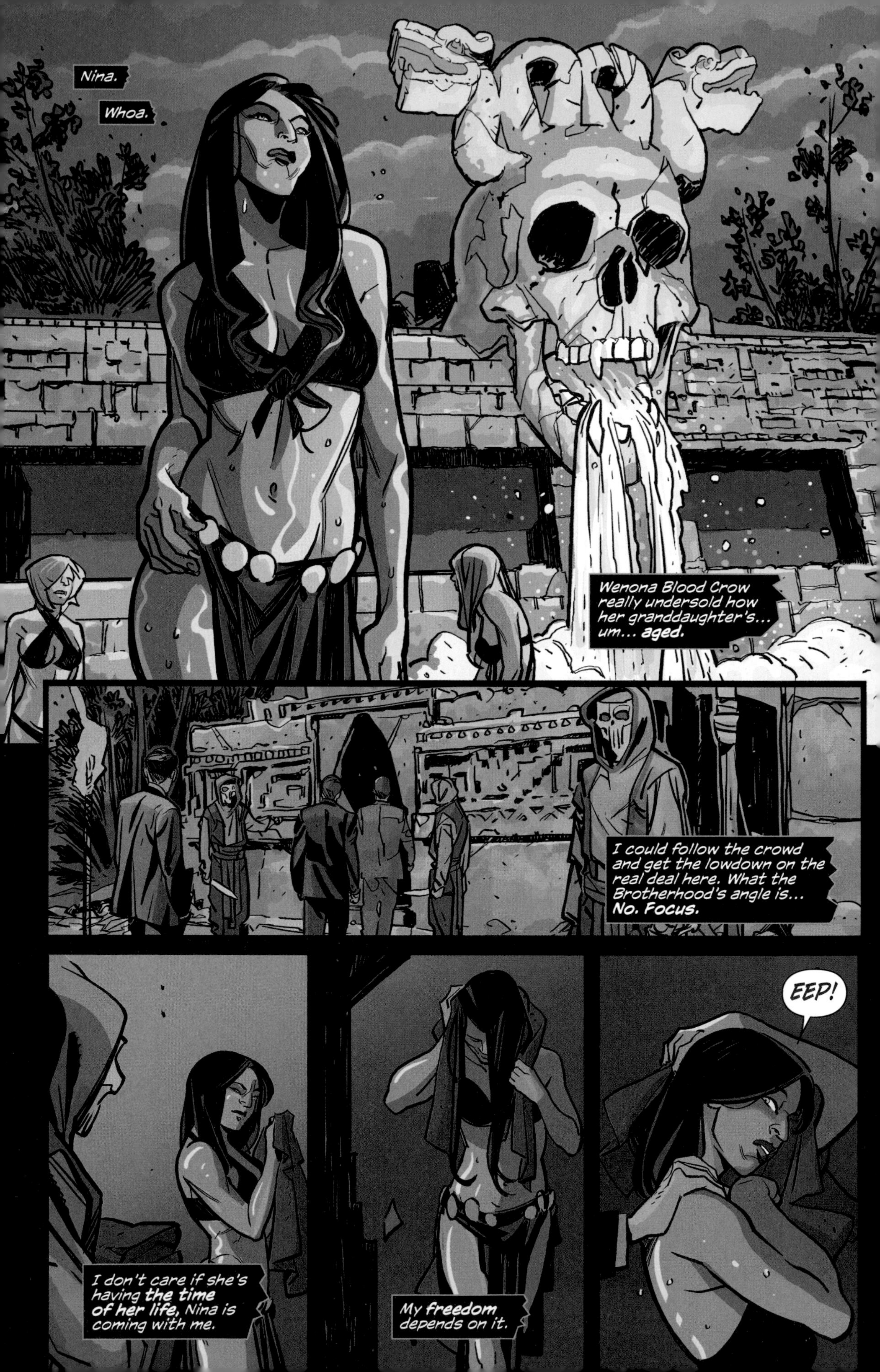
Nina.
Whoa.
Wenona Blood Crow really undersold how her granddaughter's... um... **aged.**
I could follow the crowd and get the lowdown on the real deal here. What the Brotherhood's angle is... **No. Focus.**
I don't care if she's having **the time of her life,** Nina is coming with me.
My **freedom** depends on it.
EEP!

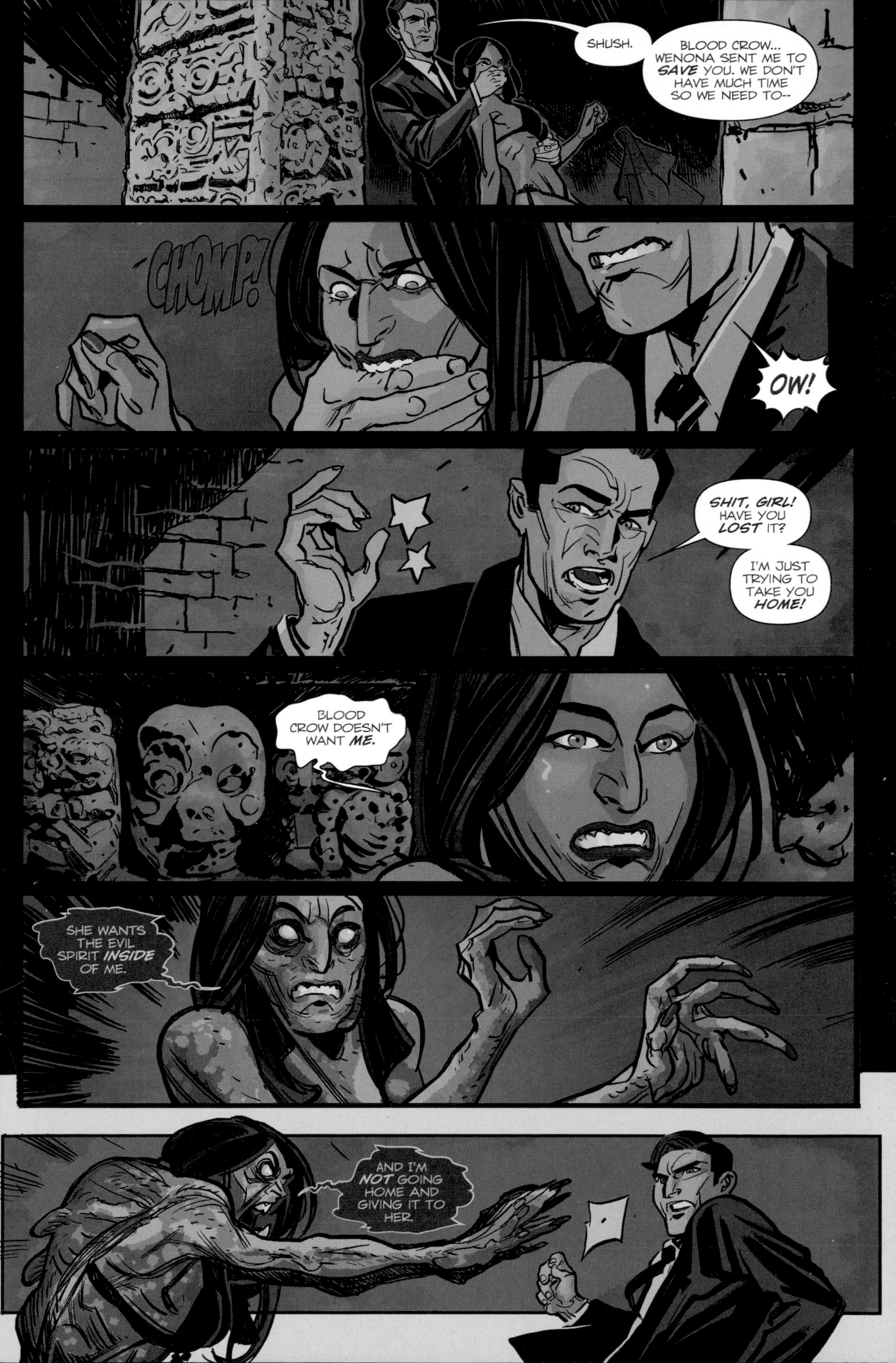
SHUSH.
BLOOD CROW... WENONA SENT ME TO SAVE YOU. WE DON'T HAVE MUCH TIME SO WE NEED TO--
CHOMP!
OW!
SHIT, GIRL! HAVE YOU LOST IT?
I'M JUST TRYING TO TAKE YOU HOME!
BLOOD CROW DOESN'T WANT ME.
SHE WANTS THE EVIL SPIRIT INSIDE OF ME.
AND I'M NOT GOING HOME AND GIVING IT TO HER.

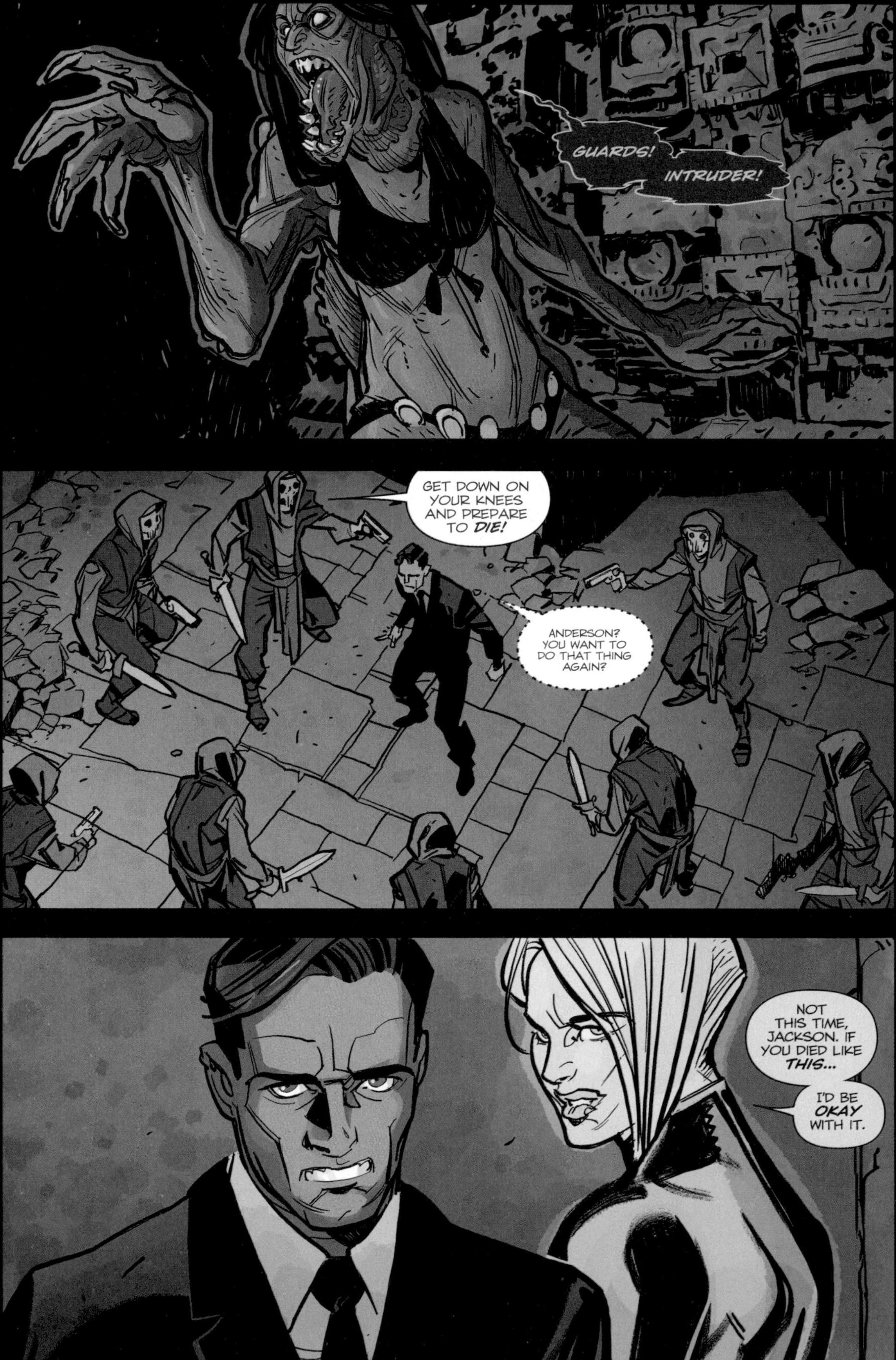
GUARDS!
INTRUDER!
GET DOWN ON YOUR KNEES AND PREPARE TO DIE!
ANDERSON? YOU WANT TO DO THAT THING AGAIN?
NOT THIS TIME, JACKSON. IF YOU DIED LIKE THIS...
I'D BE OKAY WITH IT.

CHAPTER THREE

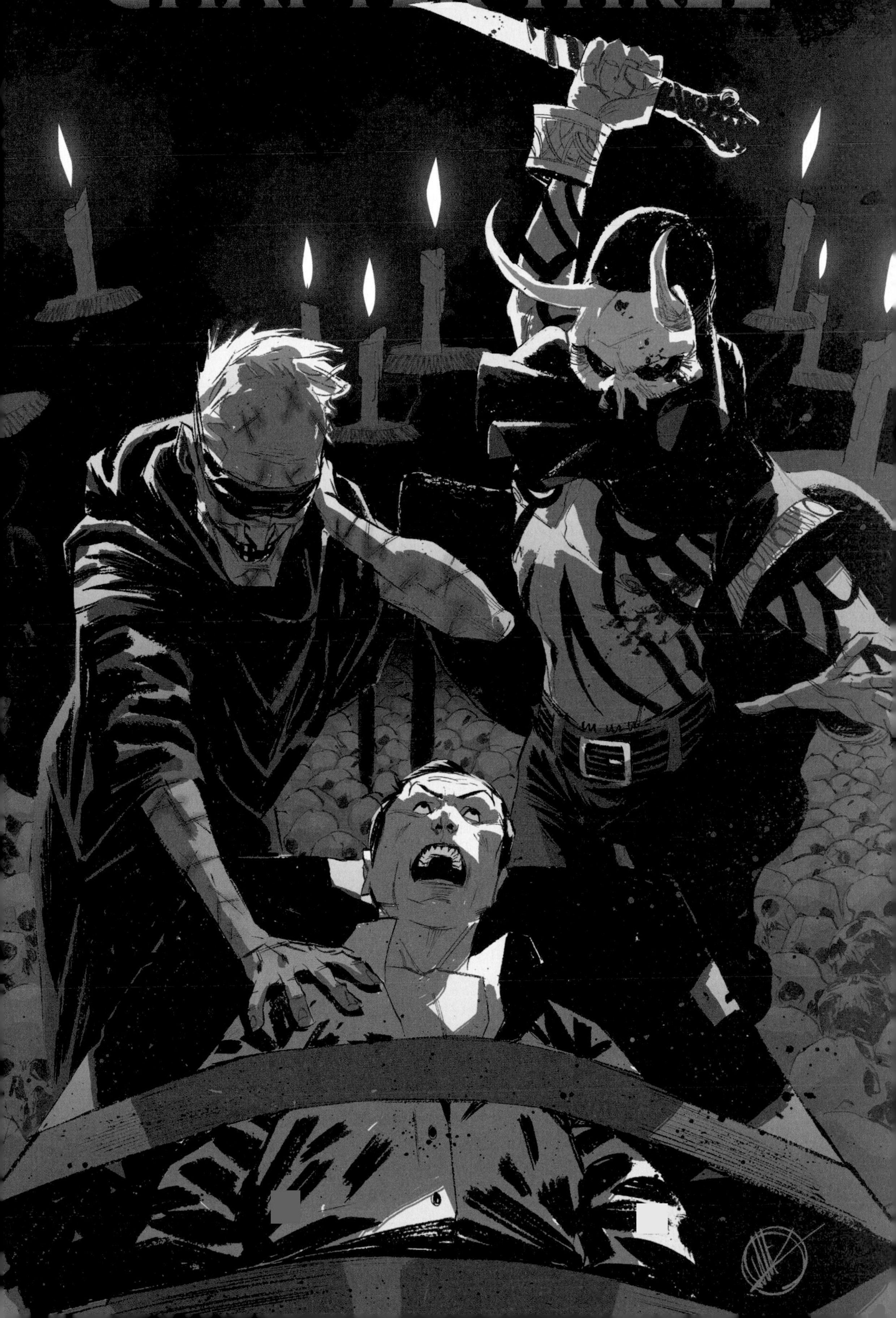

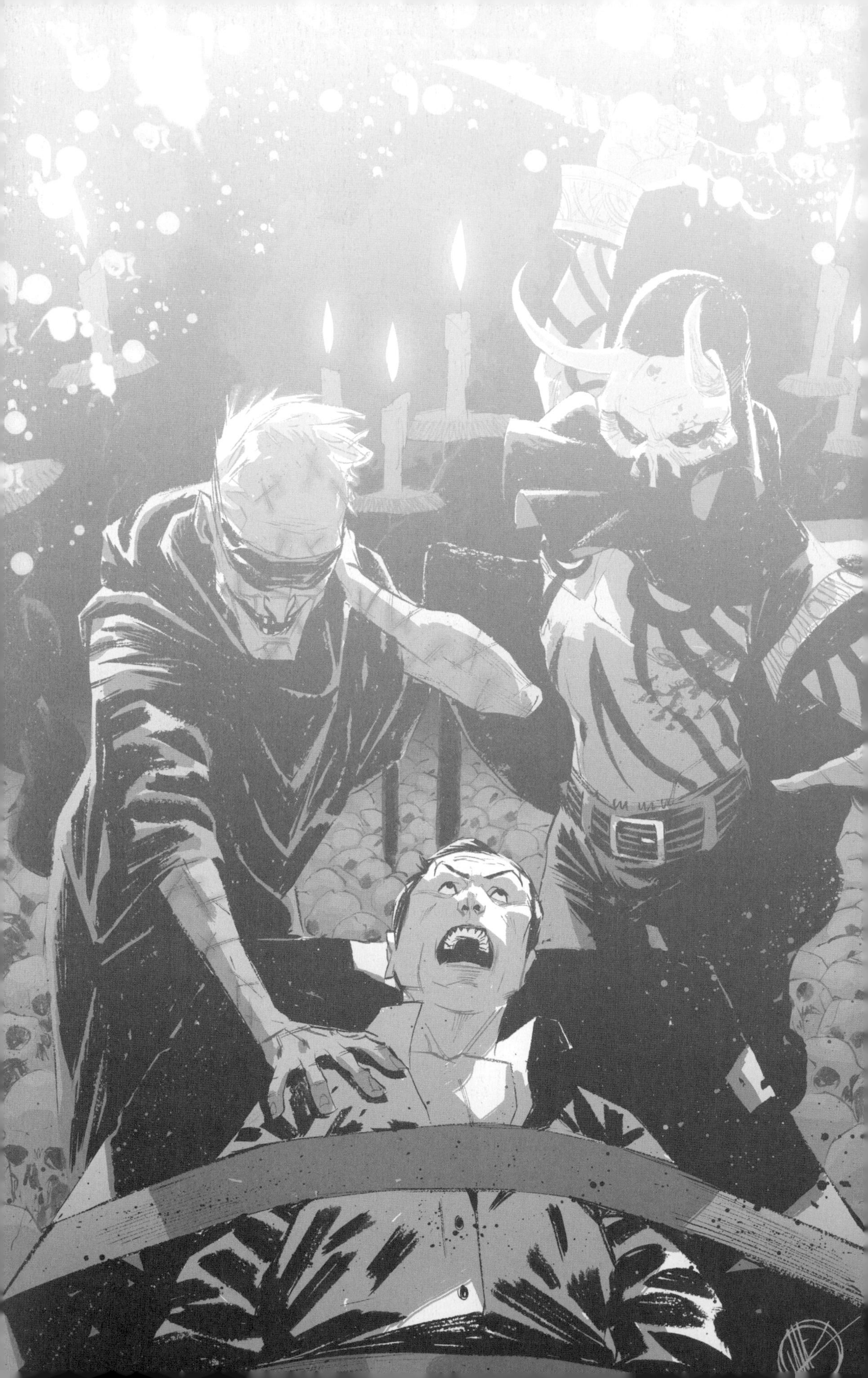

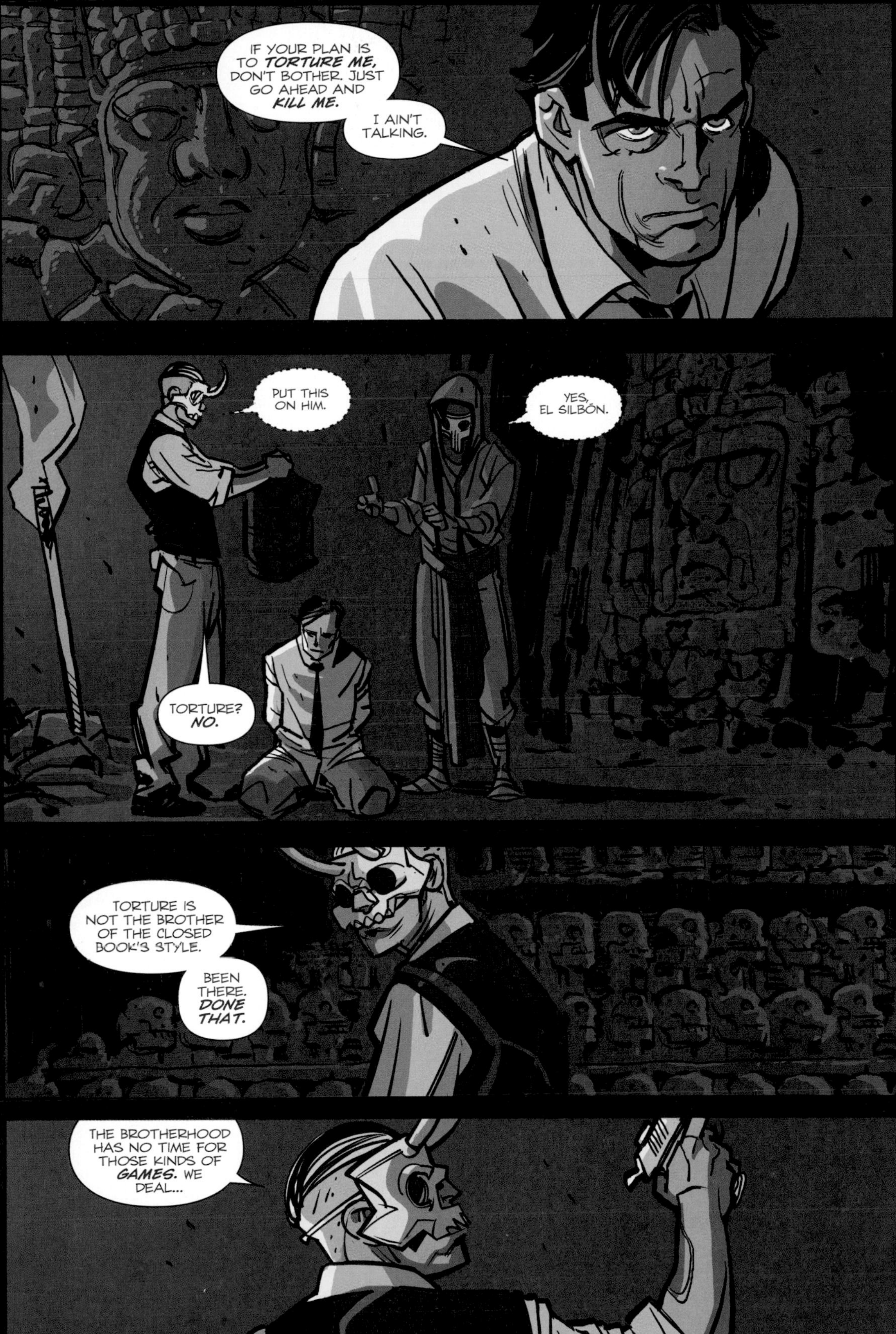
IF YOUR PLAN IS TO **TORTURE ME,** DON'T BOTHER. JUST GO AHEAD AND **KILL ME.**
I AIN'T TALKING.
PUT THIS ON HIM.
YES, EL SILBÓN.
TORTURE? **NO.**
TORTURE IS NOT THE BROTHER OF THE CLOSED BOOK'S STYLE.
BEEN THERE. **DONE THAT.**
THE BROTHERHOOD HAS NO TIME FOR THOSE KINDS OF **GAMES.** WE DEAL...

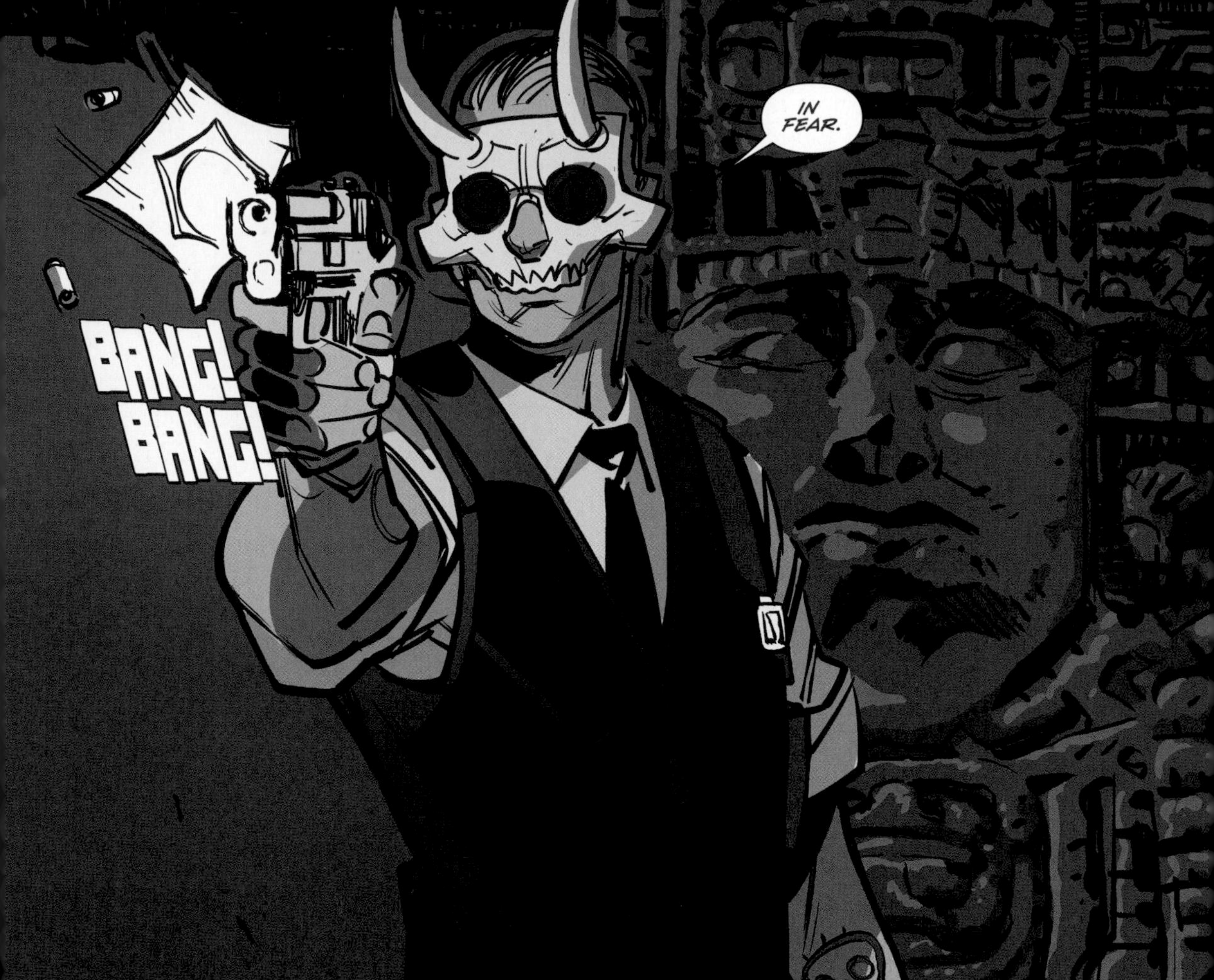
IN FEAR.
BANG! BANG!

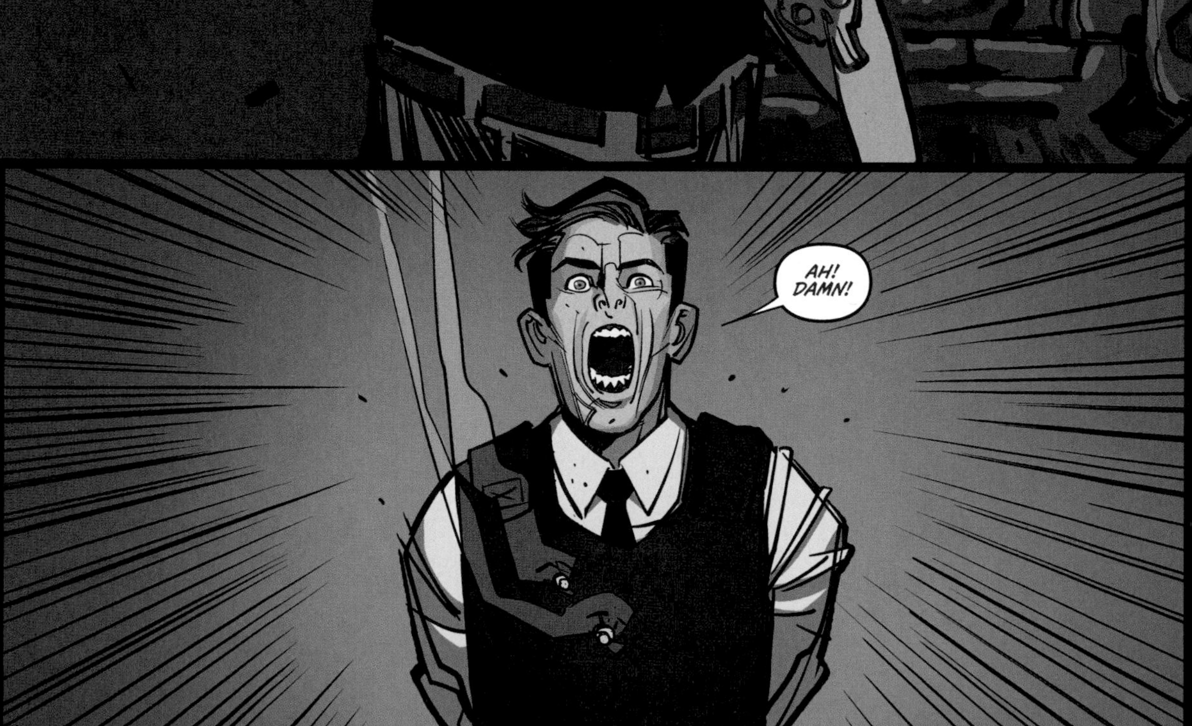
AH! DAMN!

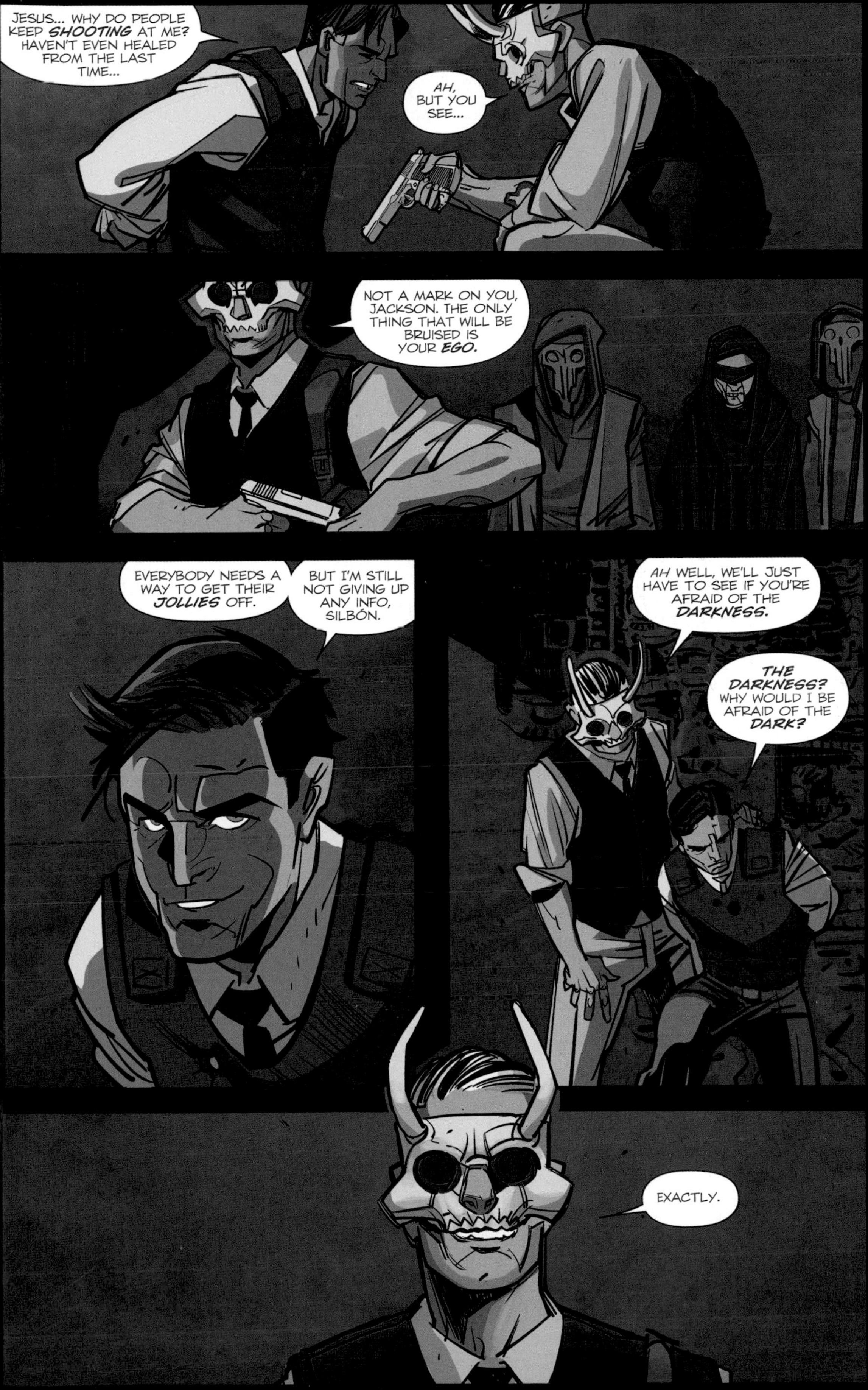
JESUS... WHY DO PEOPLE KEEP SHOOTING AT ME? HAVEN'T EVEN HEALED FROM THE LAST TIME...
AH, BUT YOU SEE...
NOT A MARK ON YOU, JACKSON. THE ONLY THING THAT WILL BE BRUISED IS YOUR EGO.
EVERYBODY NEEDS A WAY TO GET THEIR JOLLIES OFF.
BUT I'M STILL NOT GIVING UP ANY INFO, SILBÓN.
AH WELL, WE'LL JUST HAVE TO SEE IF YOU'RE AFRAID OF THE DARKNESS.
THE DARKNESS? WHY WOULD I BE AFRAID OF THE DARK?
EXACTLY.

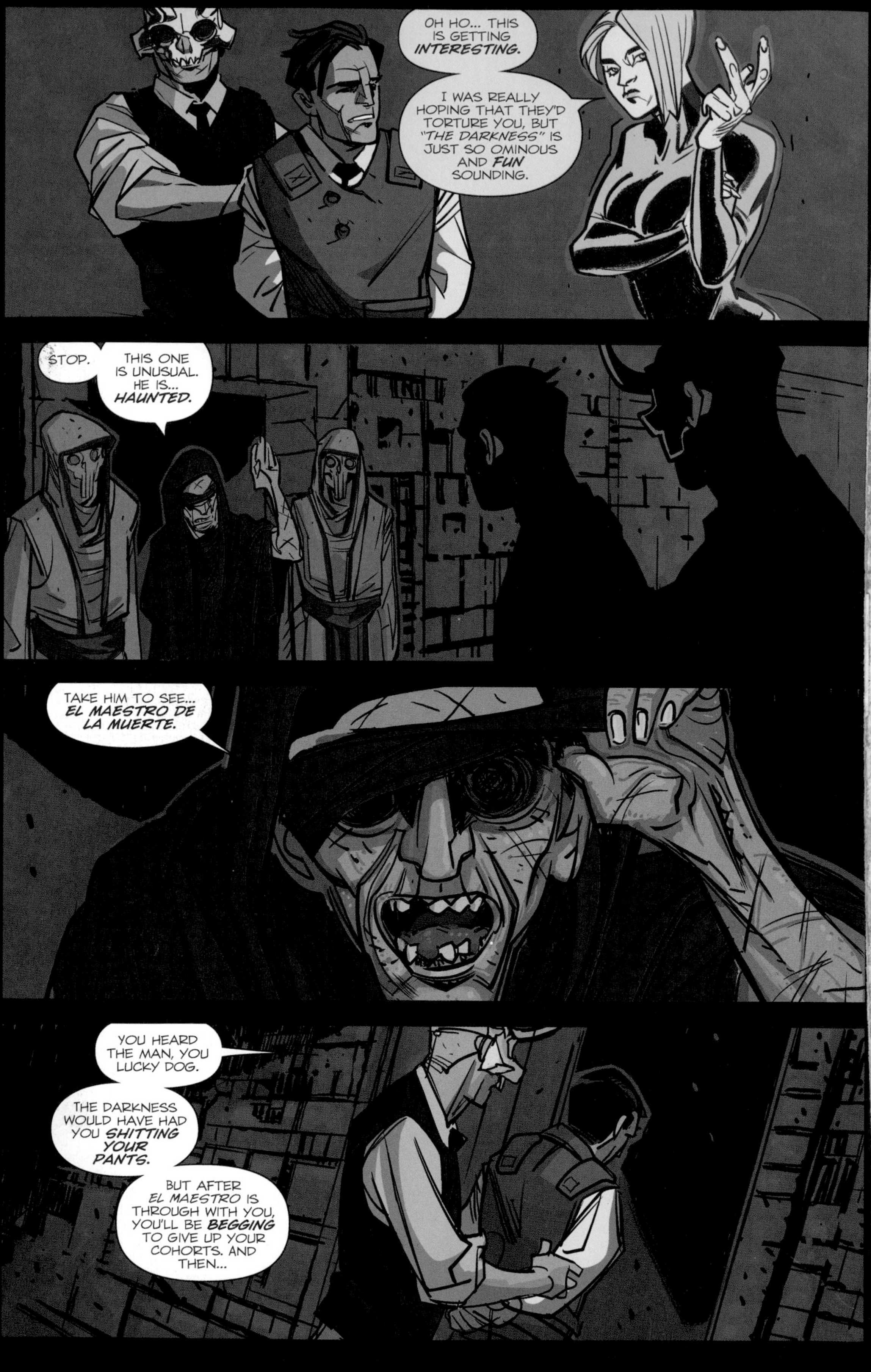
OH HO... THIS IS GETTING INTERESTING.
I WAS REALLY HOPING THAT THEY'D TORTURE YOU, BUT "THE DARKNESS" IS JUST SO OMINOUS AND FUN SOUNDING.
STOP.
THIS ONE IS UNUSUAL. HE IS... HAUNTED.
TAKE HIM TO SEE... EL MAESTRO DE LA MUERTE.
YOU HEARD THE MAN, YOU LUCKY DOG.
THE DARKNESS WOULD HAVE HAD YOU SHITTING YOUR PANTS.
BUT AFTER EL MAESTRO IS THROUGH WITH YOU, YOU'LL BE BEGGING TO GIVE UP YOUR COHORTS. AND THEN...

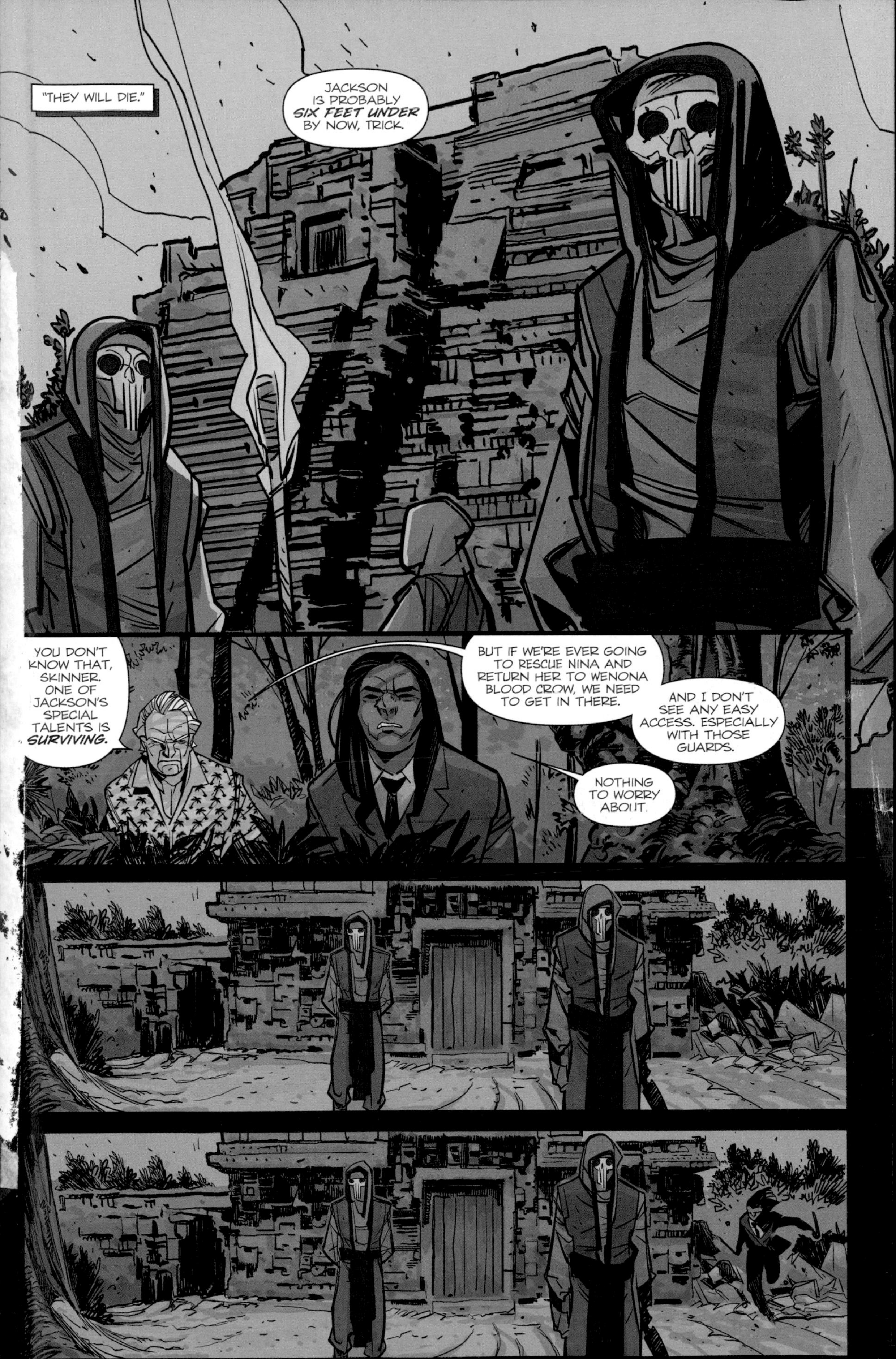
"THEY WILL DIE."
JACKSON IS PROBABLY ***SIX FEET UNDER*** BY NOW, TRICK.
YOU DON'T KNOW THAT, SKINNER. ONE OF JACKSON'S SPECIAL TALENTS IS ***SURVIVING.***
BUT IF WE'RE EVER GOING TO RESCUE NINA AND RETURN HER TO WENONA BLOOD CROW, WE NEED TO GET IN THERE.
AND I DON'T SEE ANY EASY ACCESS. ESPECIALLY WITH THOSE GUARDS.
NOTHING TO WORRY ABOUT.

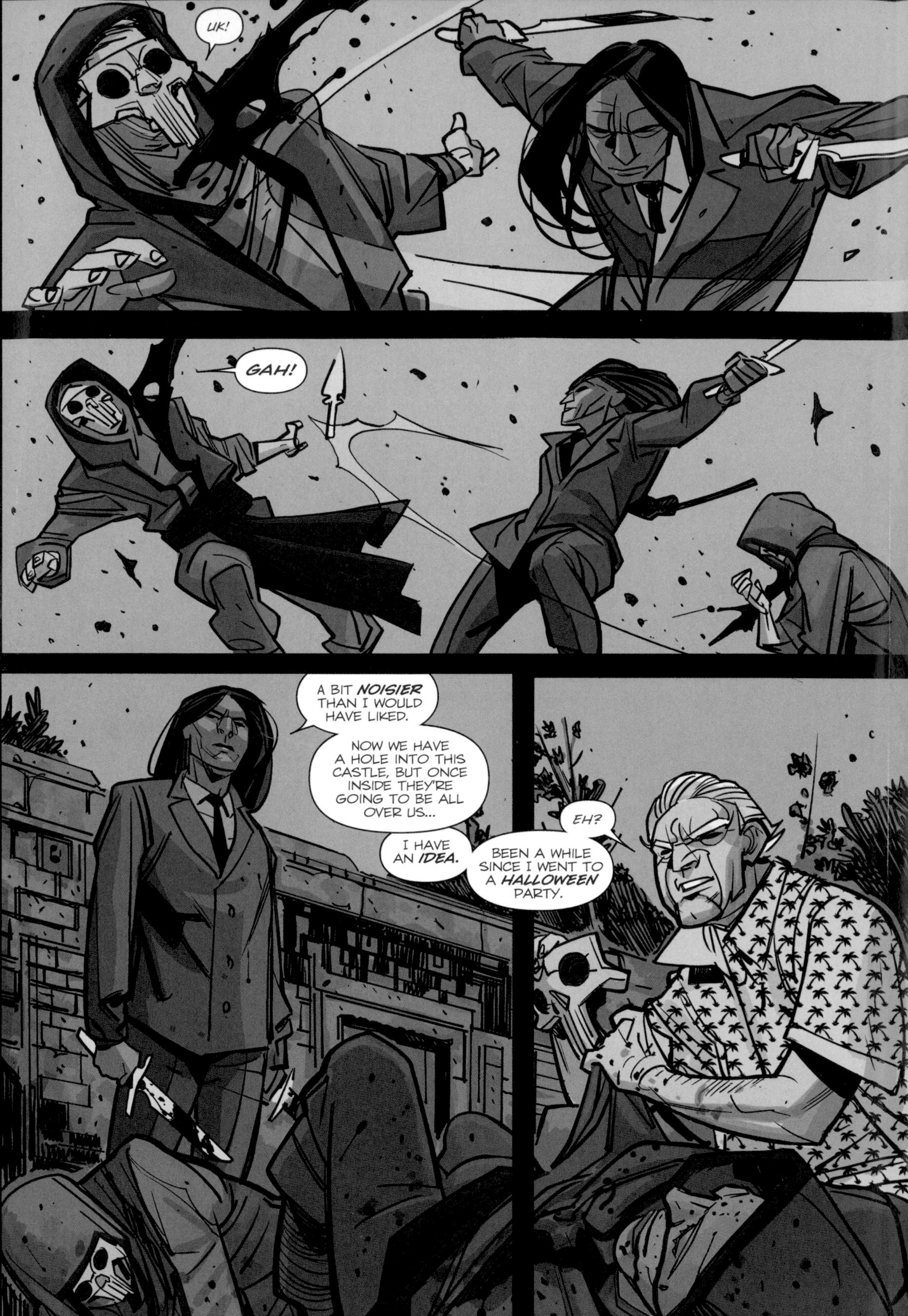
UK!
GAH!
A BIT NOISIER THAN I WOULD HAVE LIKED.
NOW WE HAVE A HOLE INTO THIS CASTLE, BUT ONCE INSIDE THEY'RE GOING TO BE ALL OVER US...
I HAVE AN IDEA.
EH?
BEEN A WHILE SINCE I WENT TO A HALLOWEEN PARTY.

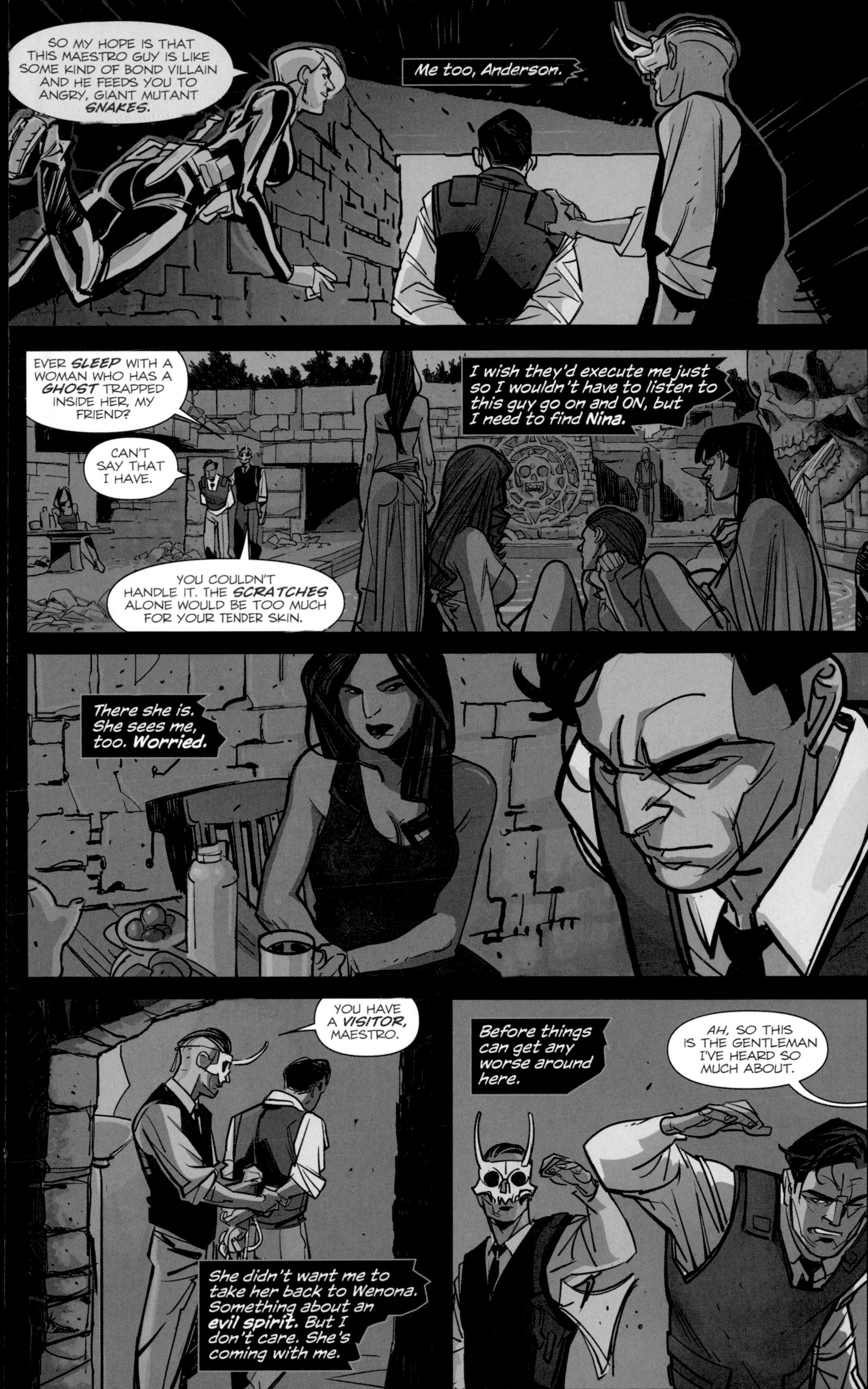
SO MY HOPE IS THAT THIS MAESTRO GUY IS LIKE SOME KIND OF BOND VILLAIN AND HE FEEDS YOU TO ANGRY, GIANT MUTANT SNAKES.
Me too, Anderson.
EVER SLEEP WITH A WOMAN WHO HAS A GHOST TRAPPED INSIDE HER, MY FRIEND?
CAN'T SAY THAT I HAVE.
YOU COULDN'T HANDLE IT. THE SCRATCHES ALONE WOULD BE TOO MUCH FOR YOUR TENDER SKIN.
I wish they'd execute me just so I wouldn't have to listen to this guy go on and ON, but I need to find Nina.
There she is. She sees me, too. Worried.
YOU HAVE A VISITOR, MAESTRO.
She didn't want me to take her back to Wenona. Something about an evil spirit. But I don't care. She's coming with me.
Before things can get any worse around here.
AH, SO THIS IS THE GENTLEMAN I'VE HEARD SO MUCH ABOUT.

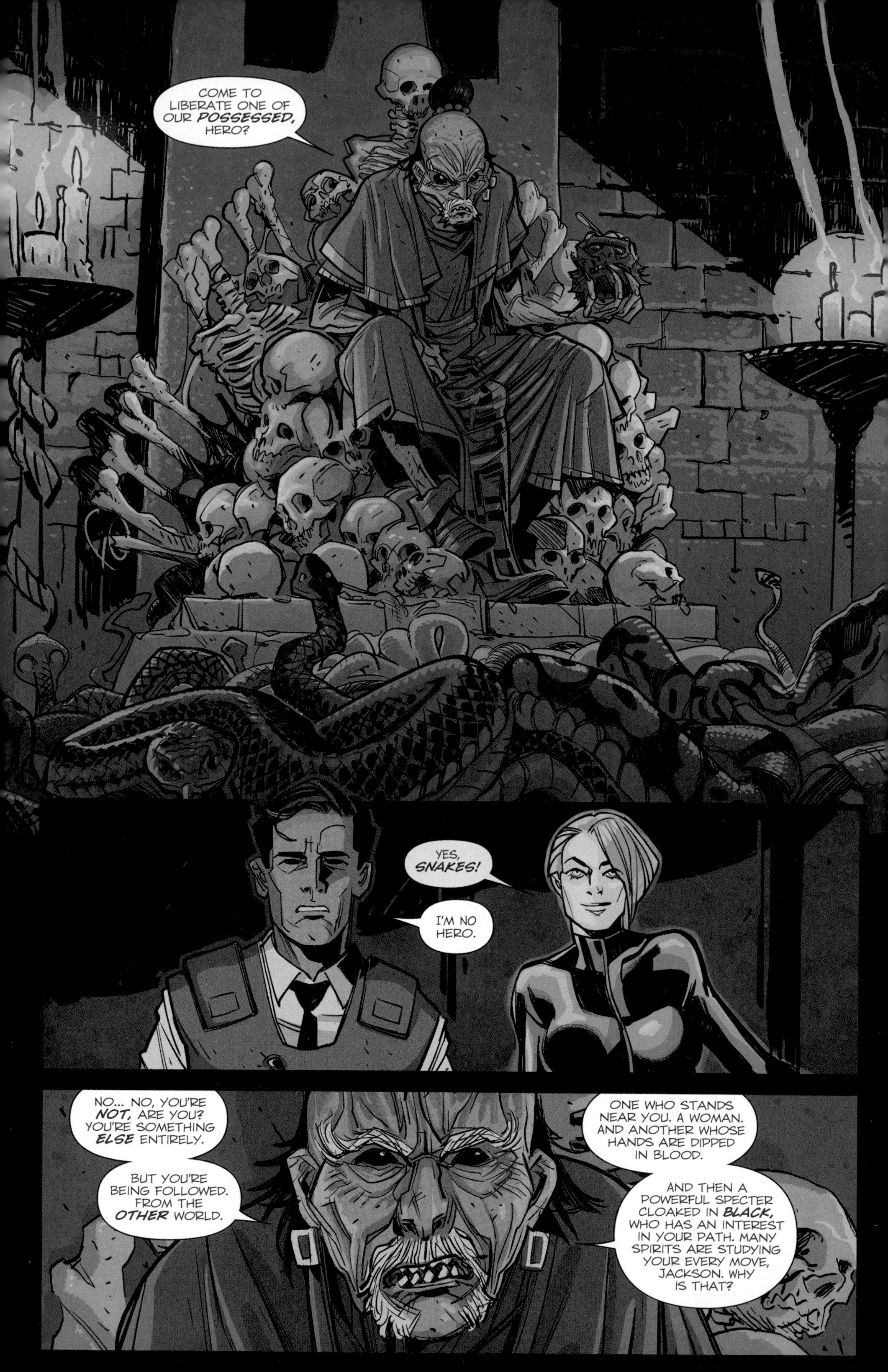
COME TO LIBERATE ONE OF OUR POSSESSED, HERO?
YES, SNAKES!
I'M NO HERO.
NO... NO, YOU'RE NOT, ARE YOU? YOU'RE SOMETHING ELSE ENTIRELY.
BUT YOU'RE BEING FOLLOWED. FROM THE OTHER WORLD.
ONE WHO STANDS NEAR YOU. A WOMAN. AND ANOTHER WHOSE HANDS ARE DIPPED IN BLOOD.
AND THEN A POWERFUL SPECTER CLOAKED IN BLACK, WHO HAS AN INTEREST IN YOUR PATH. MANY SPIRITS ARE STUDYING YOUR EVERY MOVE, JACKSON. WHY IS THAT?

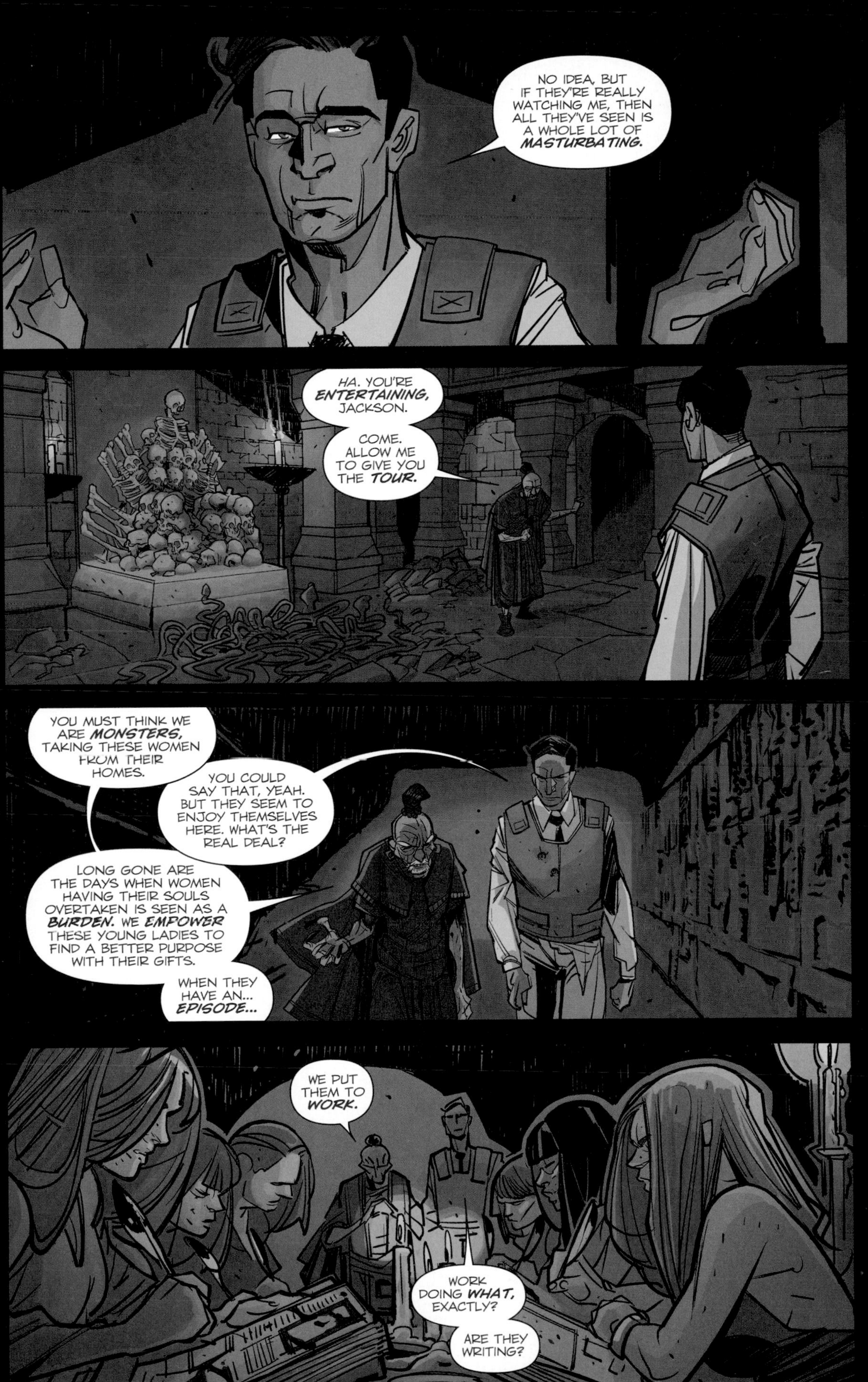
NO IDEA, BUT IF THEY'RE REALLY WATCHING ME, THEN ALL THEY'VE SEEN IS A WHOLE LOT OF MASTURBATING.
HA. YOU'RE ENTERTAINING, JACKSON.
COME. ALLOW ME TO GIVE YOU THE TOUR.
YOU MUST THINK WE ARE MONSTERS, TAKING THESE WOMEN FROM THEIR HOMES.
YOU COULD SAY THAT, YEAH. BUT THEY SEEM TO ENJOY THEMSELVES HERE. WHAT'S THE REAL DEAL?
LONG GONE ARE THE DAYS WHEN WOMEN HAVING THEIR SOULS OVERTAKEN IS SEEN AS A BURDEN. WE EMPOWER THESE YOUNG LADIES TO FIND A BETTER PURPOSE WITH THEIR GIFTS.
WHEN THEY HAVE AN... EPISODE...
WE PUT THEM TO WORK.
WORK DOING WHAT, EXACTLY?
ARE THEY WRITING?

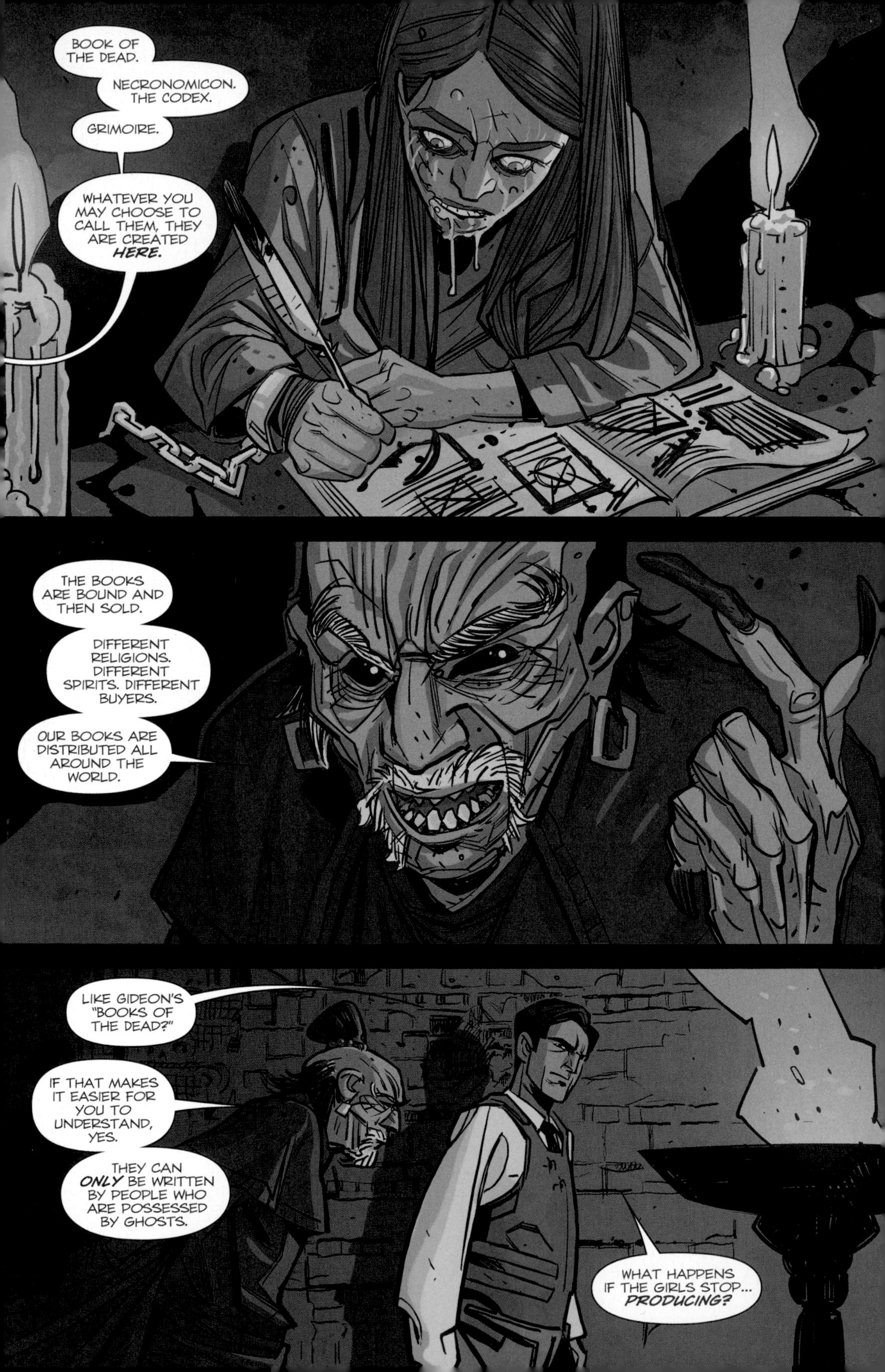
BOOK OF THE DEAD.
NECRONOMICON. THE CODEX.
GRIMOIRE.
WHATEVER YOU MAY CHOOSE TO CALL THEM, THEY ARE CREATED *HERE.*
THE BOOKS ARE BOUND AND THEN SOLD.
DIFFERENT RELIGIONS. DIFFERENT SPIRITS. DIFFERENT BUYERS.
OUR BOOKS ARE DISTRIBUTED ALL AROUND THE WORLD.
LIKE GIDEON'S "BOOKS OF THE DEAD?"
IF THAT MAKES IT EASIER FOR YOU TO UNDERSTAND, YES.
THEY CAN *ONLY* BE WRITTEN BY PEOPLE WHO ARE POSSESSED BY GHOSTS.
WHAT HAPPENS IF THE GIRLS STOP... *PRODUCING?*

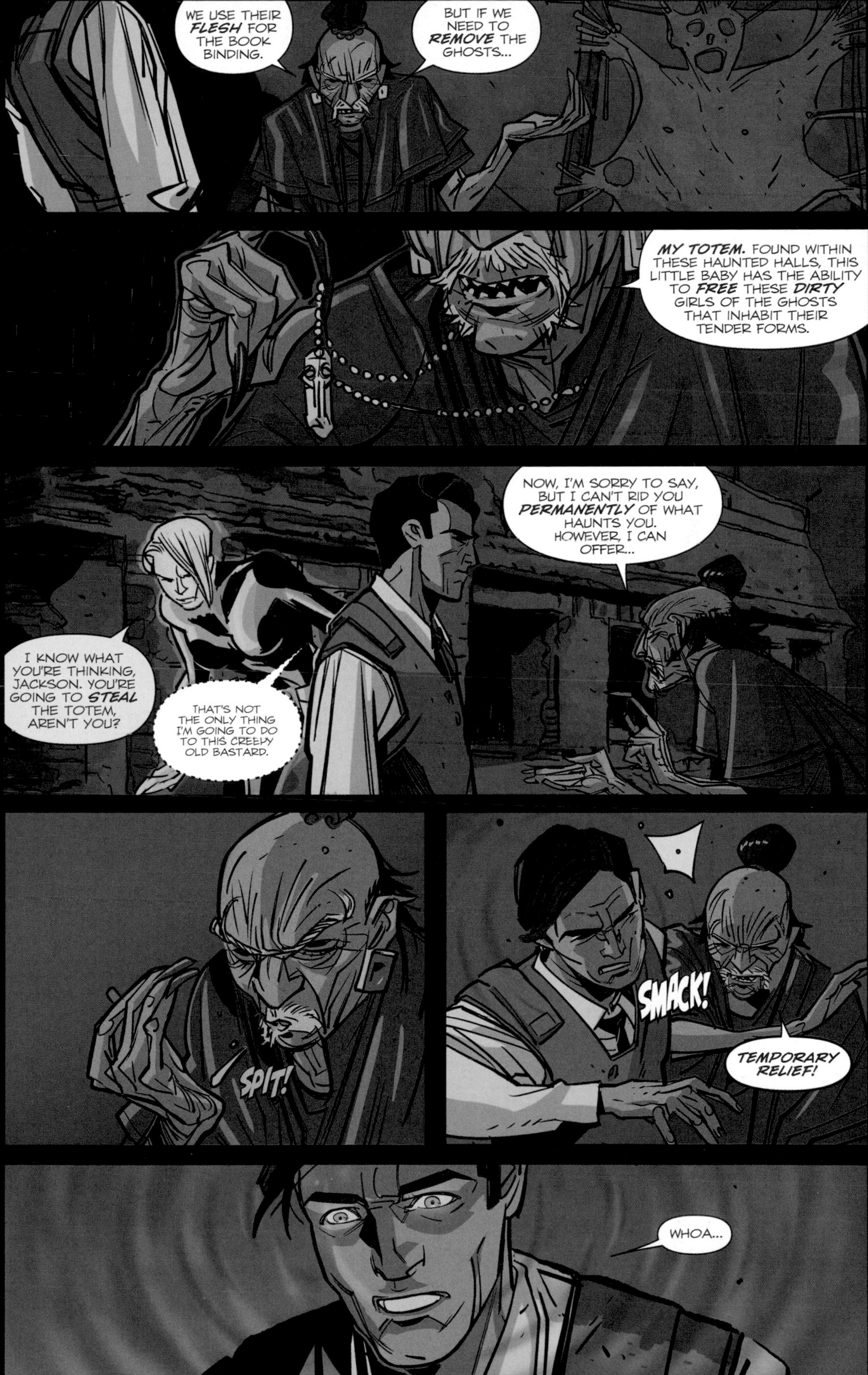
WE USE THEIR FLESH FOR THE BOOK BINDING.
BUT IF WE NEED TO REMOVE THE GHOSTS...
MY TOTEM. FOUND WITHIN THESE HAUNTED HALLS, THIS LITTLE BABY HAS THE ABILITY TO FREE THESE DIRTY GIRLS OF THE GHOSTS THAT INHABIT THEIR TENDER FORMS.
NOW, I'M SORRY TO SAY, BUT I CAN'T RID YOU PERMANENTLY OF WHAT HAUNTS YOU. HOWEVER, I CAN OFFER...
I KNOW WHAT YOU'RE THINKING, JACKSON. YOU'RE GOING TO STEAL THE TOTEM, AREN'T YOU?
THAT'S NOT THE ONLY THING I'M GOING TO DO TO THIS CREEPY OLD BASTARD.
SPIT!
SMACK!
TEMPORARY RELIEF!
WHOA...

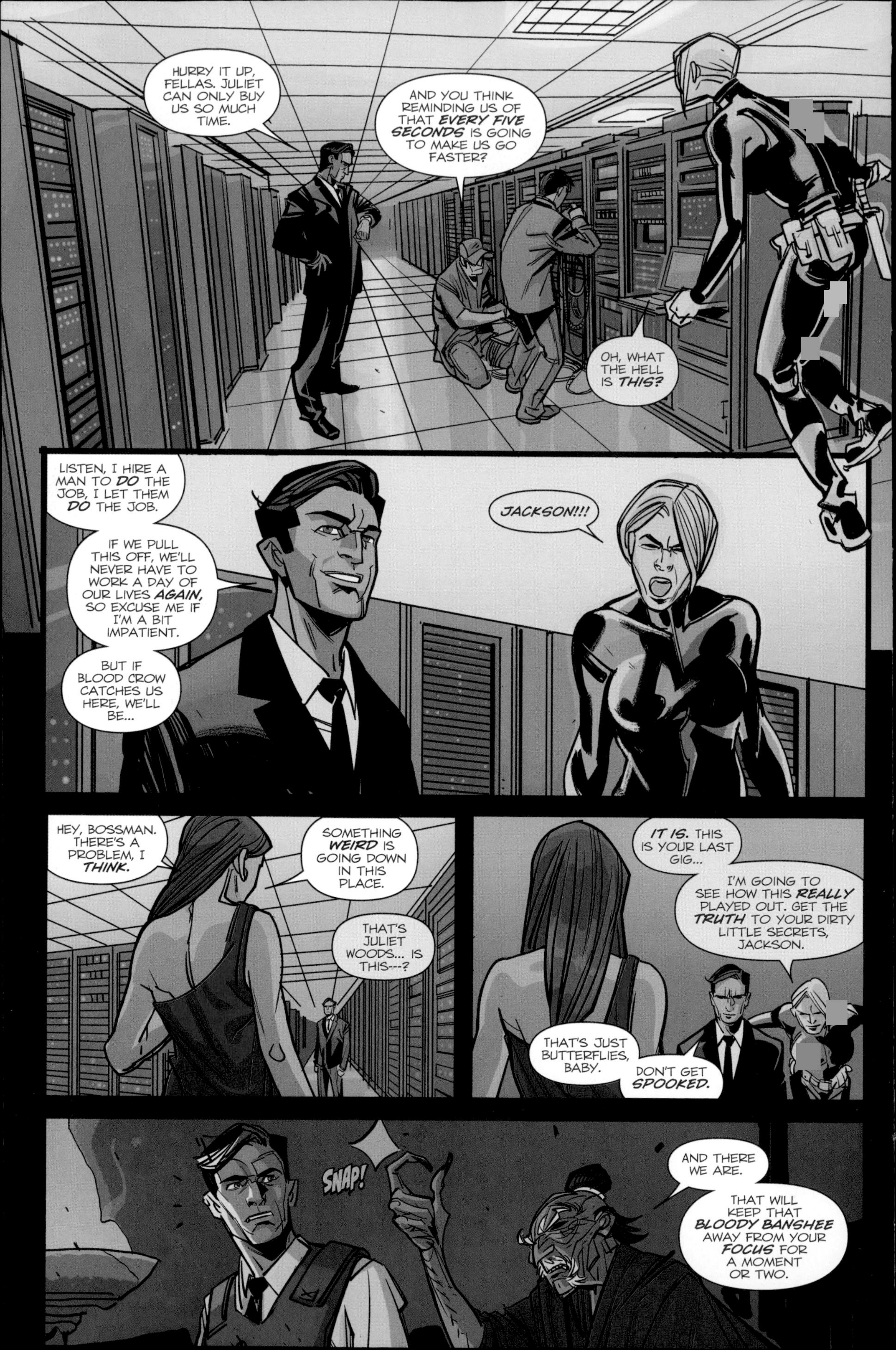
HURRY IT UP, FELLAS. JULIET CAN ONLY BUY US SO MUCH TIME.
AND YOU THINK REMINDING US OF THAT EVERY FIVE SECONDS IS GOING TO MAKE US GO FASTER?
OH, WHAT THE HELL IS THIS?
LISTEN, I HIRE A MAN TO DO THE JOB, I LET THEM DO THE JOB.
IF WE PULL THIS OFF, WE'LL NEVER HAVE TO WORK A DAY OF OUR LIVES AGAIN, SO EXCUSE ME IF I'M A BIT IMPATIENT.
BUT IF BLOOD CROW CATCHES US HERE, WE'LL BE...
JACKSON!!!
HEY, BOSSMAN. THERE'S A PROBLEM, I THINK.
SOMETHING WEIRD IS GOING DOWN IN THIS PLACE.
THAT'S JULIET WOODS... IS THIS---?
IT IS. THIS IS YOUR LAST GIG...
I'M GOING TO SEE HOW THIS REALLY PLAYED OUT. GET THE TRUTH TO YOUR DIRTY LITTLE SECRETS, JACKSON.
THAT'S JUST BUTTERFLIES, BABY.
DON'T GET SPOOKED.
SNAP!
AND THERE WE ARE.
THAT WILL KEEP THAT BLOODY BANSHEE AWAY FROM YOUR FOCUS FOR A MOMENT OR TWO.

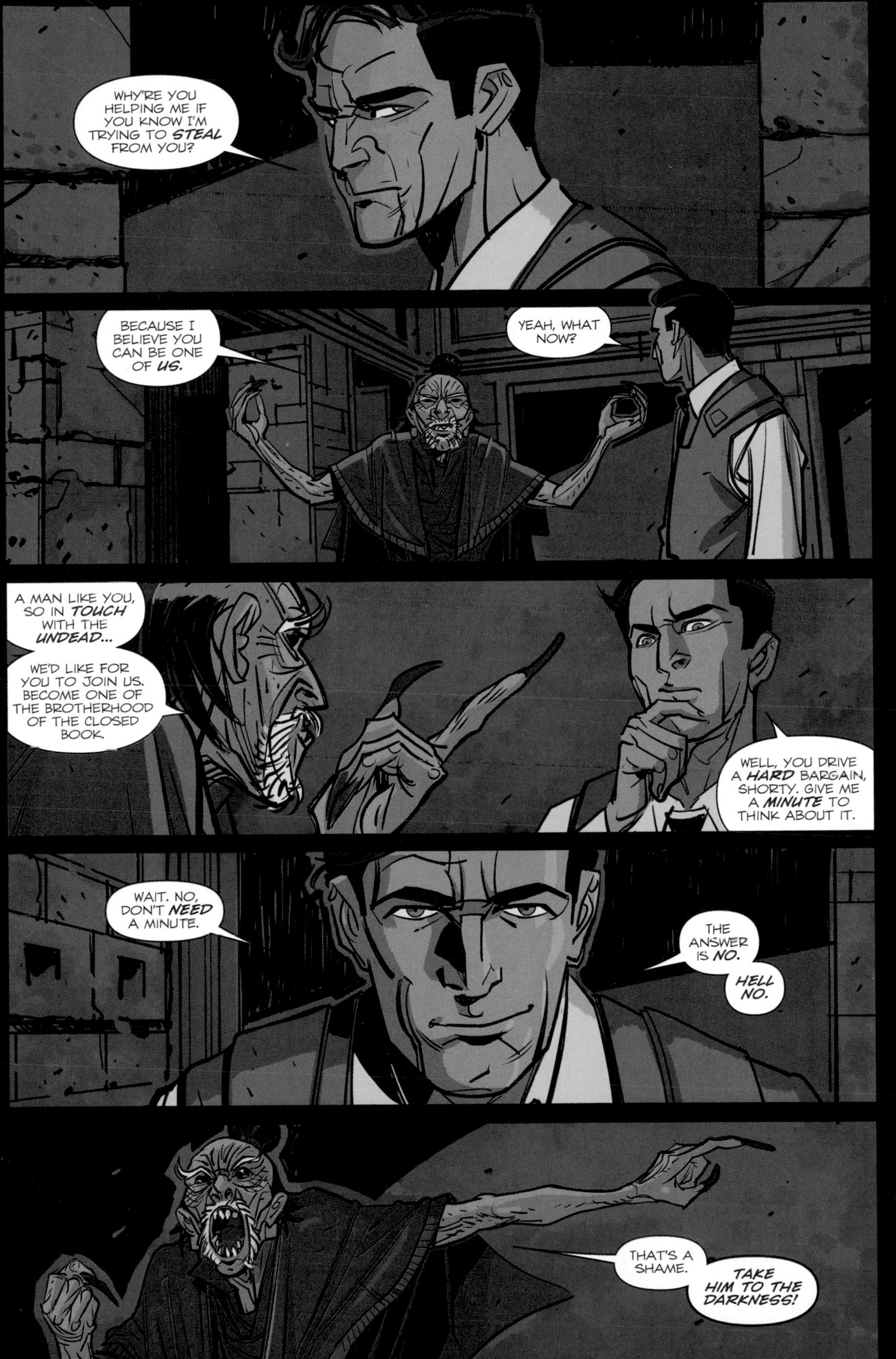

WHY'RE YOU HELPING ME IF YOU KNOW I'M TRYING TO STEAL FROM YOU?
BECAUSE I BELIEVE YOU CAN BE ONE OF US.
YEAH, WHAT NOW?
A MAN LIKE YOU, SO IN TOUCH WITH THE UNDEAD...
WE'D LIKE FOR YOU TO JOIN US. BECOME ONE OF THE BROTHERHOOD OF THE CLOSED BOOK.
WELL, YOU DRIVE A HARD BARGAIN, SHORTY. GIVE ME A MINUTE TO THINK ABOUT IT.
WAIT. NO, DON'T NEED A MINUTE.
THE ANSWER IS NO.
HELL NO.
THAT'S A SHAME.
TAKE HIM TO THE DARKNESS!

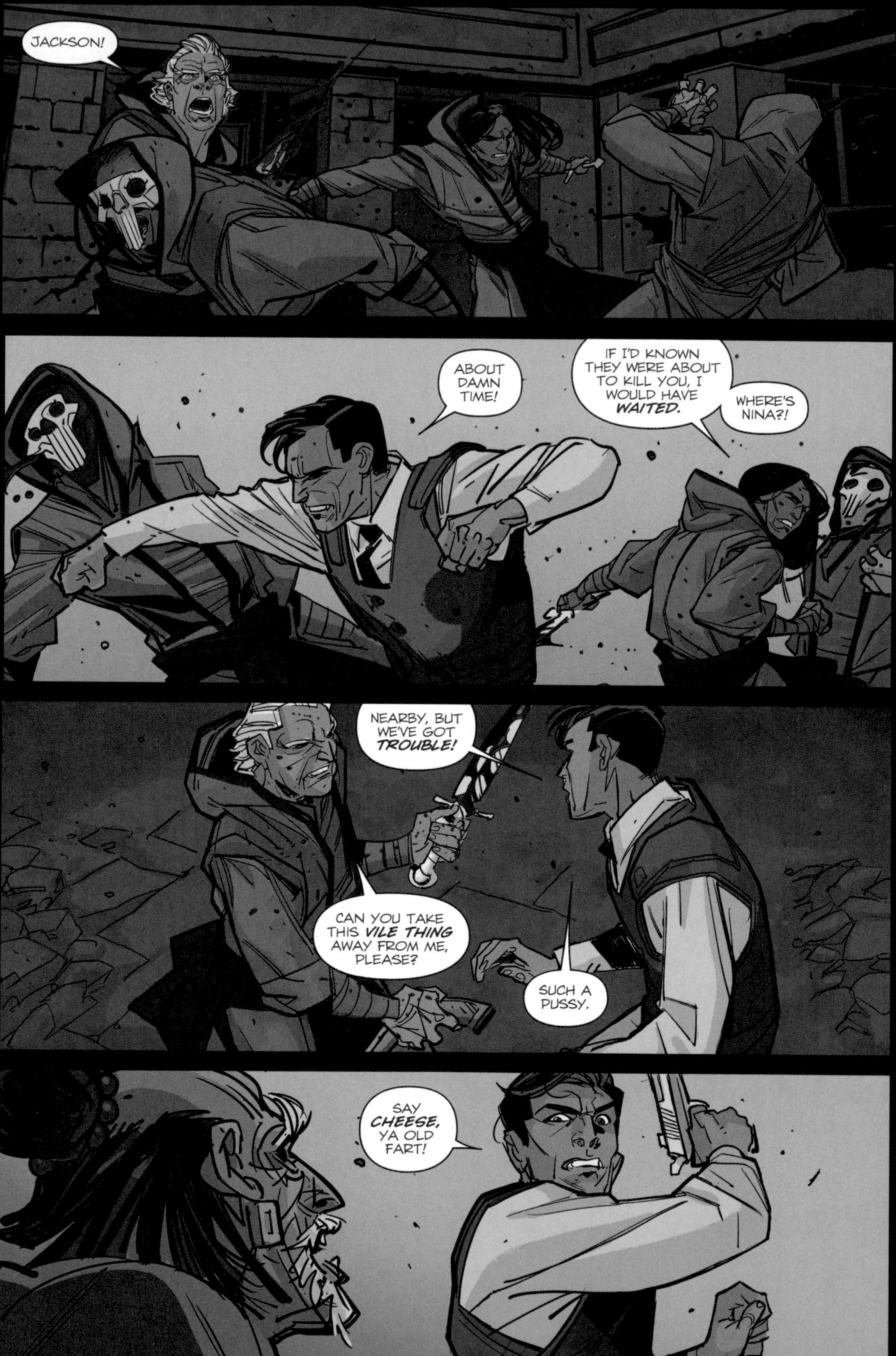
JACKSON!
ABOUT DAMN TIME!
IF I'D KNOWN THEY WERE ABOUT TO KILL YOU, I WOULD HAVE **WAITED.**
WHERE'S NINA?!
NEARBY, BUT WE'VE GOT **TROUBLE!**
CAN YOU TAKE THIS **VILE THING** AWAY FROM ME, PLEASE?
SUCH A PUSSY.
SAY **CHEESE,** YA OLD FART!

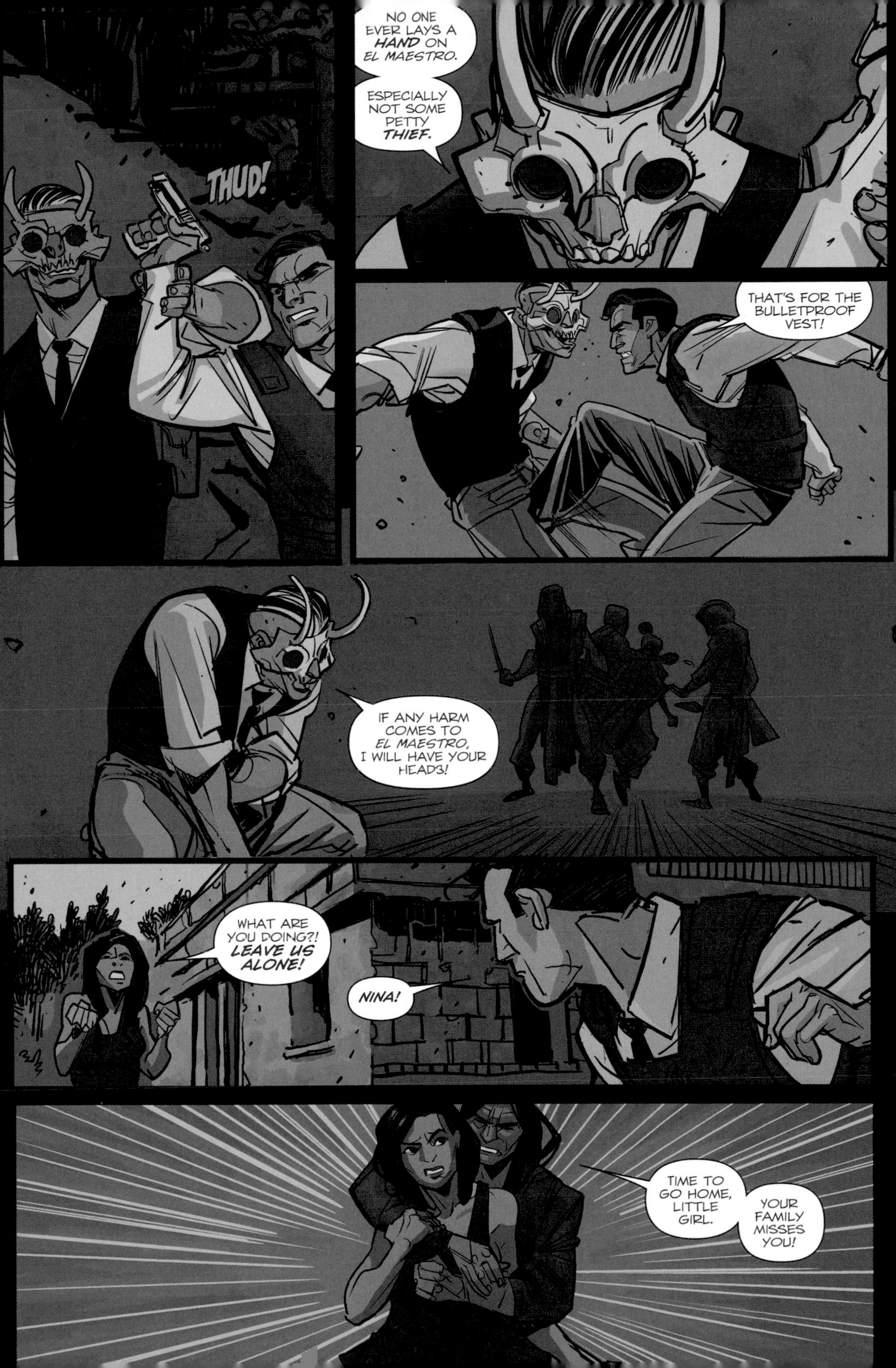
THUD!
NO ONE EVER LAYS A HAND ON EL MAESTRO.
ESPECIALLY NOT SOME PETTY THIEF.
THAT'S FOR THE BULLETPROOF VEST!
IF ANY HARM COMES TO EL MAESTRO, I WILL HAVE YOUR HEADS!
WHAT ARE YOU DOING?! LEAVE US ALONE!
NINA!
TIME TO GO HOME, LITTLE GIRL.
YOUR FAMILY MISSES YOU!

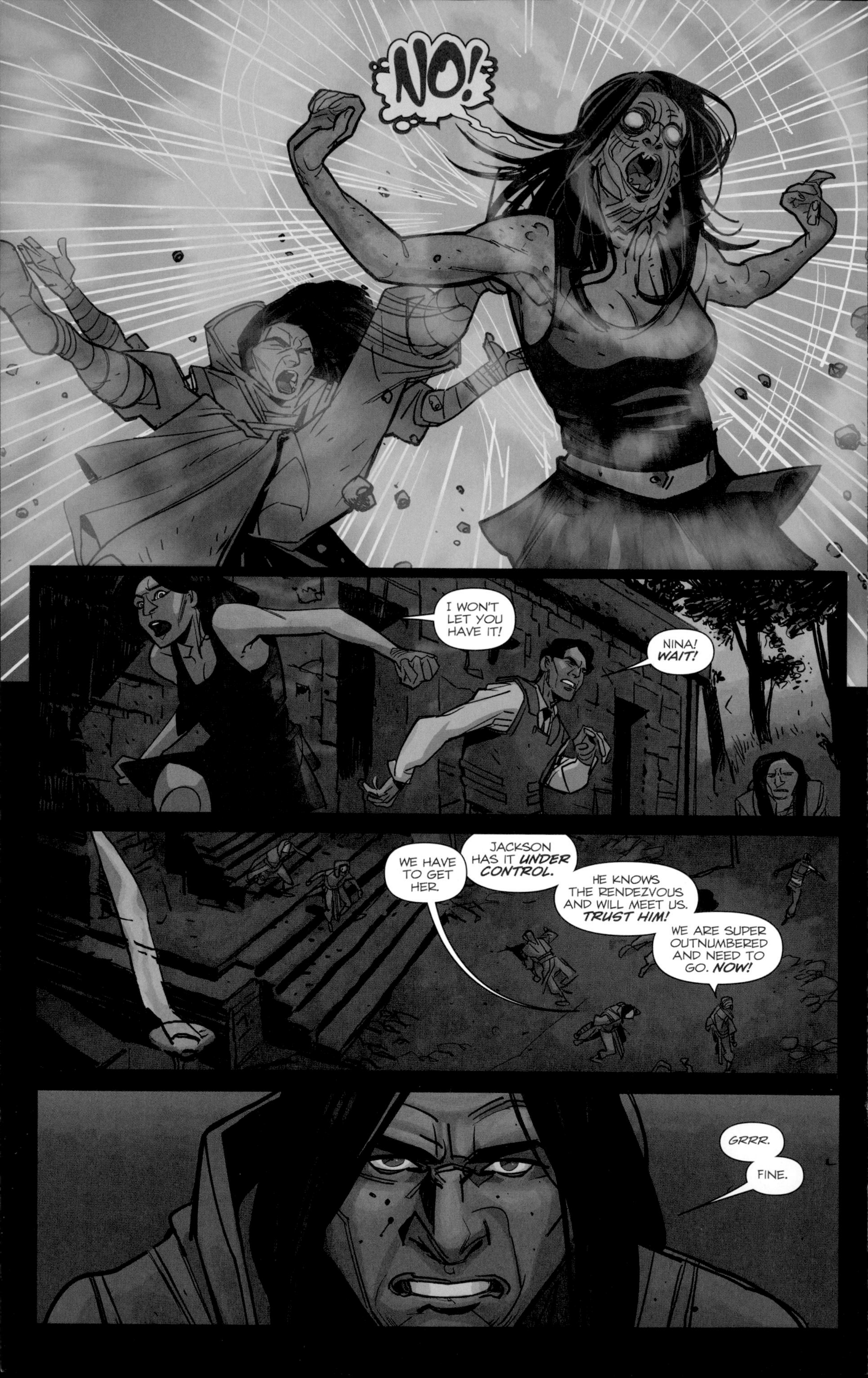
NO!
I WON'T LET YOU HAVE IT!
NINA! WAIT!
WE HAVE TO GET HER.
JACKSON HAS IT UNDER CONTROL.
HE KNOWS THE RENDEZVOUS AND WILL MEET US. TRUST HIM!
WE ARE SUPER OUTNUMBERED AND NEED TO GO. NOW!
GRRR.
FINE.

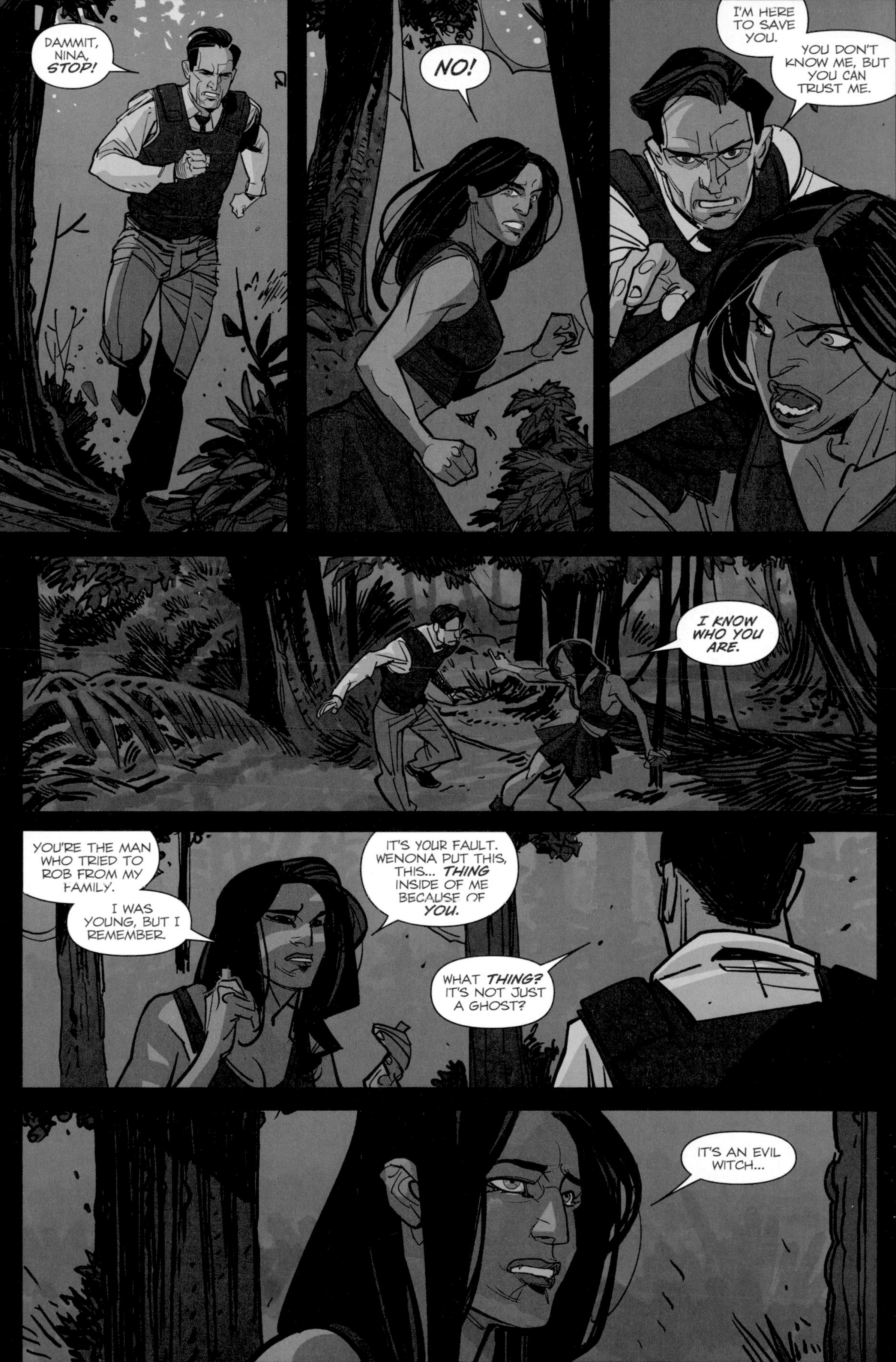
DAMMIT, NINA, STOP!
NO!
I'M HERE TO SAVE YOU.
YOU DON'T KNOW ME, BUT YOU CAN TRUST ME.
I KNOW WHO YOU ARE.
YOU'RE THE MAN WHO TRIED TO ROB FROM MY FAMILY.
I WAS YOUNG, BUT I REMEMBER.
IT'S YOUR FAULT. WENONA PUT THIS, THIS... THING INSIDE OF ME BECAUSE OF YOU.
WHAT THING? IT'S NOT JUST A GHOST?
IT'S AN EVIL WITCH...

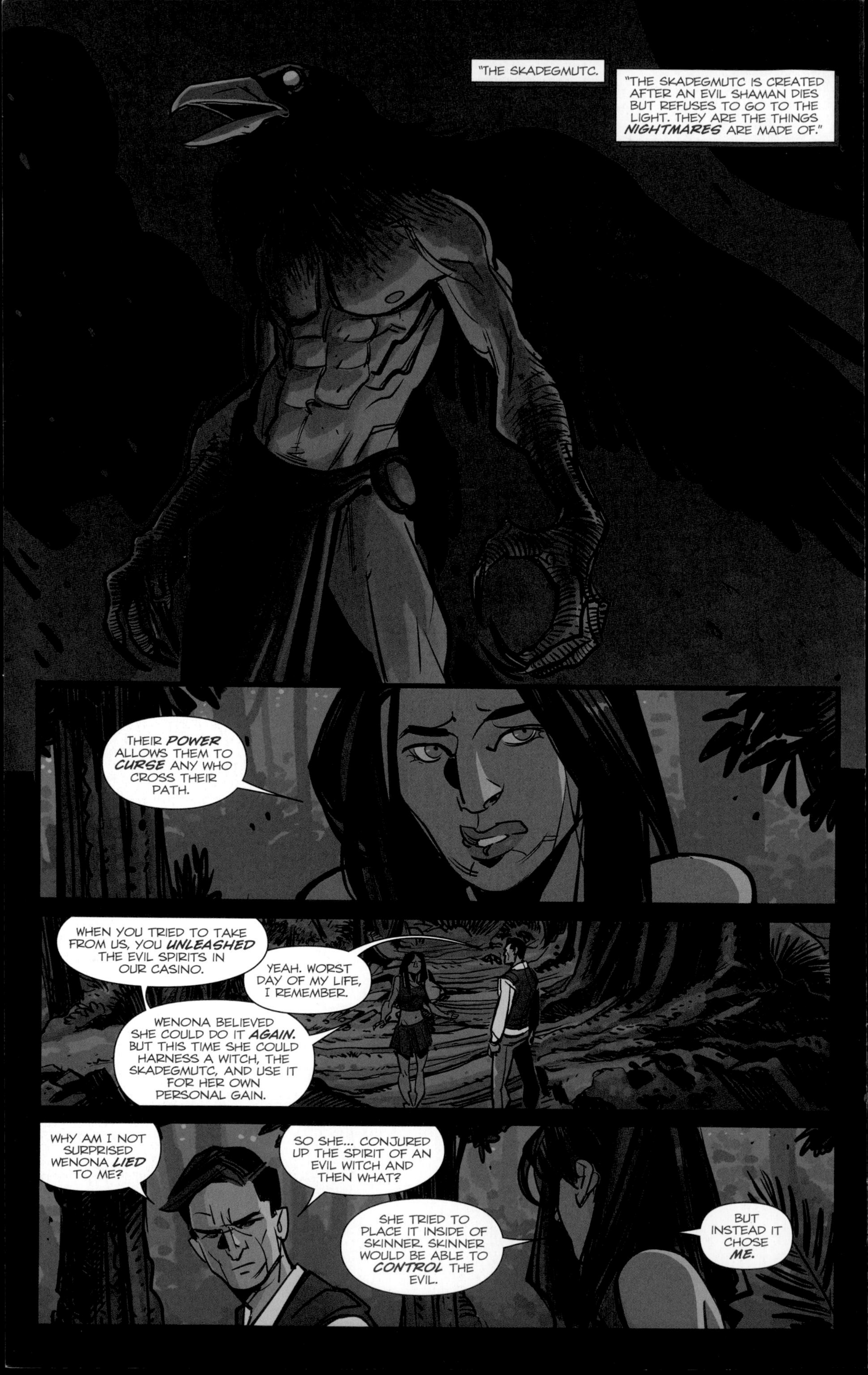
"THE SKADEGMUTC.
"THE SKADEGMUTC IS CREATED AFTER AN EVIL SHAMAN DIES BUT REFUSES TO GO TO THE LIGHT. THEY ARE THE THINGS NIGHTMARES ARE MADE OF."
THEIR POWER ALLOWS THEM TO CURSE ANY WHO CROSS THEIR PATH.
WHEN YOU TRIED TO TAKE FROM US, YOU UNLEASHED THE EVIL SPIRITS IN OUR CASINO.
YEAH. WORST DAY OF MY LIFE, I REMEMBER.
WENONA BELIEVED SHE COULD DO IT AGAIN. BUT THIS TIME SHE COULD HARNESS A WITCH, THE SKADEGMUTC, AND USE IT FOR HER OWN PERSONAL GAIN.
WHY AM I NOT SURPRISED WENONA LIED TO ME?
SO SHE... CONJURED UP THE SPIRIT OF AN EVIL WITCH AND THEN WHAT?
SHE TRIED TO PLACE IT INSIDE OF SKINNER. SKINNER WOULD BE ABLE TO CONTROL THE EVIL.
BUT INSTEAD IT CHOSE ME.

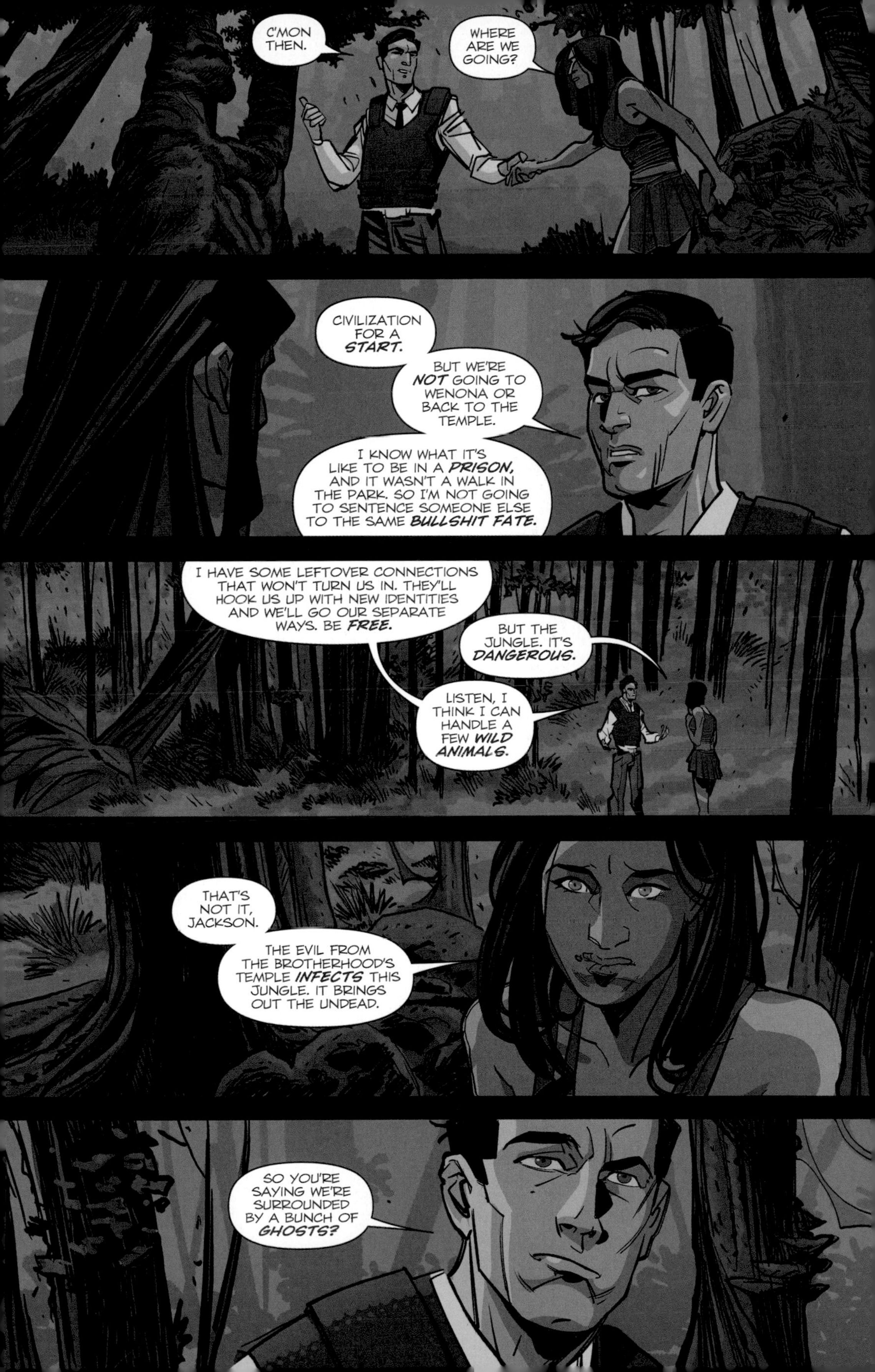

C'MON THEN.
WHERE ARE WE GOING?
CIVILIZATION FOR A START.
BUT WE'RE NOT GOING TO WENONA OR BACK TO THE TEMPLE.
I KNOW WHAT IT'S LIKE TO BE IN A PRISON, AND IT WASN'T A WALK IN THE PARK. SO I'M NOT GOING TO SENTENCE SOMEONE ELSE TO THE SAME BULLSHIT FATE.
I HAVE SOME LEFTOVER CONNECTIONS THAT WON'T TURN US IN. THEY'LL HOOK US UP WITH NEW IDENTITIES AND WE'LL GO OUR SEPARATE WAYS. BE FREE.
BUT THE JUNGLE. IT'S DANGEROUS.
LISTEN, I THINK I CAN HANDLE A FEW WILD ANIMALS.
THAT'S NOT IT, JACKSON.
THE EVIL FROM THE BROTHERHOOD'S TEMPLE INFECTS THIS JUNGLE. IT BRINGS OUT THE UNDEAD.
SO YOU'RE SAYING WE'RE SURROUNDED BY A BUNCH OF GHOSTS?

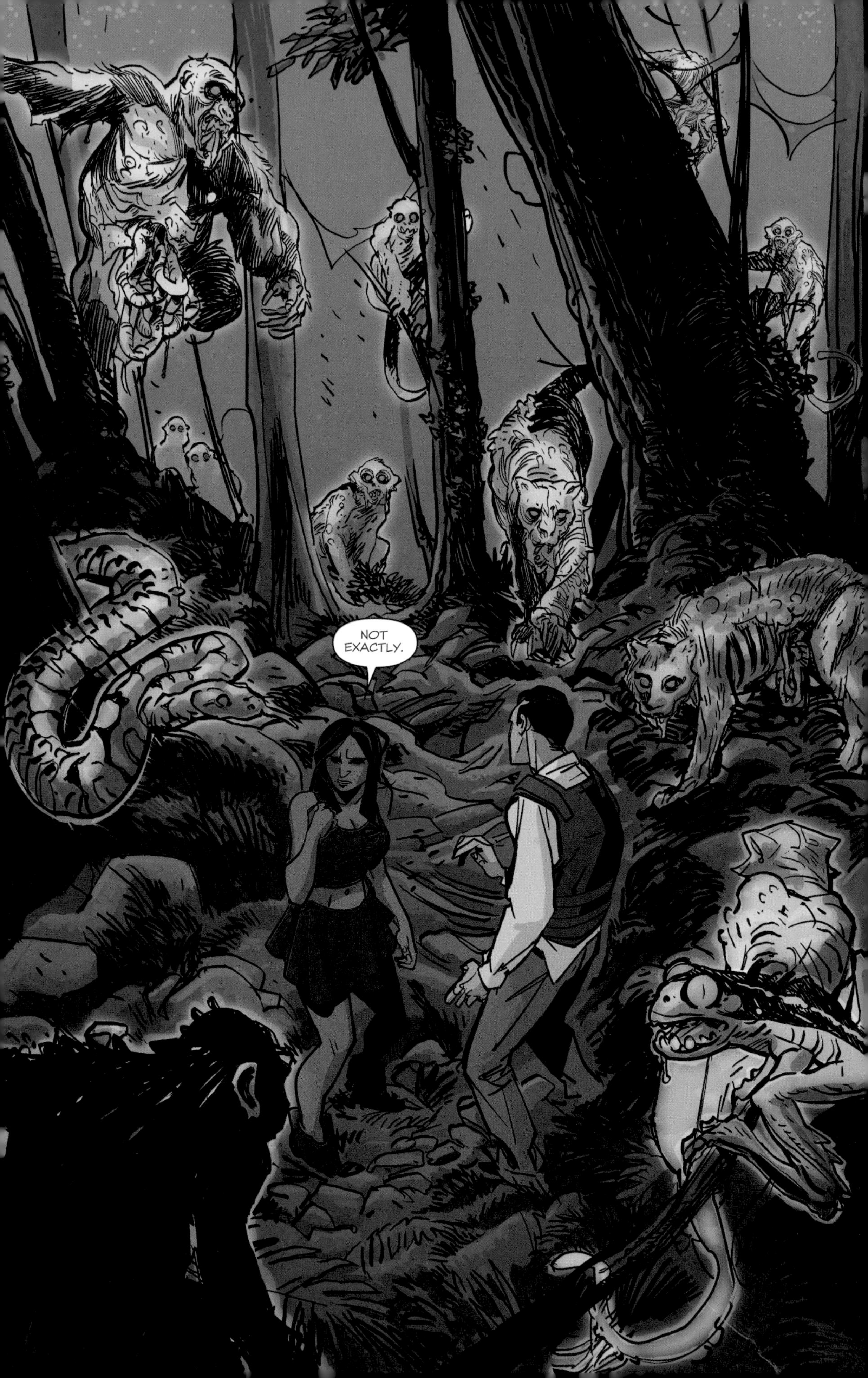
NOT EXACTLY.

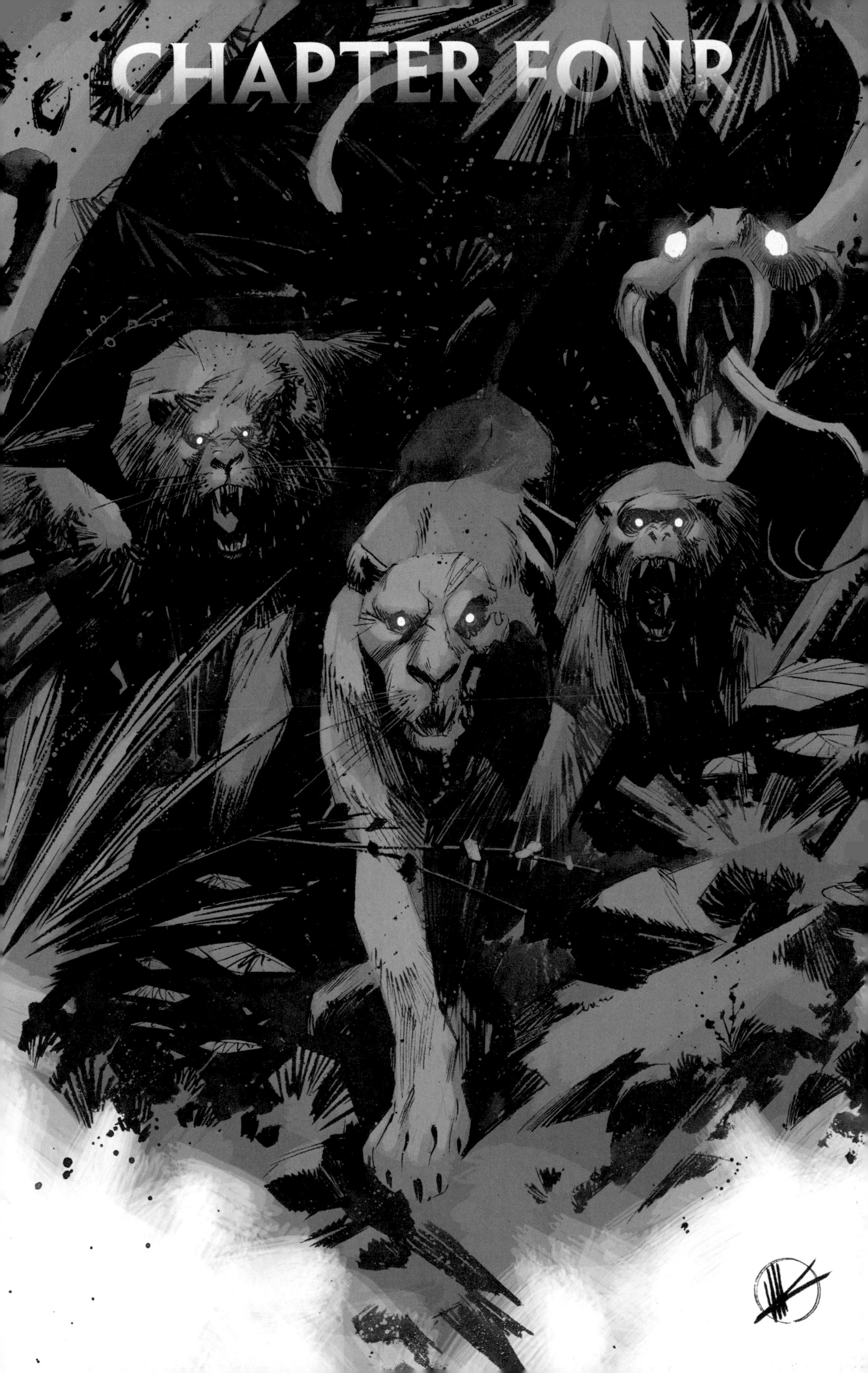
CHAPTER FOUR

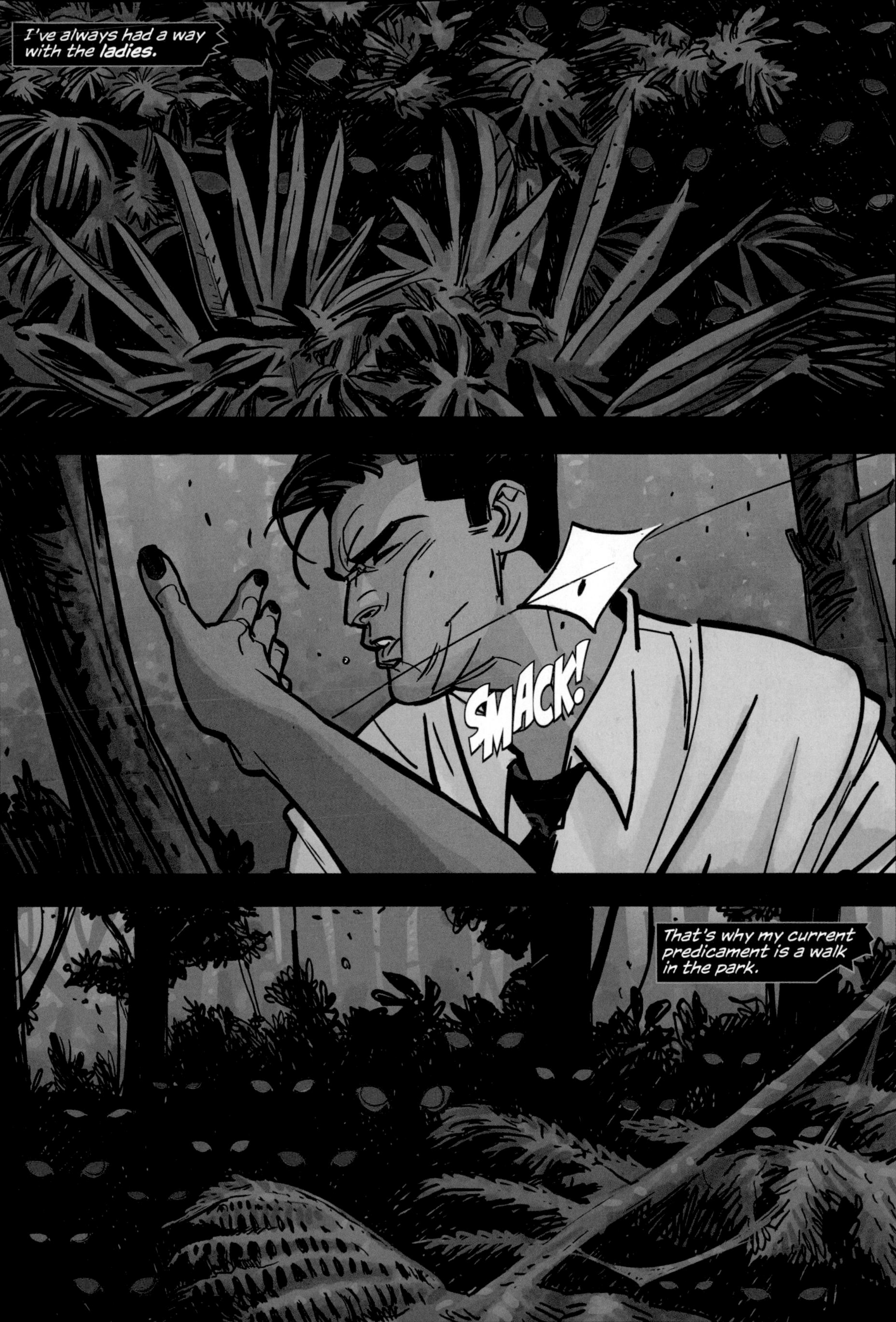
I've always had a way with the ladies.
SMACK!
That's why my current predicament is a walk in the park.

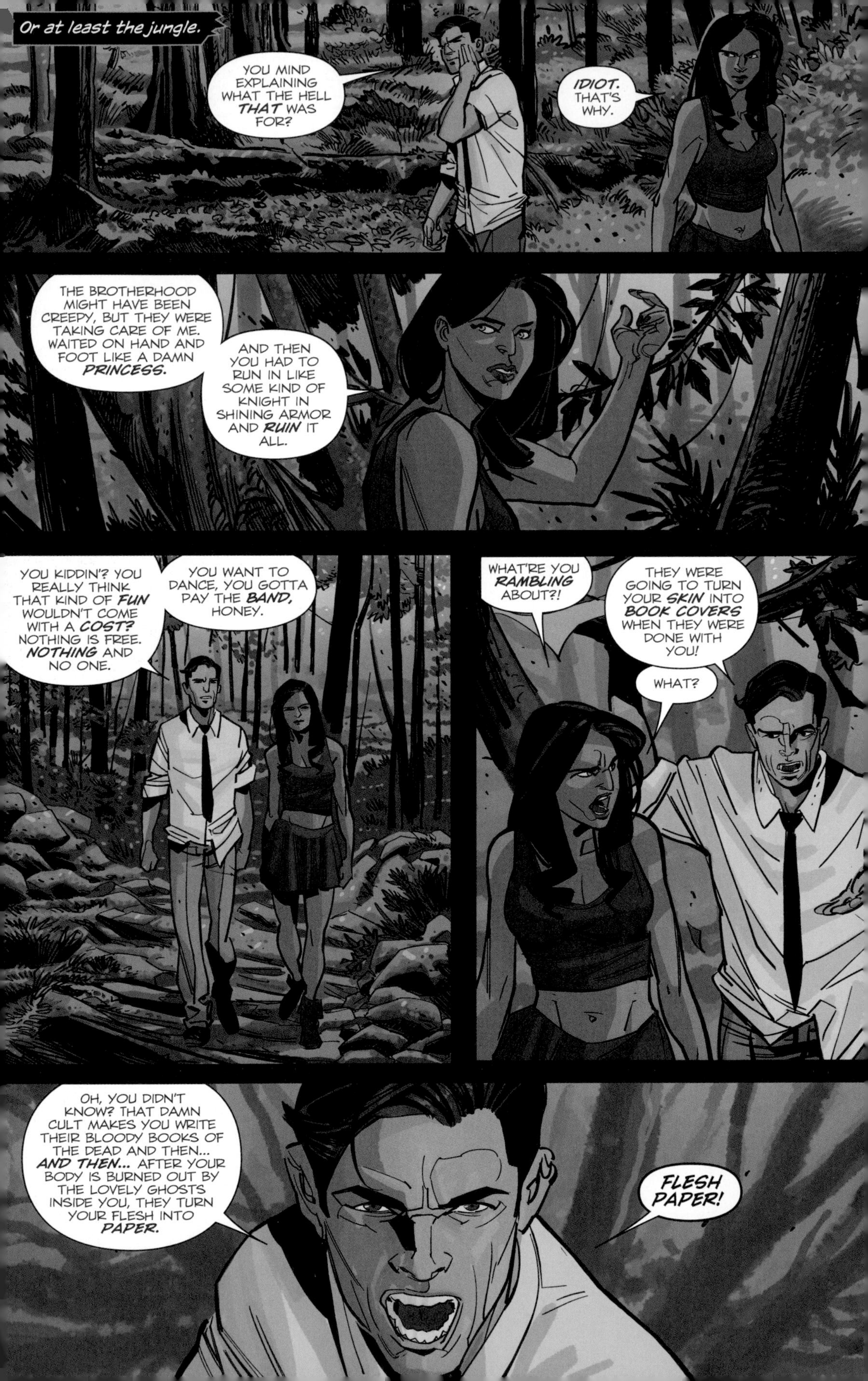
Or at least the jungle.
YOU MIND EXPLAINING WHAT THE HELL THAT WAS FOR?
IDIOT. THAT'S WHY.
THE BROTHERHOOD MIGHT HAVE BEEN CREEPY, BUT THEY WERE TAKING CARE OF ME. WAITED ON HAND AND FOOT LIKE A DAMN PRINCESS.
AND THEN YOU HAD TO RUN IN LIKE SOME KIND OF KNIGHT IN SHINING ARMOR AND RUIN IT ALL.
YOU KIDDIN'? YOU REALLY THINK THAT KIND OF FUN WOULDN'T COME WITH A COST? NOTHING IS FREE. NOTHING AND NO ONE.
YOU WANT TO DANCE, YOU GOTTA PAY THE BAND, HONEY.
WHAT'RE YOU RAMBLING ABOUT?!
THEY WERE GOING TO TURN YOUR SKIN INTO BOOK COVERS WHEN THEY WERE DONE WITH YOU!
WHAT?
OH, YOU DIDN'T KNOW? THAT DAMN CULT MAKES YOU WRITE THEIR BLOODY BOOKS OF THE DEAD AND THEN... AND THEN... AFTER YOUR BODY IS BURNED OUT BY THE LOVELY GHOSTS INSIDE YOU, THEY TURN YOUR FLESH INTO PAPER.
FLESH PAPER!

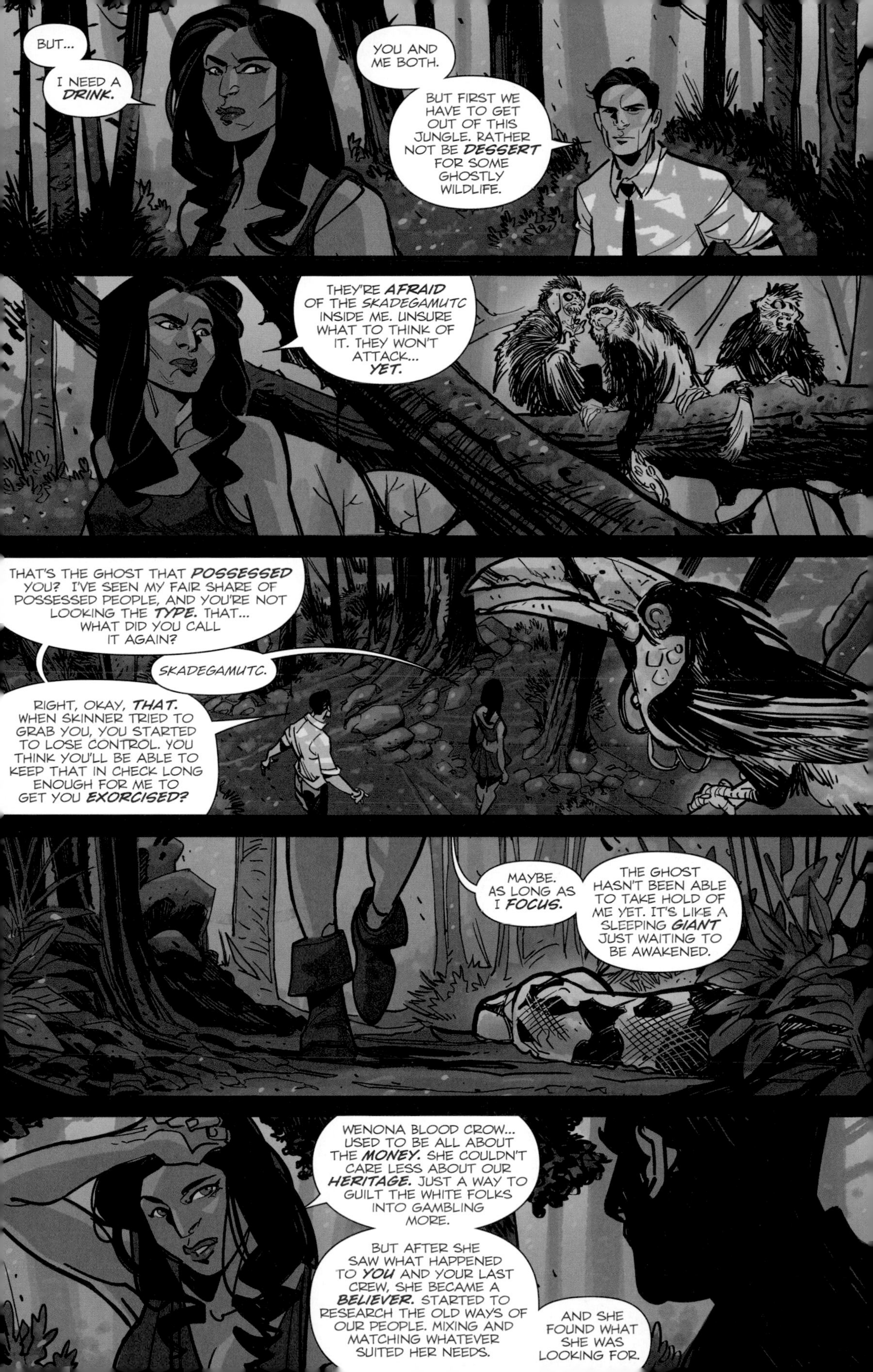
BUT...
I NEED A *DRINK.*
YOU AND ME BOTH.
BUT FIRST WE HAVE TO GET OUT OF THIS JUNGLE. RATHER NOT BE *DESSERT* FOR SOME GHOSTLY WILDLIFE.
THEY'RE *AFRAID* OF THE *SKADEGAMUTC* INSIDE ME. UNSURE WHAT TO THINK OF IT. THEY WON'T ATTACK... *YET.*
THAT'S THE GHOST THAT *POSSESSED* YOU? I'VE SEEN MY FAIR SHARE OF POSSESSED PEOPLE, AND YOU'RE NOT LOOKING THE *TYPE.* THAT... WHAT DID YOU CALL IT AGAIN?
SKADEGAMUTC.
RIGHT, OKAY, *THAT.* WHEN SKINNER TRIED TO GRAB YOU, YOU STARTED TO LOSE CONTROL. YOU THINK YOU'LL BE ABLE TO KEEP THAT IN CHECK LONG ENOUGH FOR ME TO GET YOU *EXORCISED?*
MAYBE. AS LONG AS I *FOCUS.*
THE GHOST HASN'T BEEN ABLE TO TAKE HOLD OF ME YET. IT'S LIKE A SLEEPING *GIANT* JUST WAITING TO BE AWAKENED.
WENONA BLOOD CROW... USED TO BE ALL ABOUT THE *MONEY.* SHE COULDN'T CARE LESS ABOUT OUR *HERITAGE.* JUST A WAY TO GUILT THE WHITE FOLKS INTO GAMBLING MORE.
BUT AFTER SHE SAW WHAT HAPPENED TO *YOU* AND YOUR LAST CREW, SHE BECAME A *BELIEVER.* STARTED TO RESEARCH THE OLD WAYS OF OUR PEOPLE. MIXING AND MATCHING WHATEVER SUITED HER NEEDS.
AND SHE FOUND WHAT SHE WAS LOOKING FOR.

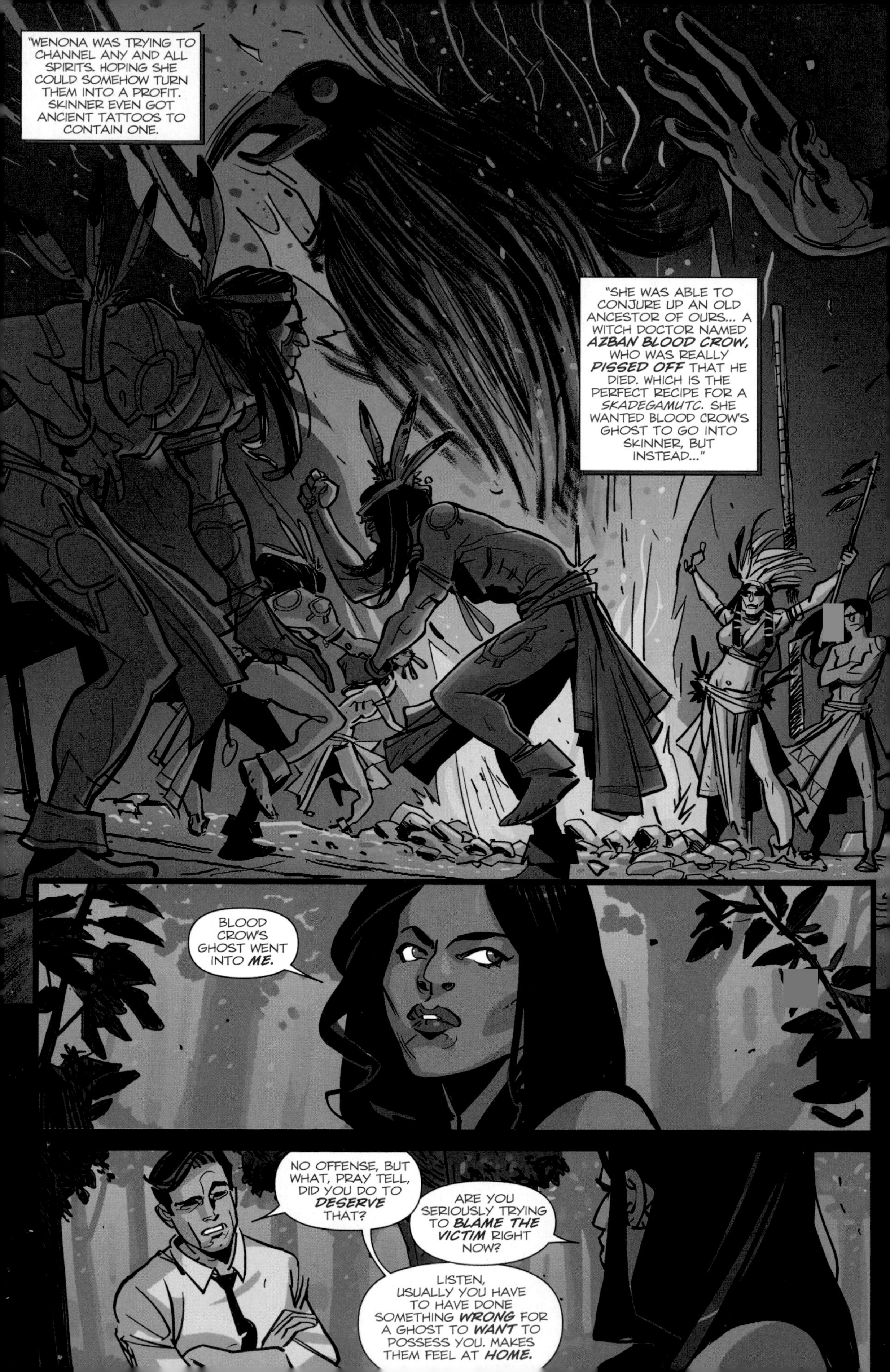
"WENONA WAS TRYING TO CHANNEL ANY AND ALL SPIRITS. HOPING SHE COULD SOMEHOW TURN THEM INTO A PROFIT. SKINNER EVEN GOT ANCIENT TATTOOS TO CONTAIN ONE.
"SHE WAS ABLE TO CONJURE UP AN OLD ANCESTOR OF OURS... A WITCH DOCTOR NAMED AZBAN BLOOD CROW, WHO WAS REALLY PISSED OFF THAT HE DIED. WHICH IS THE PERFECT RECIPE FOR A SKADEGAMUTC. SHE WANTED BLOOD CROW'S GHOST TO GO INTO SKINNER, BUT INSTEAD..."
BLOOD CROW'S GHOST WENT INTO ME.
NO OFFENSE, BUT WHAT, PRAY TELL, DID YOU DO TO DESERVE THAT?
ARE YOU SERIOUSLY TRYING TO BLAME THE VICTIM RIGHT NOW?
LISTEN, USUALLY YOU HAVE TO HAVE DONE SOMETHING WRONG FOR A GHOST TO WANT TO POSSESS YOU. MAKES THEM FEEL AT HOME.

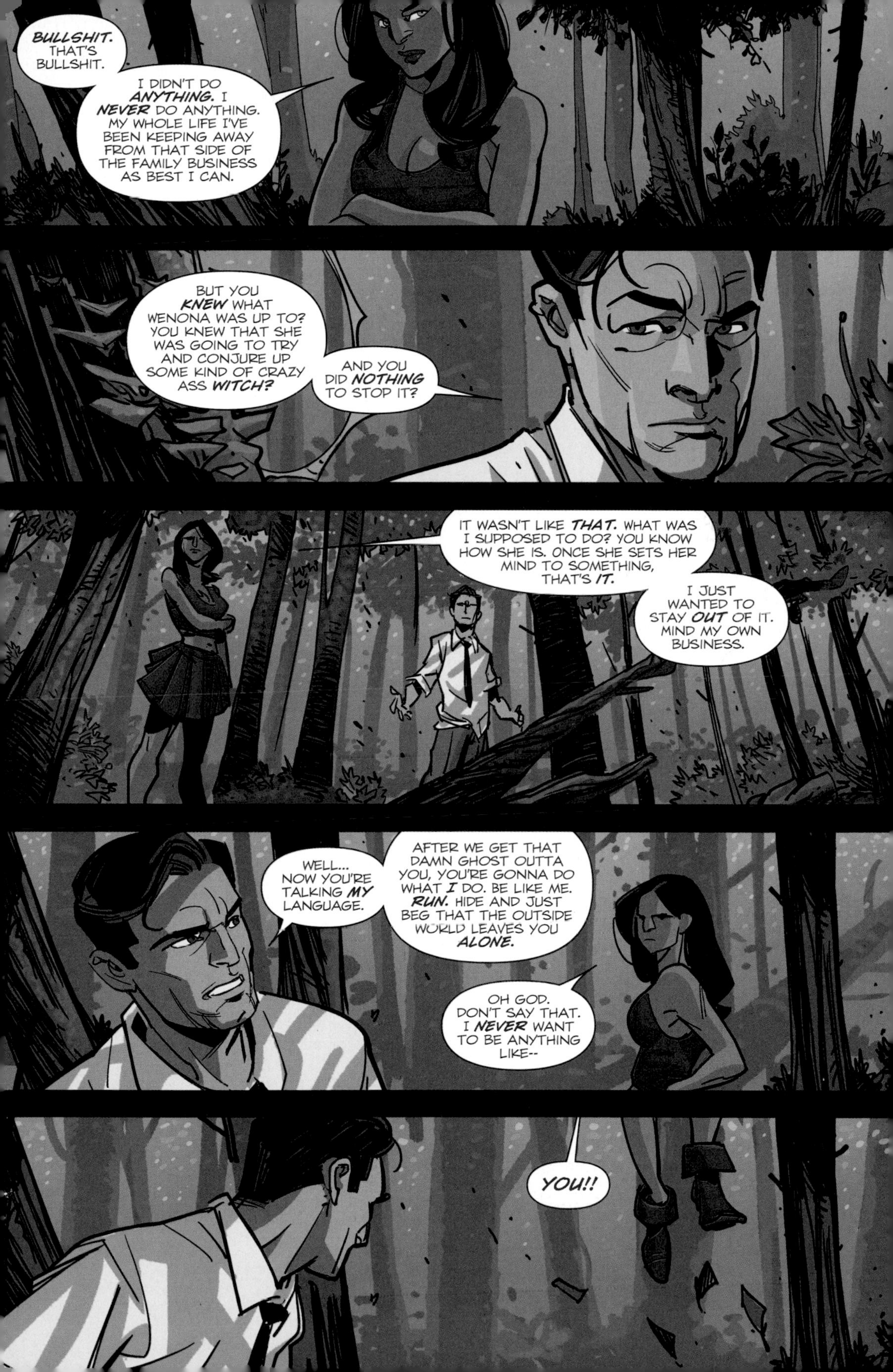
BULLSHIT. THAT'S BULLSHIT.
I DIDN'T DO ANYTHING. I NEVER DO ANYTHING. MY WHOLE LIFE I'VE BEEN KEEPING AWAY FROM THAT SIDE OF THE FAMILY BUSINESS AS BEST I CAN.
BUT YOU KNEW WHAT WENONA WAS UP TO? YOU KNEW THAT SHE WAS GOING TO TRY AND CONJURE UP SOME KIND OF CRAZY ASS WITCH?
AND YOU DID NOTHING TO STOP IT?
IT WASN'T LIKE THAT. WHAT WAS I SUPPOSED TO DO? YOU KNOW HOW SHE IS. ONCE SHE SETS HER MIND TO SOMETHING, THAT'S IT.
I JUST WANTED TO STAY OUT OF IT. MIND MY OWN BUSINESS.
WELL... NOW YOU'RE TALKING MY LANGUAGE.
AFTER WE GET THAT DAMN GHOST OUTTA YOU, YOU'RE GONNA DO WHAT I DO. BE LIKE ME. RUN. HIDE AND JUST BEG THAT THE OUTSIDE WORLD LEAVES YOU ALONE.
OH GOD. DON'T SAY THAT. I NEVER WANT TO BE ANYTHING LIKE--
YOU!!

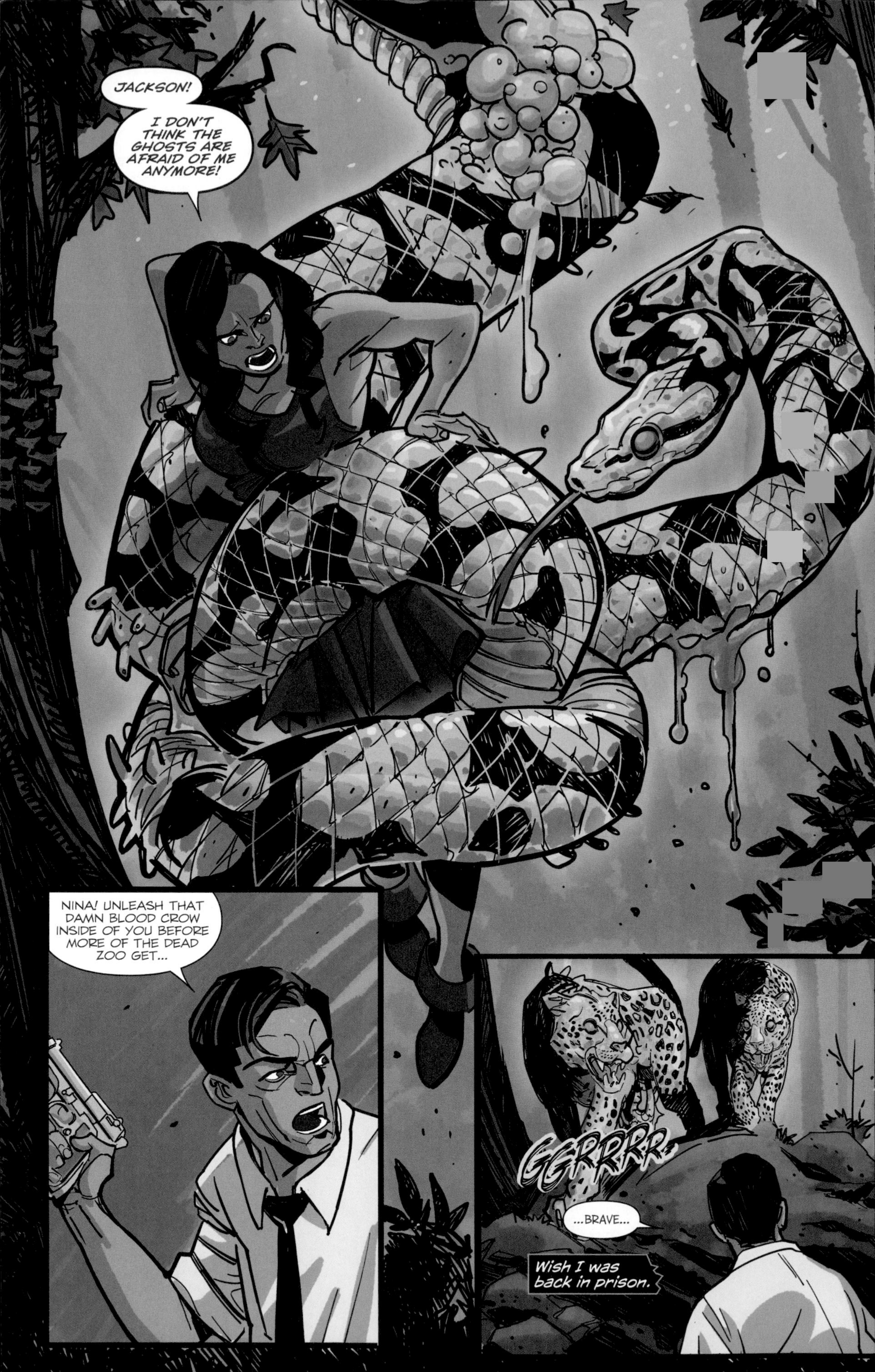
JACKSON!
I DON'T THINK THE GHOSTS ARE AFRAID OF ME ANYMORE!
NINA! UNLEASH THAT DAMN BLOOD CROW INSIDE OF YOU BEFORE MORE OF THE DEAD ZOO GET...
GGRRRR
...BRAVE...
Wish I was back in prison.

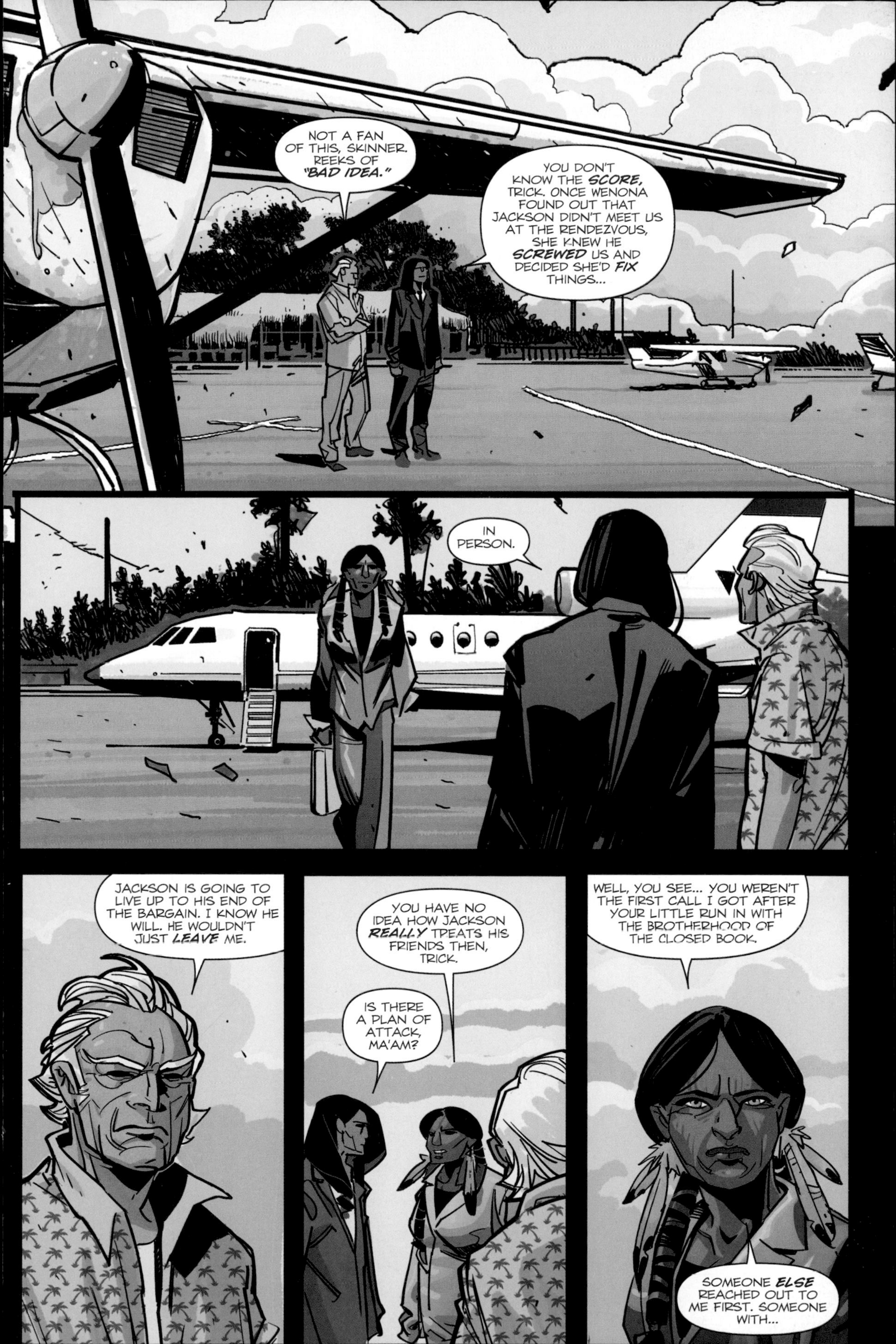
NOT A FAN OF THIS, SKINNER. REEKS OF "BAD IDEA."
YOU DON'T KNOW THE SCORE, TRICK. ONCE WENONA FOUND OUT THAT JACKSON DIDN'T MEET US AT THE RENDEZVOUS, SHE KNEW HE SCREWED US AND DECIDED SHE'D FIX THINGS...
IN PERSON.
JACKSON IS GOING TO LIVE UP TO HIS END OF THE BARGAIN. I KNOW HE WILL. HE WOULDN'T JUST LEAVE ME.
YOU HAVE NO IDEA HOW JACKSON REALLY TREATS HIS FRIENDS THEN, TRICK.
IS THERE A PLAN OF ATTACK, MA'AM?
WELL, YOU SEE... YOU WEREN'T THE FIRST CALL I GOT AFTER YOUR LITTLE RUN IN WITH THE BROTHERHOOD OF THE CLOSED BOOK.
SOMEONE ELSE REACHED OUT TO ME FIRST. SOMEONE WITH...

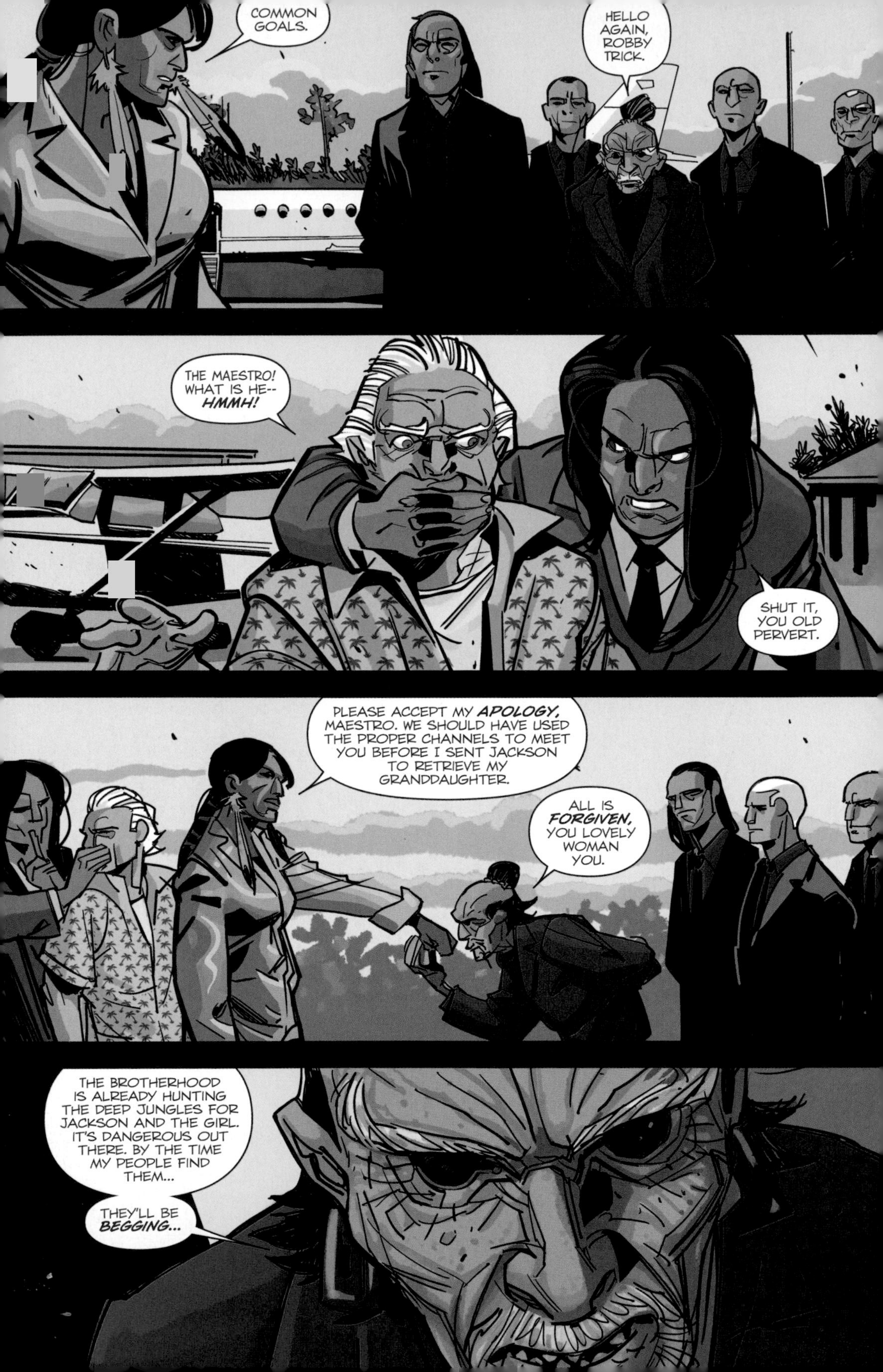
COMMON GOALS.
HELLO AGAIN, ROBBY TRICK.
THE MAESTRO! WHAT IS HE-- HMMH!
SHUT IT, YOU OLD PERVERT.
PLEASE ACCEPT MY APOLOGY, MAESTRO. WE SHOULD HAVE USED THE PROPER CHANNELS TO MEET YOU BEFORE I SENT JACKSON TO RETRIEVE MY GRANDDAUGHTER.
ALL IS FORGIVEN, YOU LOVELY WOMAN YOU.
THE BROTHERHOOD IS ALREADY HUNTING THE DEEP JUNGLES FOR JACKSON AND THE GIRL. IT'S DANGEROUS OUT THERE. BY THE TIME MY PEOPLE FIND THEM...
THEY'LL BE BEGGING...

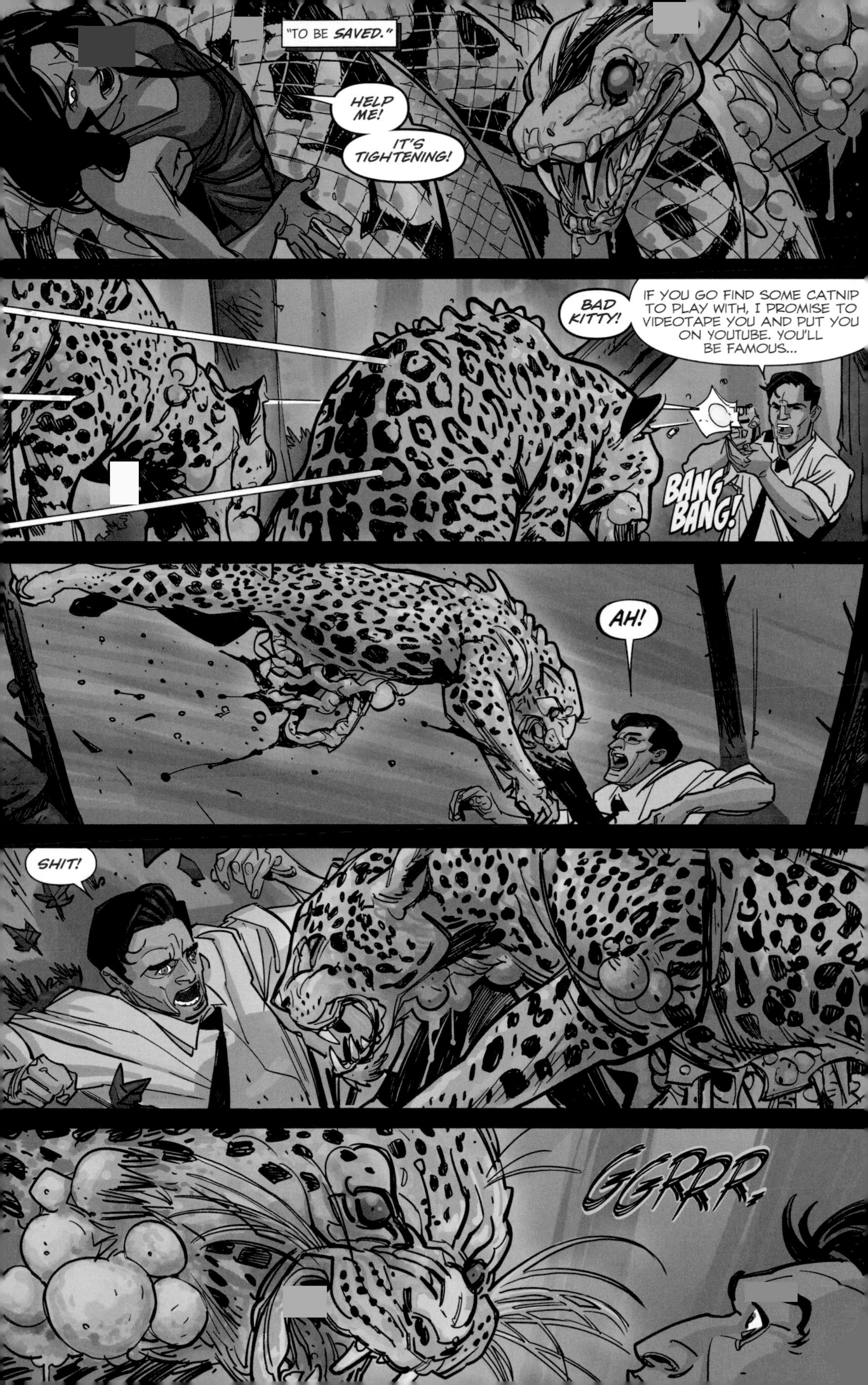
"TO BE SAVED."
HELP ME!
IT'S TIGHTENING!
BAD KITTY!
IF YOU GO FIND SOME CATNIP TO PLAY WITH, I PROMISE TO VIDEOTAPE YOU AND PUT YOU ON YOUTUBE. YOU'LL BE FAMOUS...
BANG BANG!
AH!
SHIT!
GGRRR.

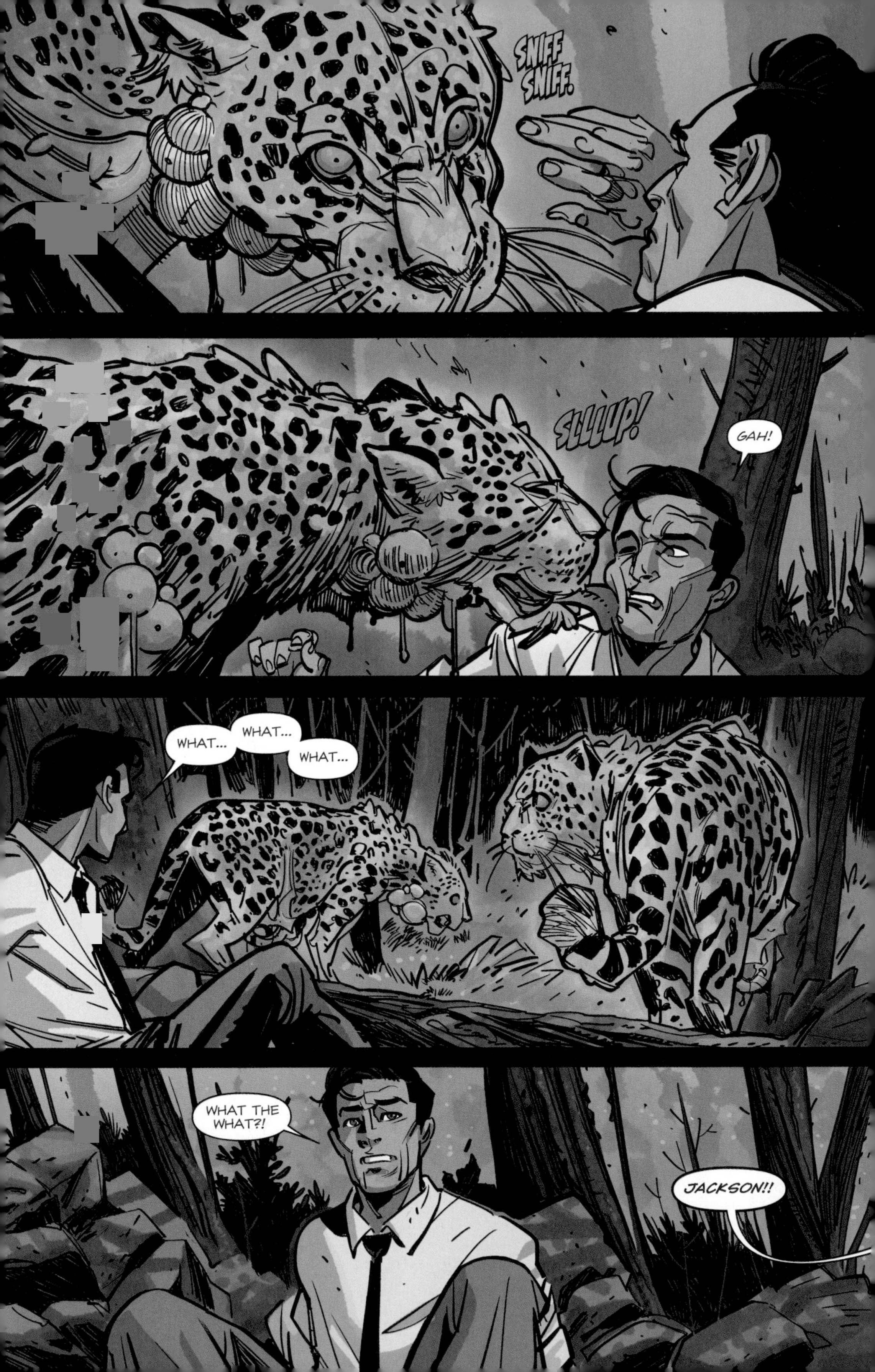

SNIFF SNIFF.
SLLLUP!
GAH!
WHAT...
WHAT...
WHAT...
WHAT THE WHAT?!
JACKSON!!

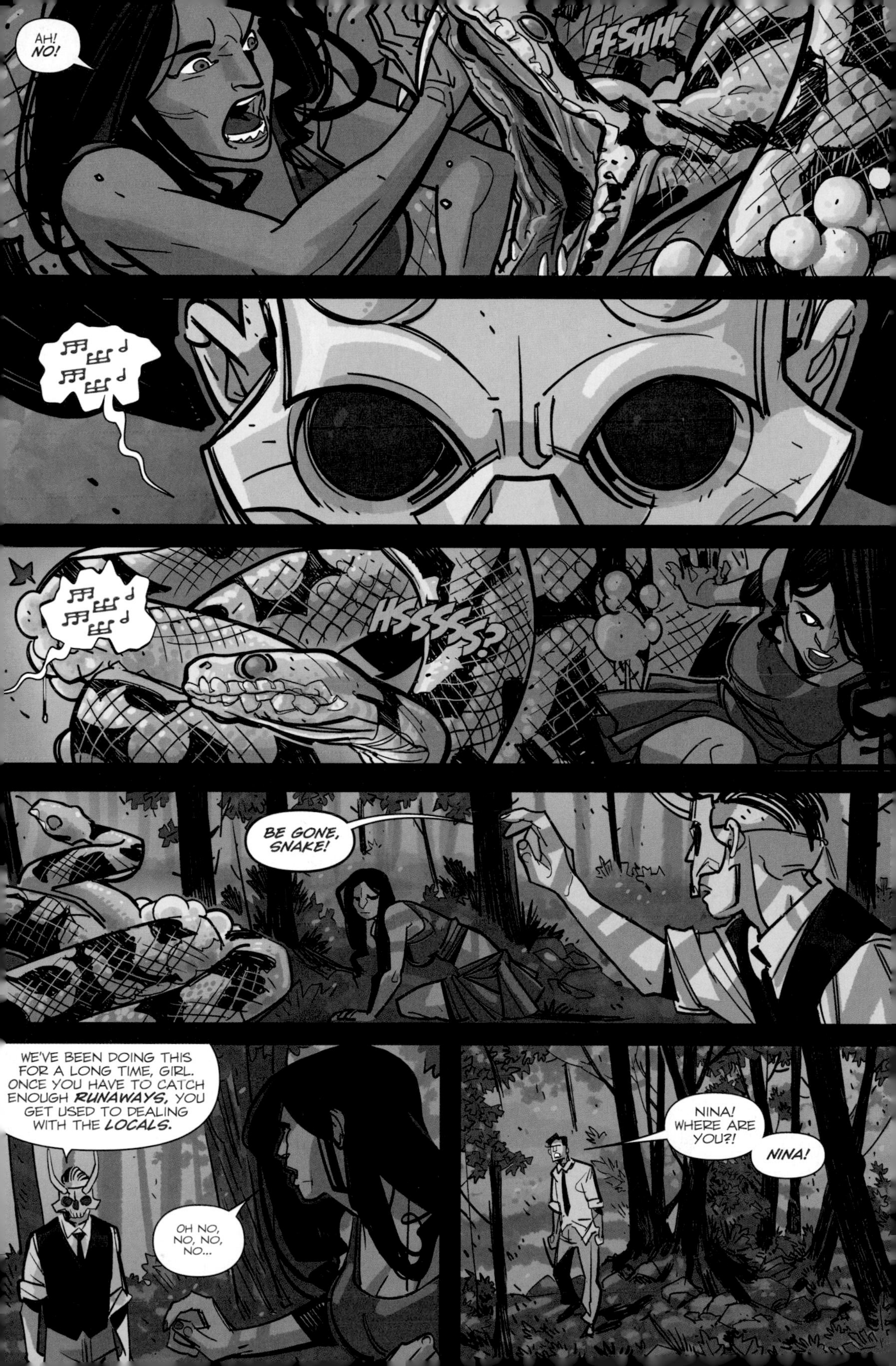
AH! NO!
FFSHH!
HSSSSS?
BE GONE, SNAKE!
WE'VE BEEN DOING THIS FOR A LONG TIME, GIRL. ONCE YOU HAVE TO CATCH ENOUGH RUNAWAYS, YOU GET USED TO DEALING WITH THE LOCALS.
OH NO, NO, NO, NO...
NINA! WHERE ARE YOU?!
NINA!

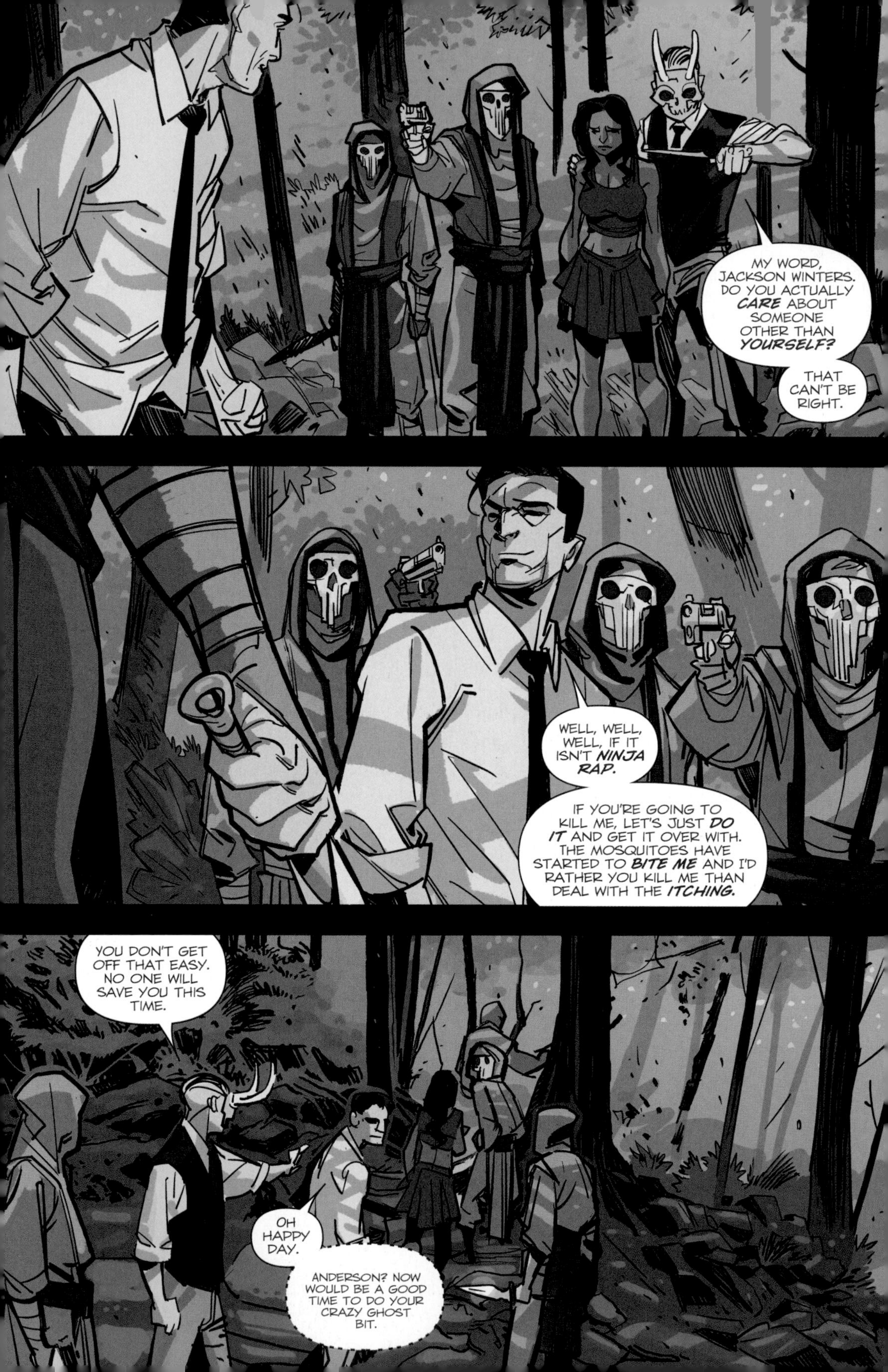
MY WORD, JACKSON WINTERS. DO YOU ACTUALLY CARE ABOUT SOMEONE OTHER THAN YOURSELF?
THAT CAN'T BE RIGHT.
WELL, WELL, WELL, IF IT ISN'T NINJA RAP.
IF YOU'RE GOING TO KILL ME, LET'S JUST DO IT AND GET IT OVER WITH. THE MOSQUITOES HAVE STARTED TO BITE ME AND I'D RATHER YOU KILL ME THAN DEAL WITH THE ITCHING.
YOU DON'T GET OFF THAT EASY. NO ONE WILL SAVE YOU THIS TIME.
OH HAPPY DAY.
ANDERSON? NOW WOULD BE A GOOD TIME TO DO YOUR CRAZY GHOST BIT.

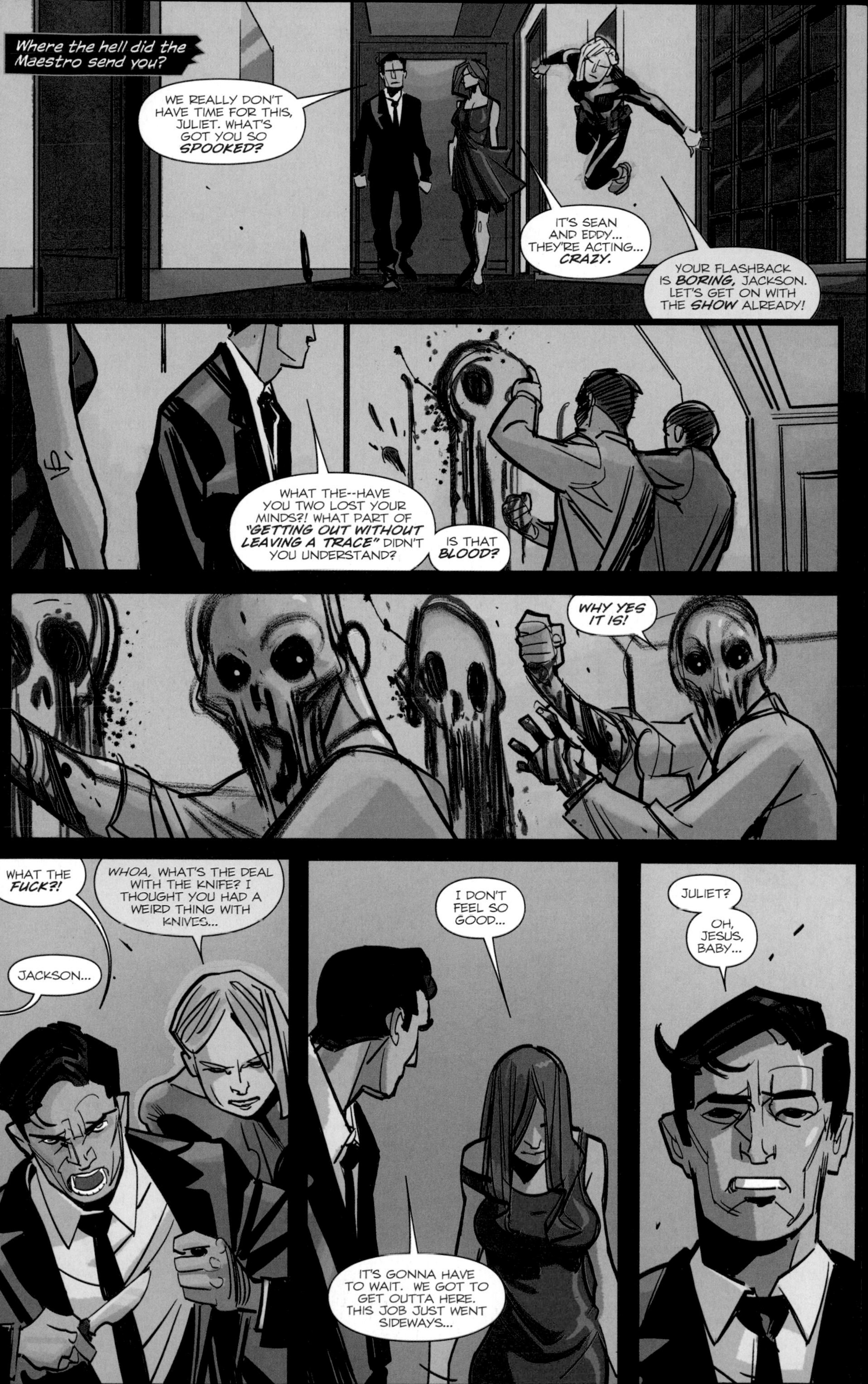
Where the hell did the Maestro send you?
WE REALLY DON'T HAVE TIME FOR THIS, JULIET. WHAT'S GOT YOU SO SPOOKED?
IT'S SEAN AND EDDY... THEY'RE ACTING... CRAZY.
YOUR FLASHBACK IS BORING, JACKSON. LET'S GET ON WITH THE SHOW ALREADY!
WHAT THE--HAVE YOU TWO LOST YOUR MINDS?! WHAT PART OF "GETTING OUT WITHOUT LEAVING A TRACE" DIDN'T YOU UNDERSTAND?
IS THAT BLOOD?
WHY YES IT IS!
WHAT THE FUCK?!
WHOA, WHAT'S THE DEAL WITH THE KNIFE? I THOUGHT YOU HAD A WEIRD THING WITH KNIVES...
JACKSON...
I DON'T FEEL SO GOOD...
IT'S GONNA HAVE TO WAIT. WE GOT TO GET OUTTA HERE. THIS JOB JUST WENT SIDEWAYS...
JULIET?
OH, JESUS, BABY...

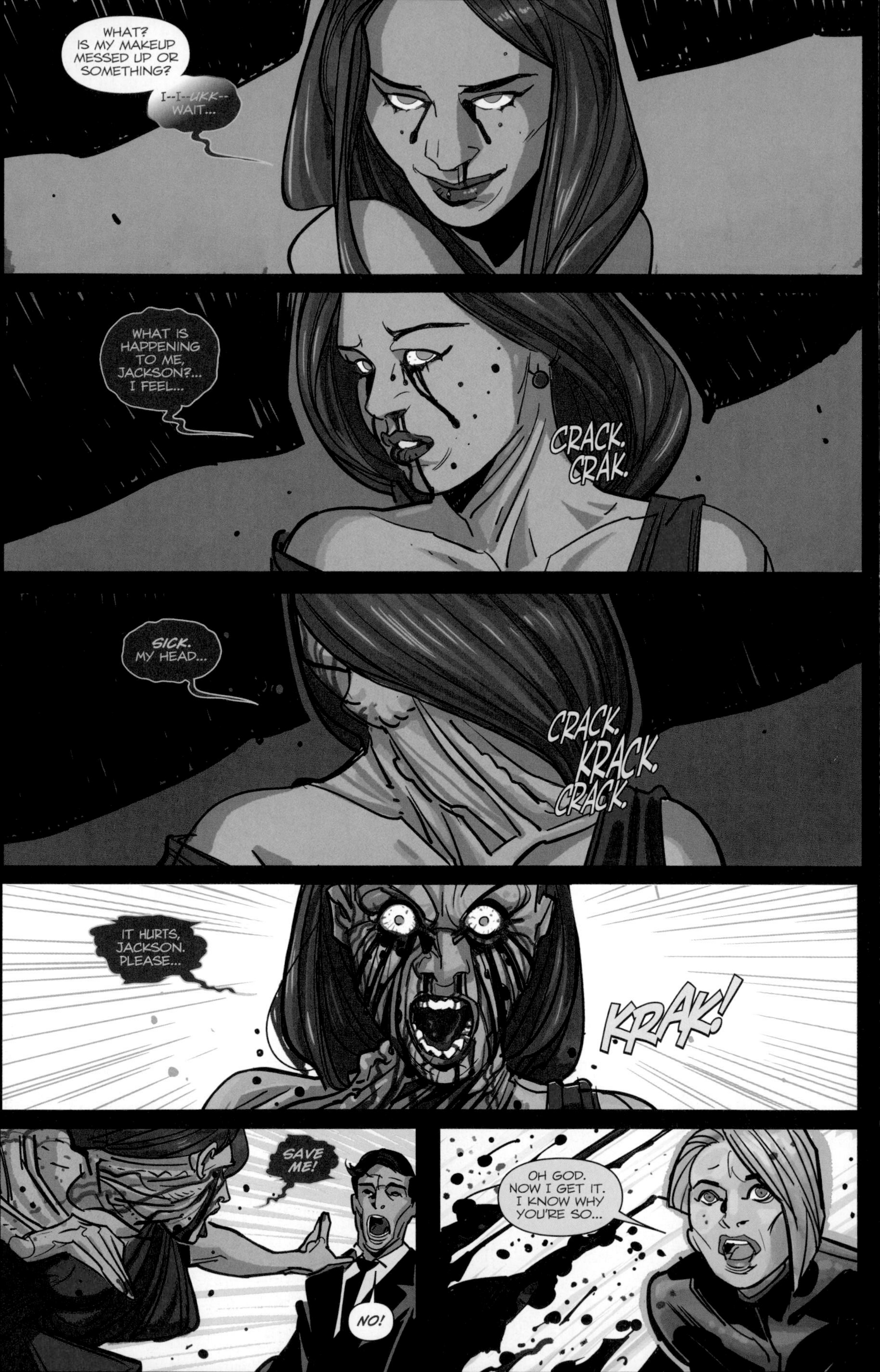
WHAT? IS MY MAKEUP MESSED UP OR SOMETHING?
I--I--UKK-- WAIT...
WHAT IS HAPPENING TO ME, JACKSON?... I FEEL...
CRACK. CRAK.
SICK. MY HEAD...
CRACK. KRACK. CRACK.
IT HURTS, JACKSON. PLEASE...
KRAK!
SAVE ME!
NO!
OH GOD. NOW I GET IT. I KNOW WHY YOU'RE SO...

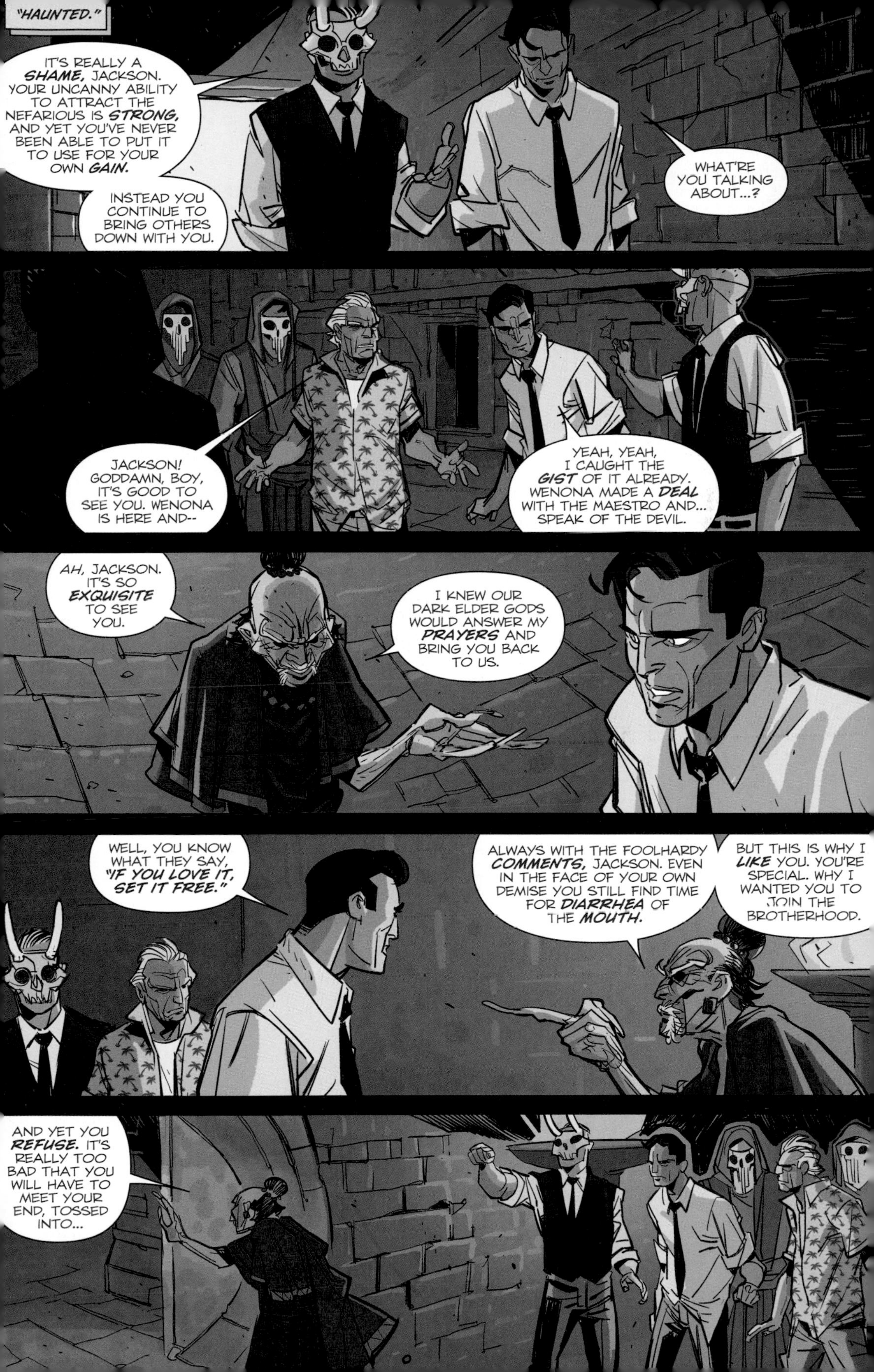
"HAUNTED."
IT'S REALLY A SHAME, JACKSON. YOUR UNCANNY ABILITY TO ATTRACT THE NEFARIOUS IS STRONG, AND YET YOU'VE NEVER BEEN ABLE TO PUT IT TO USE FOR YOUR OWN GAIN.
INSTEAD YOU CONTINUE TO BRING OTHERS DOWN WITH YOU.
WHAT'RE YOU TALKING ABOUT...?
JACKSON! GODDAMN, BOY, IT'S GOOD TO SEE YOU. WENONA IS HERE AND--
YEAH, YEAH, I CAUGHT THE GIST OF IT ALREADY. WENONA MADE A DEAL WITH THE MAESTRO AND... SPEAK OF THE DEVIL.
AH, JACKSON. IT'S SO EXQUISITE TO SEE YOU.
I KNEW OUR DARK ELDER GODS WOULD ANSWER MY PRAYERS AND BRING YOU BACK TO US.
WELL, YOU KNOW WHAT THEY SAY, "IF YOU LOVE IT, SET IT FREE."
ALWAYS WITH THE FOOLHARDY COMMENTS, JACKSON. EVEN IN THE FACE OF YOUR OWN DEMISE YOU STILL FIND TIME FOR DIARRHEA OF THE MOUTH.
BUT THIS IS WHY I LIKE YOU. YOU'RE SPECIAL. WHY I WANTED YOU TO JOIN THE BROTHERHOOD.
AND YET YOU REFUSE. IT'S REALLY TOO BAD THAT YOU WILL HAVE TO MEET YOUR END, TOSSED INTO...

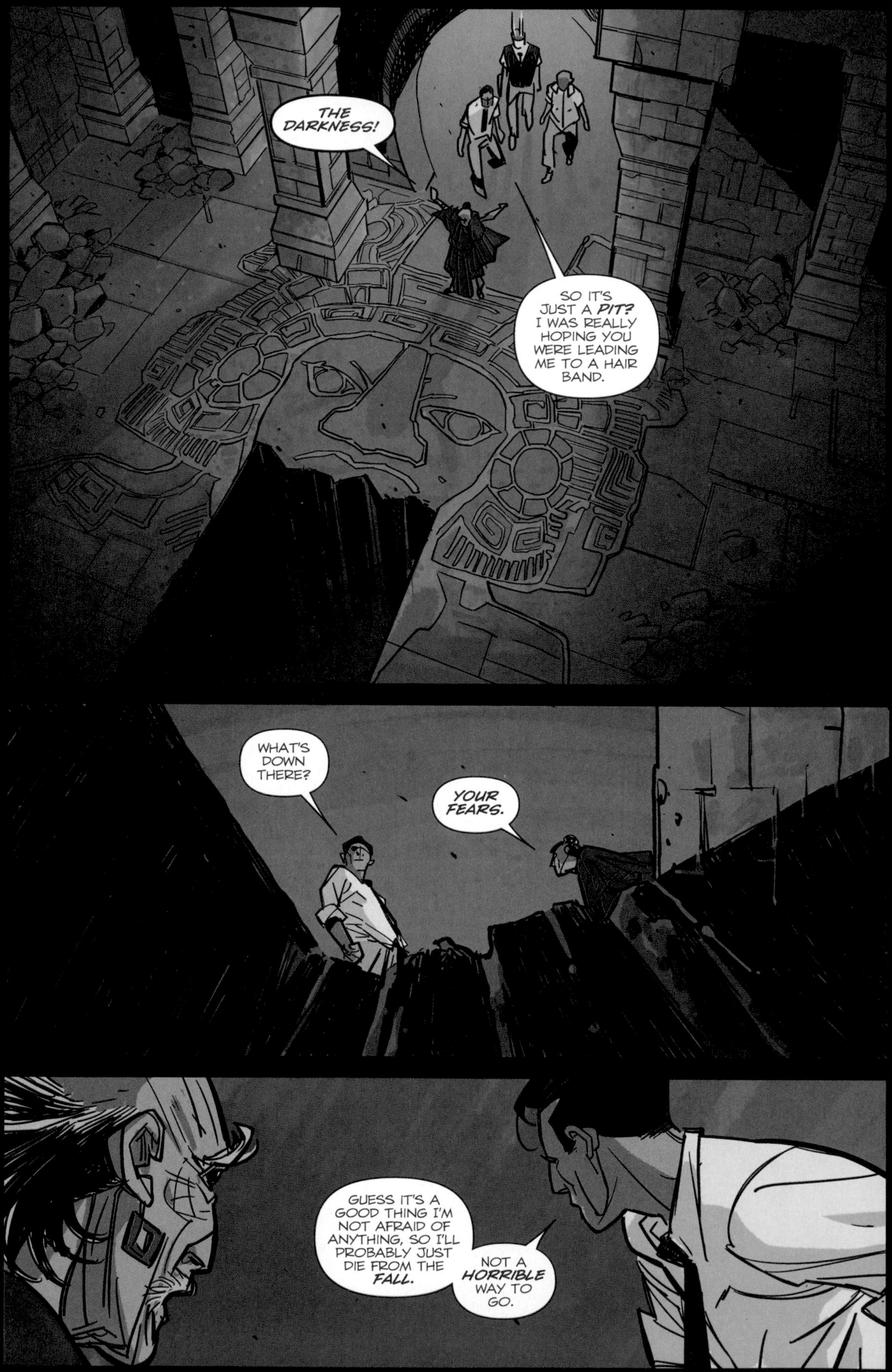
THE DARKNESS!
SO IT'S JUST A PIT? I WAS REALLY HOPING YOU WERE LEADING ME TO A HAIR BAND.
WHAT'S DOWN THERE?
YOUR FEARS.
GUESS IT'S A GOOD THING I'M NOT AFRAID OF ANYTHING, SO I'LL PROBABLY JUST DIE FROM THE FALL.
NOT A HORRIBLE WAY TO GO.

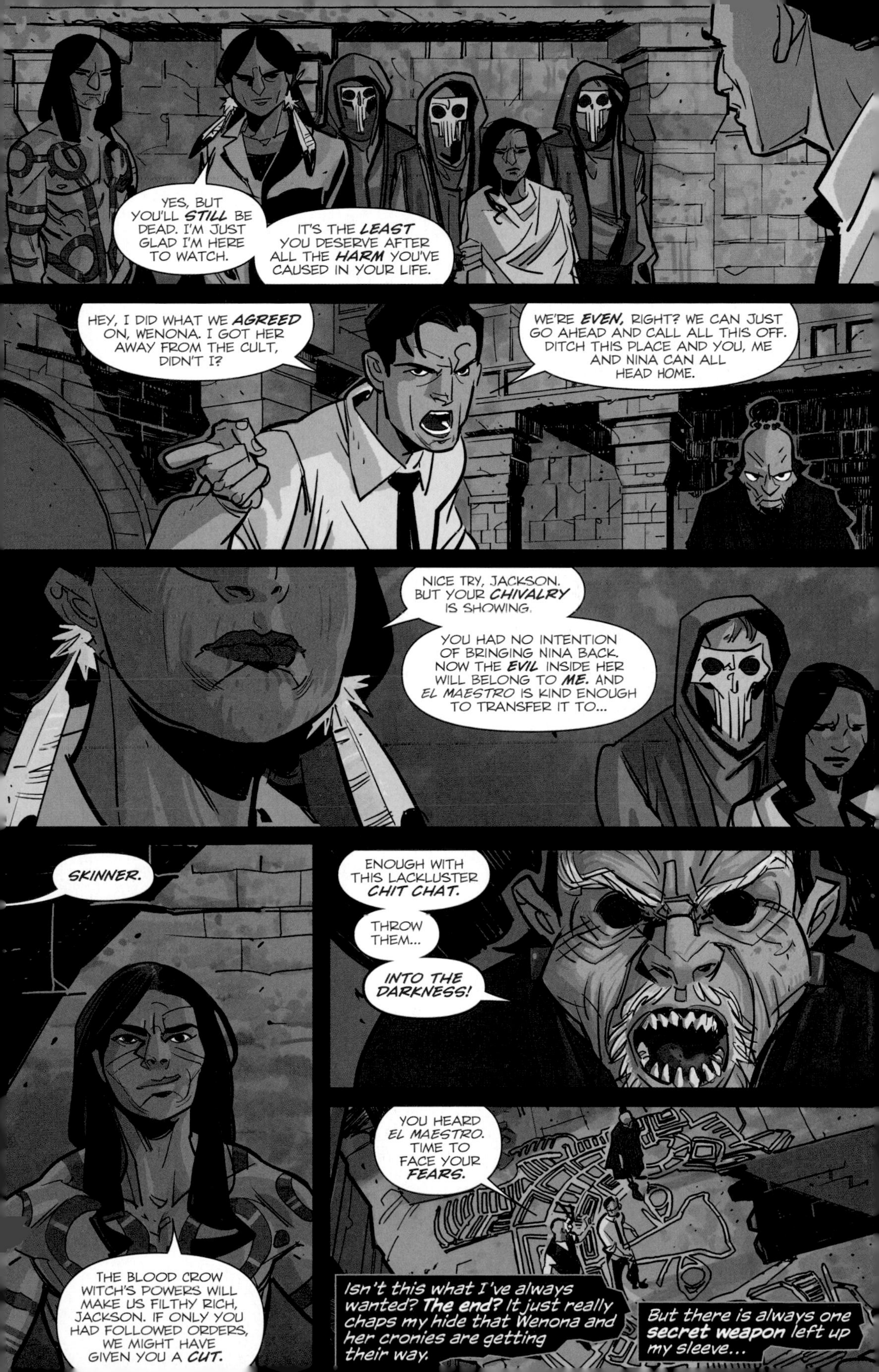
YES, BUT YOU'LL STILL BE DEAD. I'M JUST GLAD I'M HERE TO WATCH.
IT'S THE LEAST YOU DESERVE AFTER ALL THE HARM YOU'VE CAUSED IN YOUR LIFE.
HEY, I DID WHAT WE AGREED ON, WENONA. I GOT HER AWAY FROM THE CULT, DIDN'T I?
WE'RE EVEN, RIGHT? WE CAN JUST GO AHEAD AND CALL ALL THIS OFF. DITCH THIS PLACE AND YOU, ME AND NINA CAN ALL HEAD HOME.
NICE TRY, JACKSON. BUT YOUR CHIVALRY IS SHOWING.
YOU HAD NO INTENTION OF BRINGING NINA BACK. NOW THE EVIL INSIDE HER WILL BELONG TO ME. AND EL MAESTRO IS KIND ENOUGH TO TRANSFER IT TO...
SKINNER.
THE BLOOD CROW WITCH'S POWERS WILL MAKE US FILTHY RICH, JACKSON. IF ONLY YOU HAD FOLLOWED ORDERS, WE MIGHT HAVE GIVEN YOU A CUT.
ENOUGH WITH THIS LACKLUSTER CHIT CHAT.
THROW THEM...
INTO THE DARKNESS!
YOU HEARD EL MAESTRO. TIME TO FACE YOUR FEARS.
Isn't this what I've always wanted? The end? It just really chaps my hide that Wenona and her cronies are getting their way.
But there is always one secret weapon left up my sleeve...

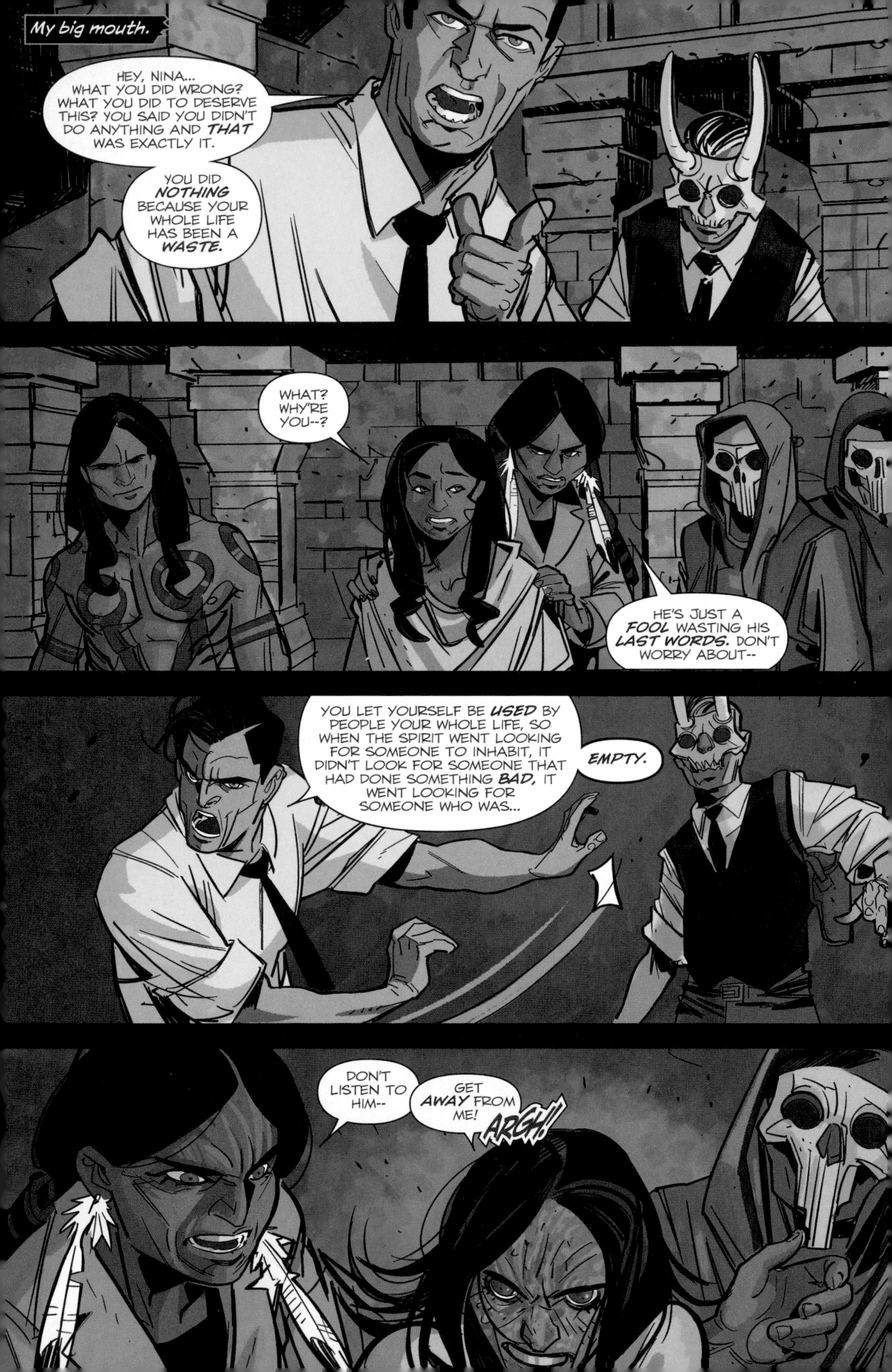
My big mouth.
HEY, NINA... WHAT YOU DID WRONG? WHAT YOU DID TO DESERVE THIS? YOU SAID YOU DIDN'T DO ANYTHING AND THAT WAS EXACTLY IT.
YOU DID NOTHING BECAUSE YOUR WHOLE LIFE HAS BEEN A WASTE.
WHAT? WHY'RE YOU--?
HE'S JUST A FOOL WASTING HIS LAST WORDS. DON'T WORRY ABOUT--
YOU LET YOURSELF BE USED BY PEOPLE YOUR WHOLE LIFE, SO WHEN THE SPIRIT WENT LOOKING FOR SOMEONE TO INHABIT, IT DIDN'T LOOK FOR SOMEONE THAT HAD DONE SOMETHING BAD, IT WENT LOOKING FOR SOMEONE WHO WAS...
EMPTY.
DON'T LISTEN TO HIM--
GET AWAY FROM ME!
ARGH!

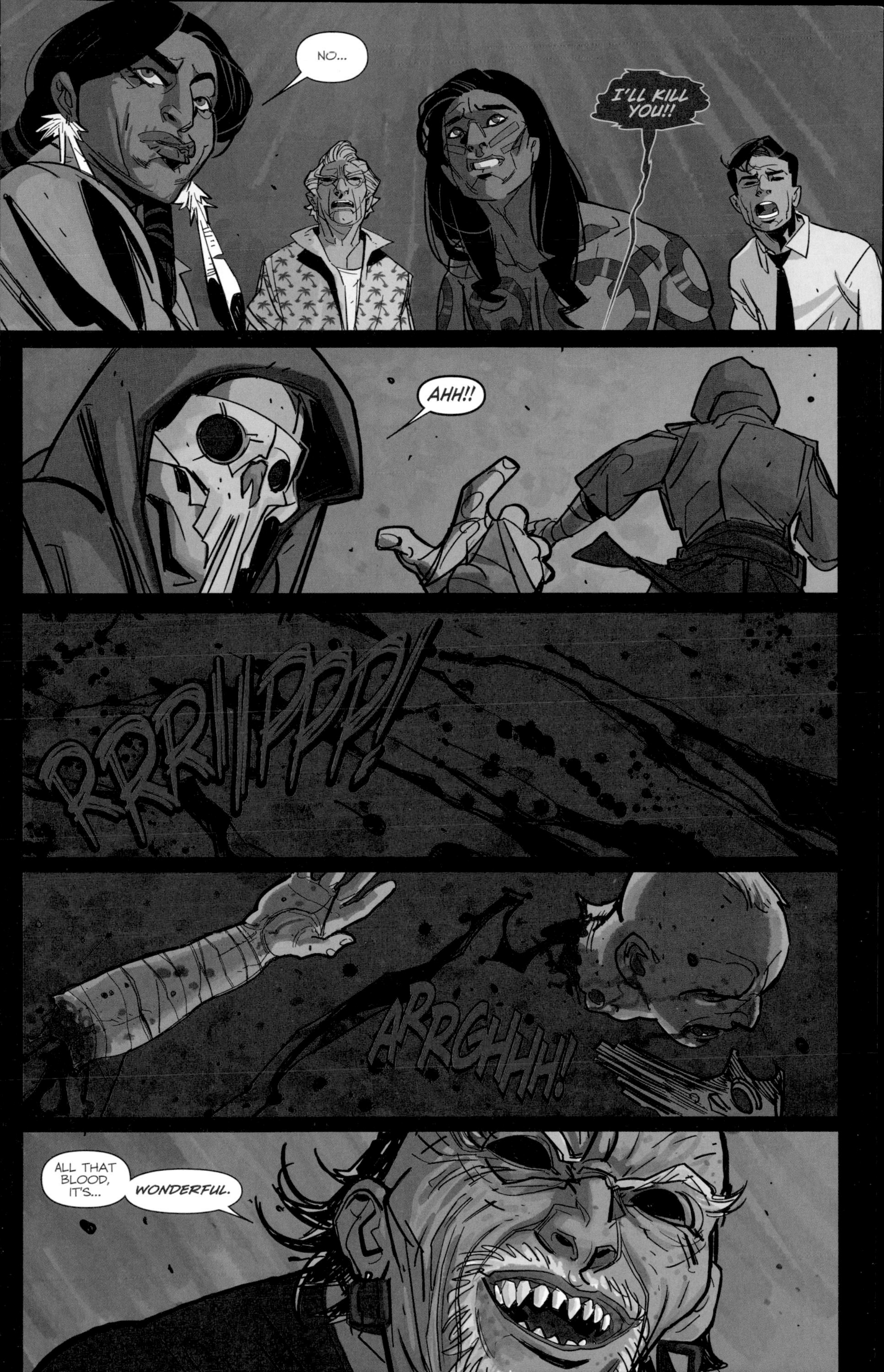
NO...
I'LL KILL YOU!!
AHH!!
RRRIIPPP!
ARRGHHH!
ALL THAT BLOOD, IT'S...
WONDERFUL.

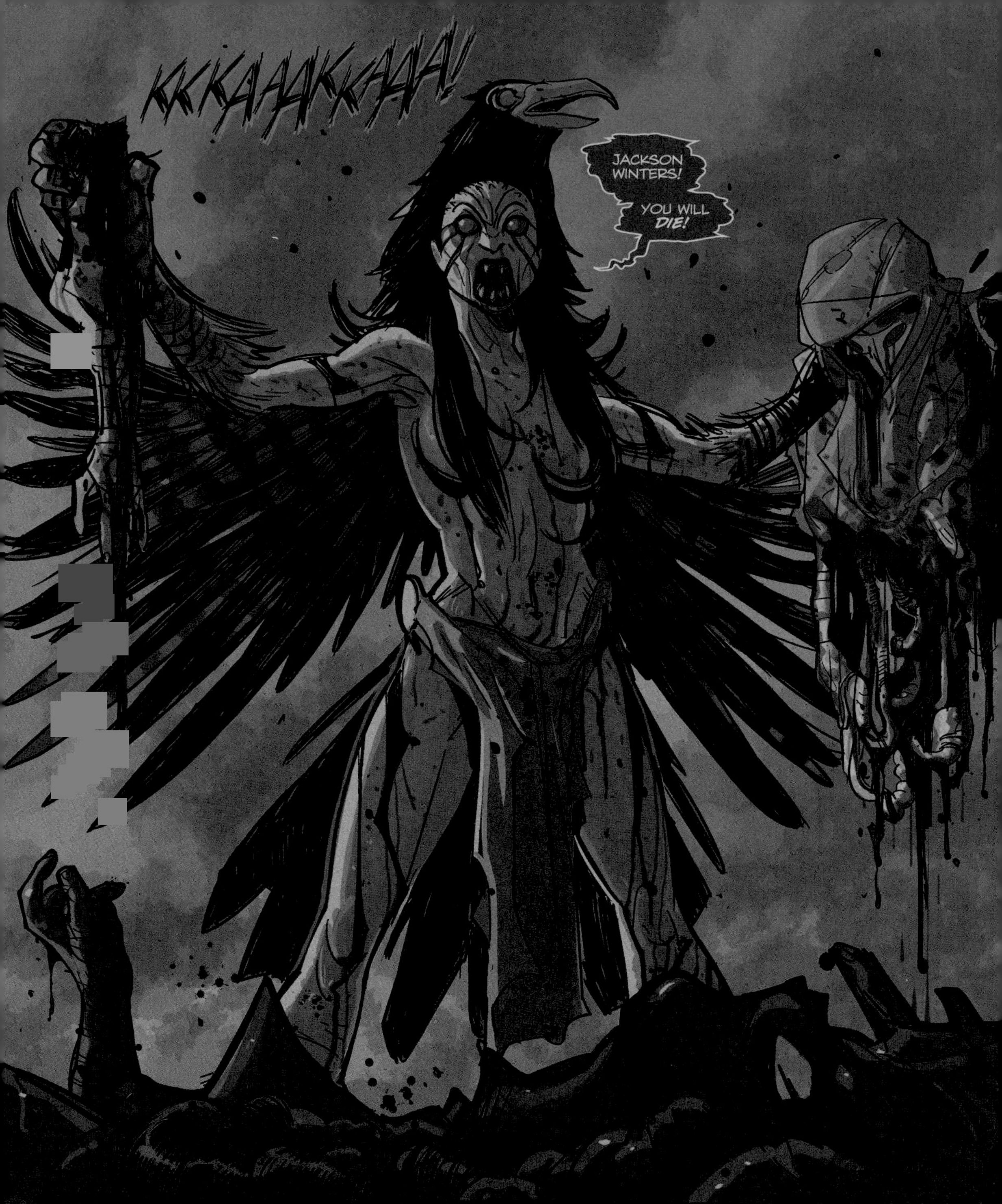
KKKAAAAKKAAA!
JACKSON WINTERS!
YOU WILL DIE!
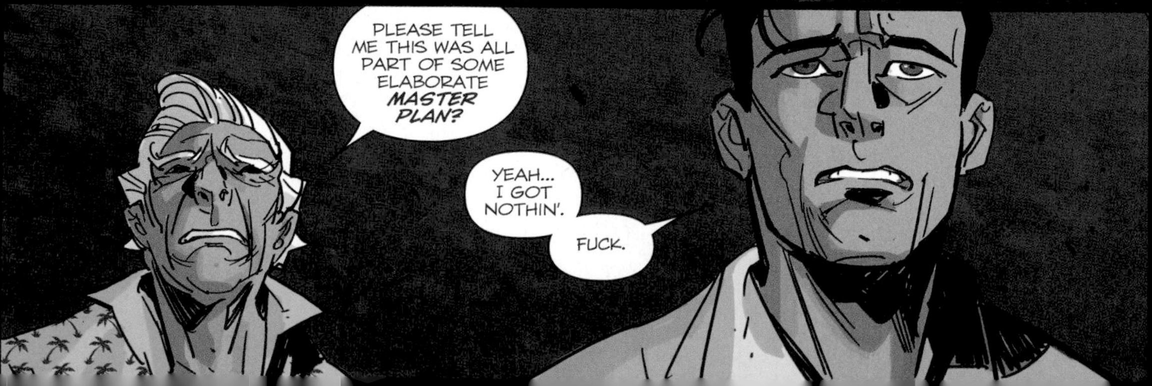
PLEASE TELL ME THIS WAS ALL PART OF SOME ELABORATE MASTER PLAN?
YEAH... I GOT NOTHIN'.
FUCK.

CHAPTER FIVE

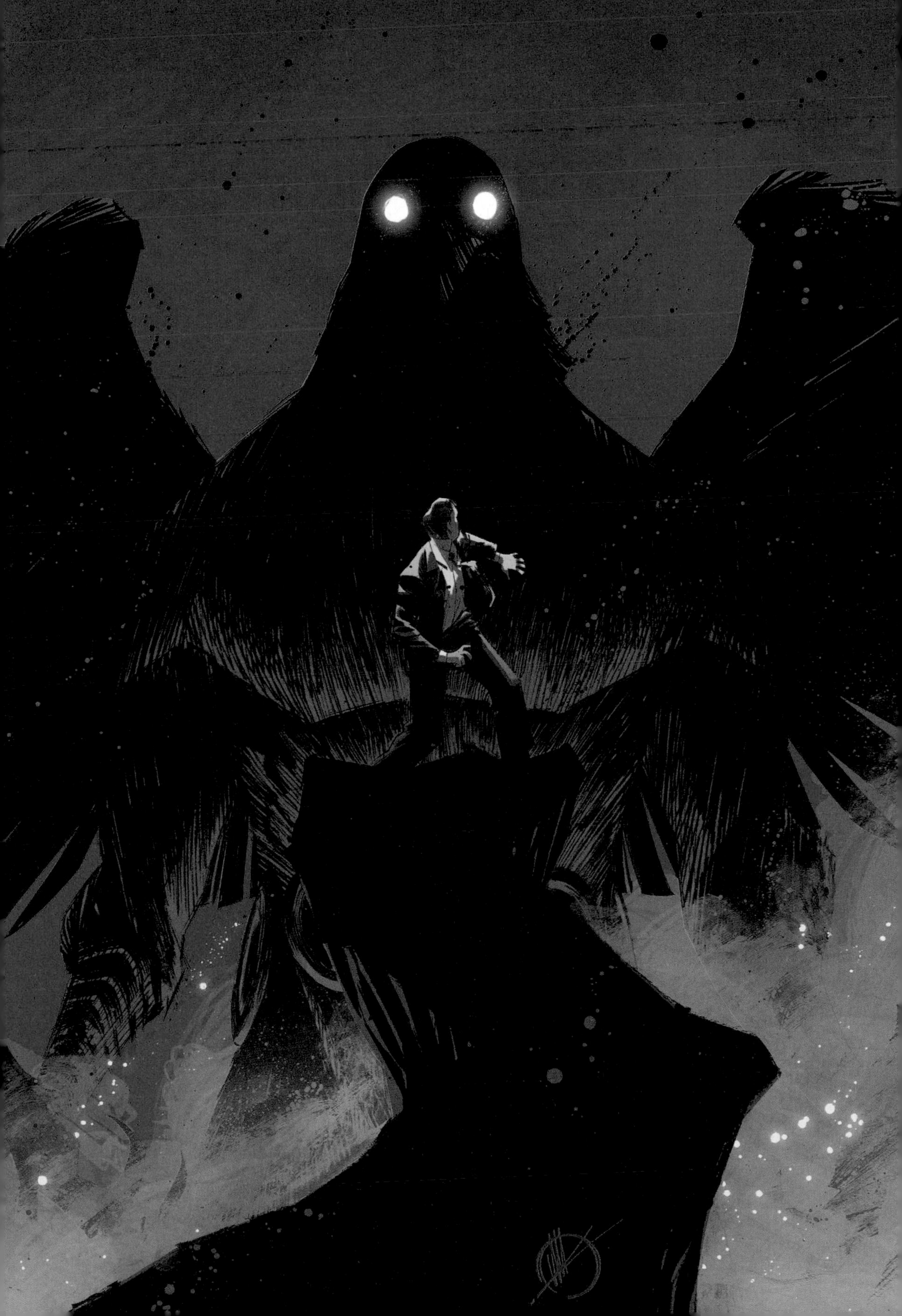

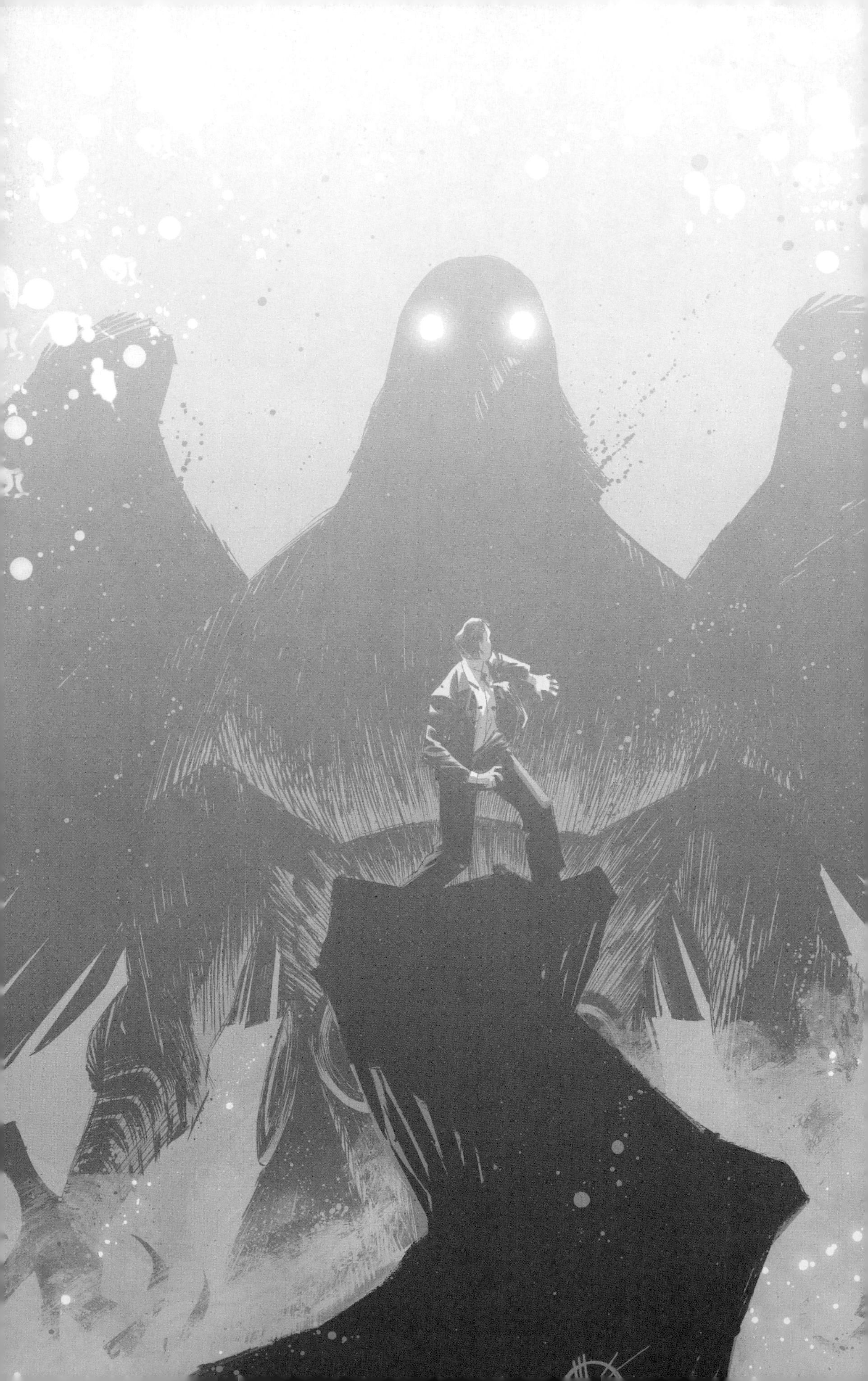

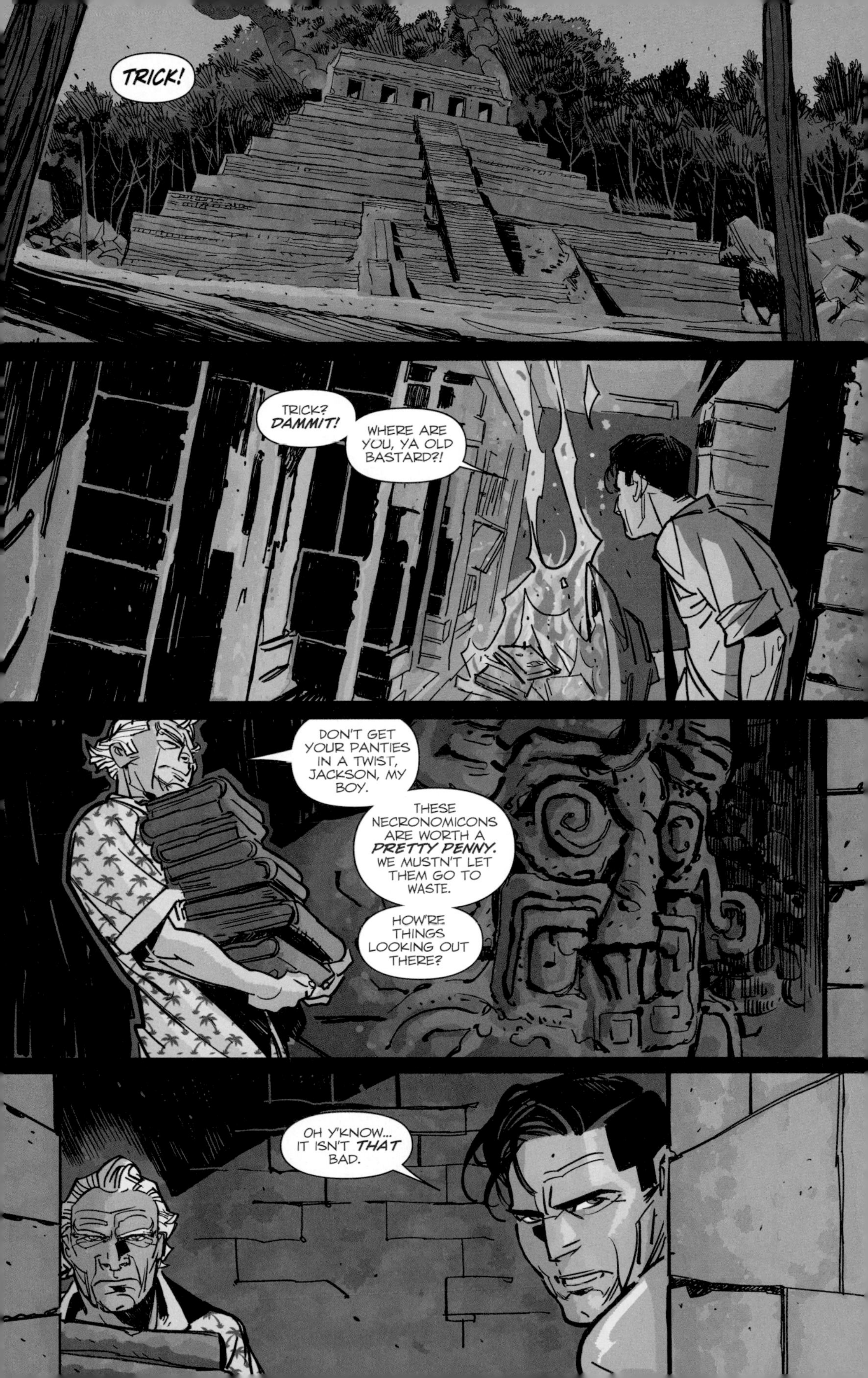
TRICK!
TRICK? DAMMIT!
WHERE ARE YOU, YA OLD BASTARD?!
DON'T GET YOUR PANTIES IN A TWIST, JACKSON, MY BOY.
THESE NECRONOMICONS ARE WORTH A PRETTY PENNY. WE MUSTN'T LET THEM GO TO WASTE.
HOW'RE THINGS LOOKING OUT THERE?
OH Y'KNOW... IT ISN'T THAT BAD.

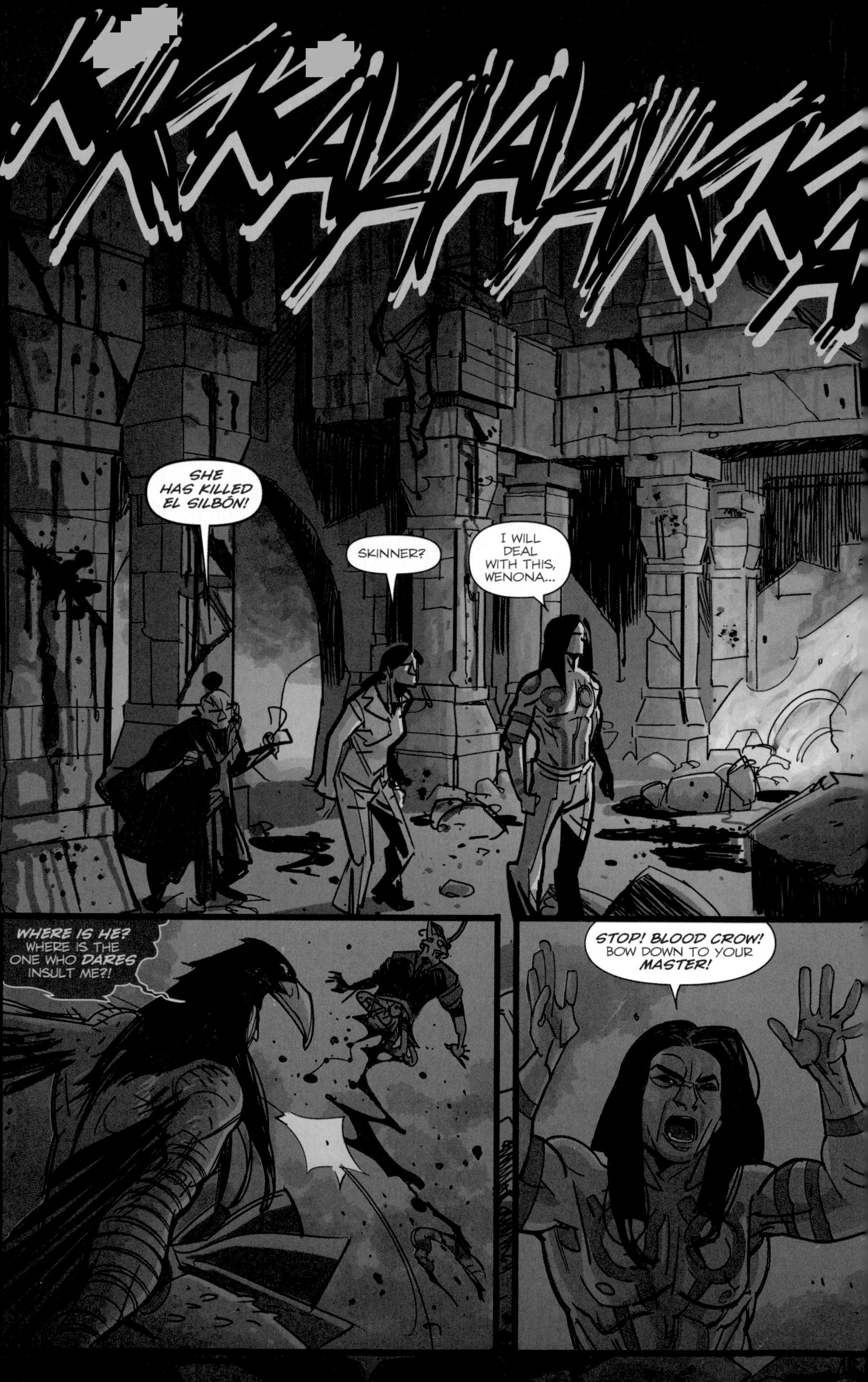
SHE HAS KILLED EL SILBÓN!
SKINNER?
I WILL DEAL WITH THIS, WENONA...
WHERE IS HE? WHERE IS THE ONE WHO DARES INSULT ME?!
STOP! BLOOD CROW! BOW DOWN TO YOUR MASTER!

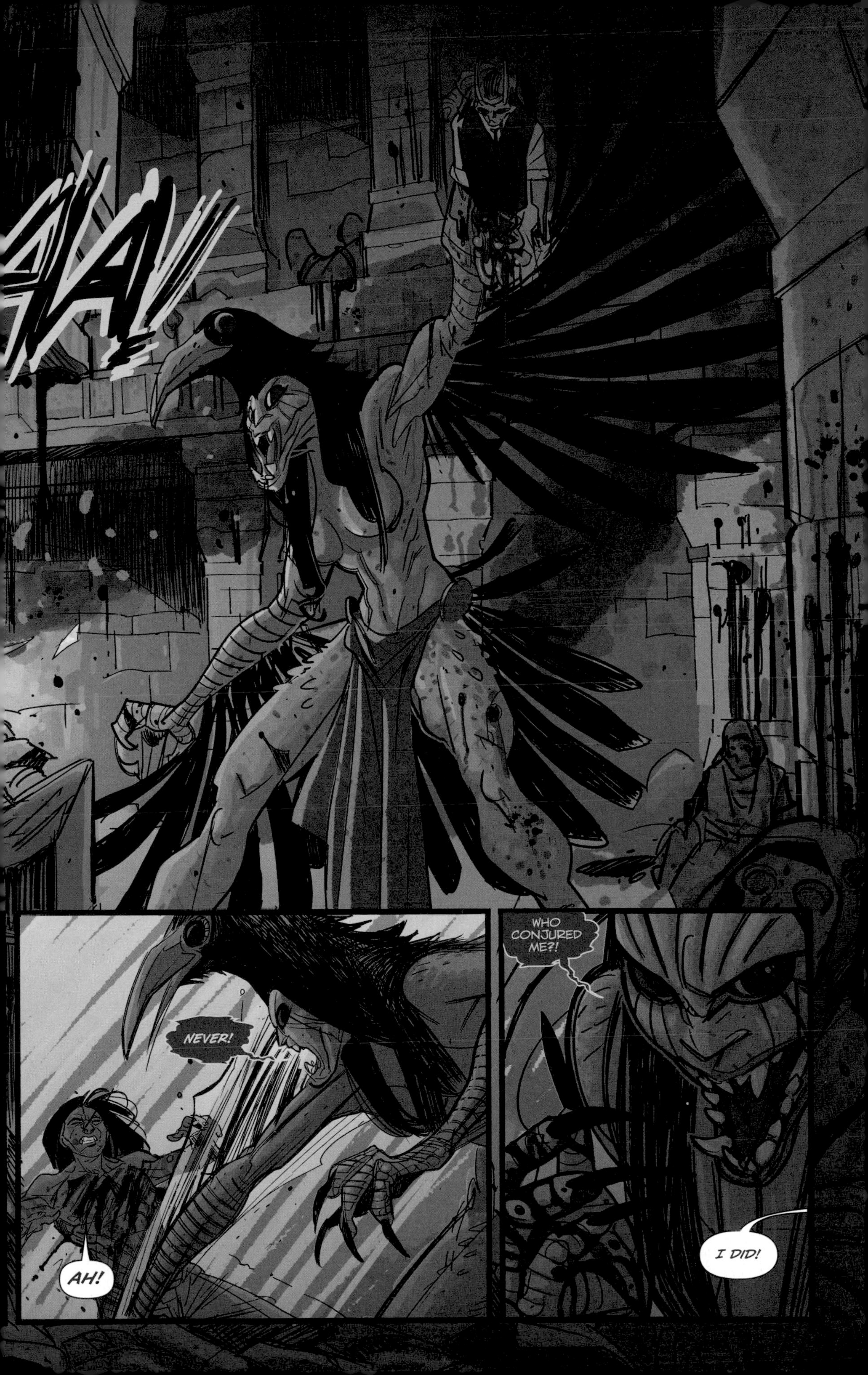

KAAW!
NEVER!
AH!
WHO CONJURED ME?!
I DID!

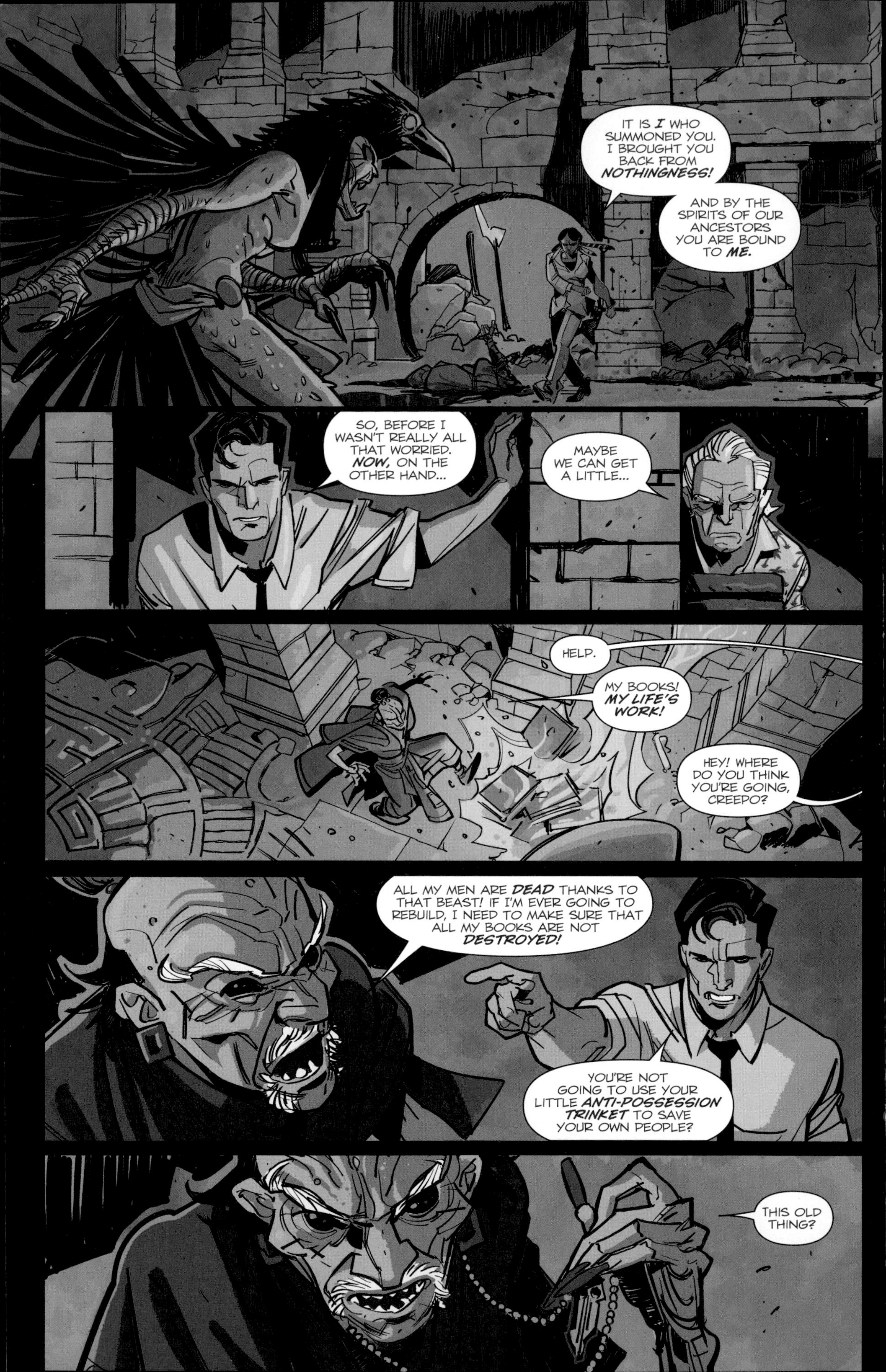
IT IS I WHO SUMMONED YOU. I BROUGHT YOU BACK FROM NOTHINGNESS!
AND BY THE SPIRITS OF OUR ANCESTORS YOU ARE BOUND TO ME.
SO, BEFORE I WASN'T REALLY ALL THAT WORRIED. NOW, ON THE OTHER HAND...
MAYBE WE CAN GET A LITTLE...
HELP.
MY BOOKS! MY LIFE'S WORK!
HEY! WHERE DO YOU THINK YOU'RE GOING, CREEPO?
ALL MY MEN ARE DEAD THANKS TO THAT BEAST! IF I'M EVER GOING TO REBUILD, I NEED TO MAKE SURE THAT ALL MY BOOKS ARE NOT DESTROYED!
YOU'RE NOT GOING TO USE YOUR LITTLE ANTI-POSSESSION TRINKET TO SAVE YOUR OWN PEOPLE?
THIS OLD THING?

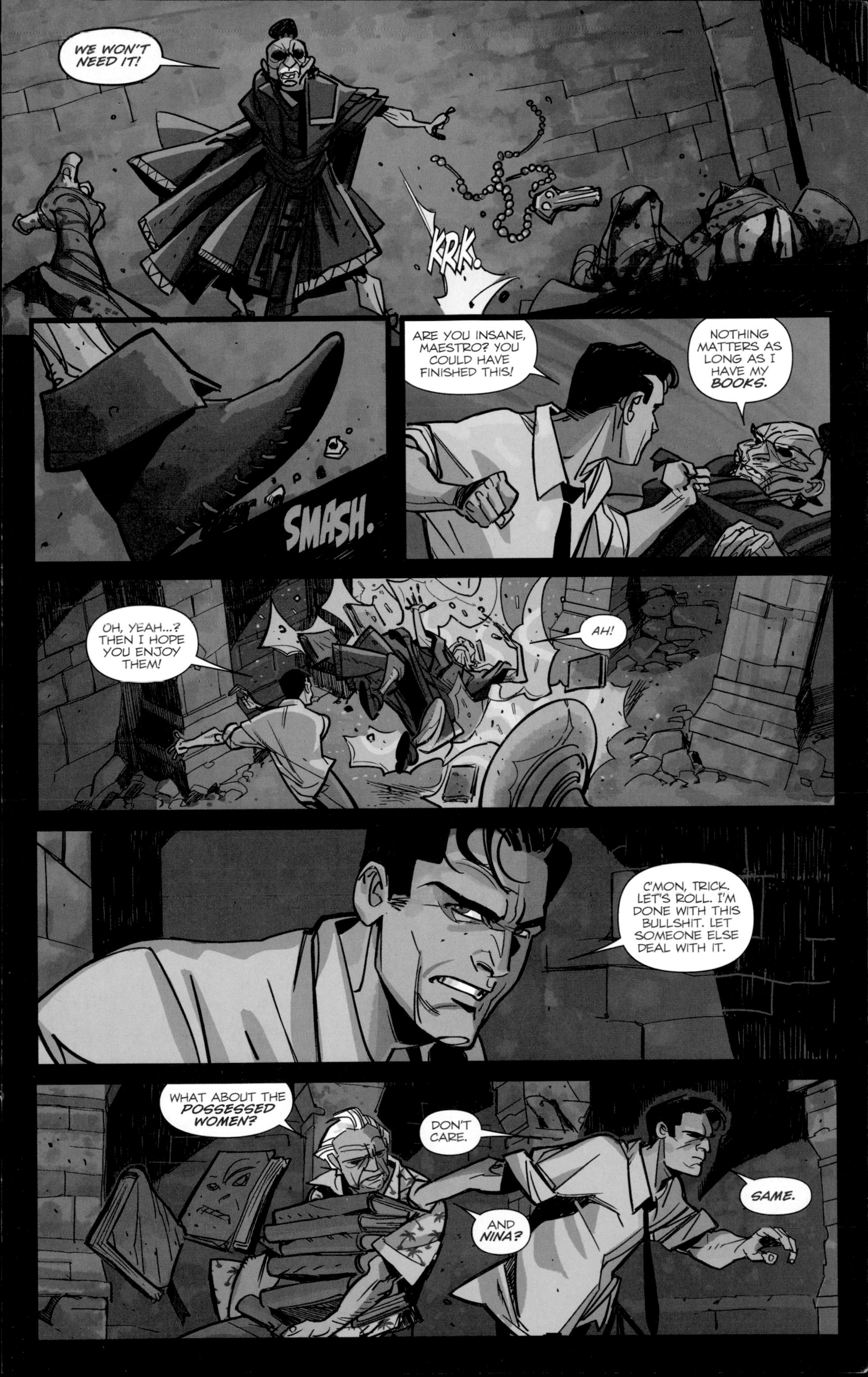
WE WON'T NEED IT!
KRK.
SMASH.
ARE YOU INSANE, MAESTRO? YOU COULD HAVE FINISHED THIS!
NOTHING MATTERS AS LONG AS I HAVE MY BOOKS.
OH, YEAH...? THEN I HOPE YOU ENJOY THEM!
AH!
C'MON, TRICK. LET'S ROLL. I'M DONE WITH THIS BULLSHIT. LET SOMEONE ELSE DEAL WITH IT.
WHAT ABOUT THE POSSESSED WOMEN?
DON'T CARE.
AND NINA?
SAME.

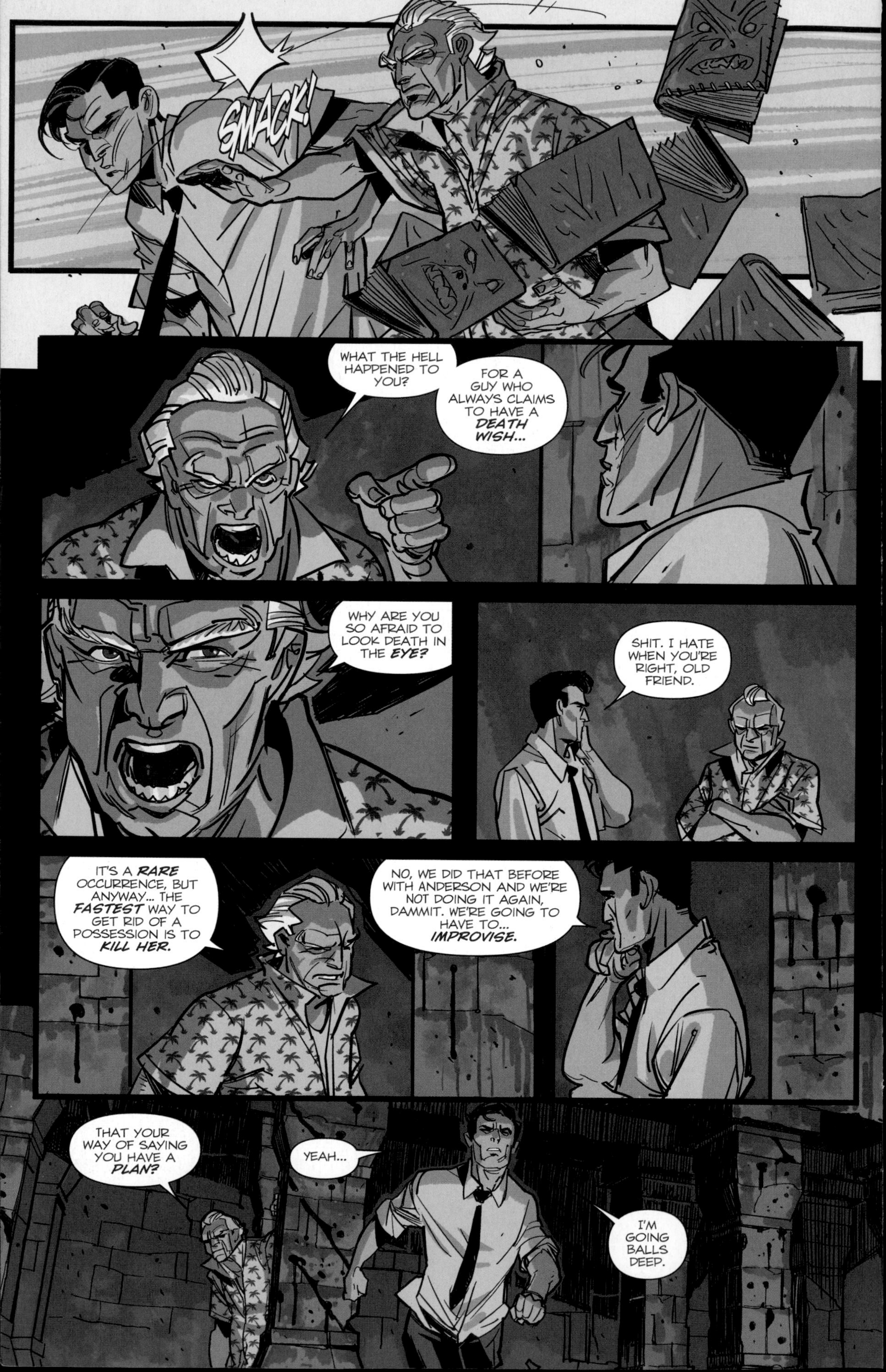
SMACK!
WHAT THE HELL HAPPENED TO YOU?
FOR A GUY WHO ALWAYS CLAIMS TO HAVE A DEATH WISH...
WHY ARE YOU SO AFRAID TO LOOK DEATH IN THE EYE?
SHIT. I HATE WHEN YOU'RE RIGHT, OLD FRIEND.
IT'S A RARE OCCURRENCE, BUT ANYWAY... THE FASTEST WAY TO GET RID OF A POSSESSION IS TO KILL HER.
NO, WE DID THAT BEFORE WITH ANDERSON AND WE'RE NOT DOING IT AGAIN, DAMMIT. WE'RE GOING TO HAVE TO... IMPROVISE.
THAT YOUR WAY OF SAYING YOU HAVE A PLAN?
YEAH...
I'M GOING BALLS DEEP.

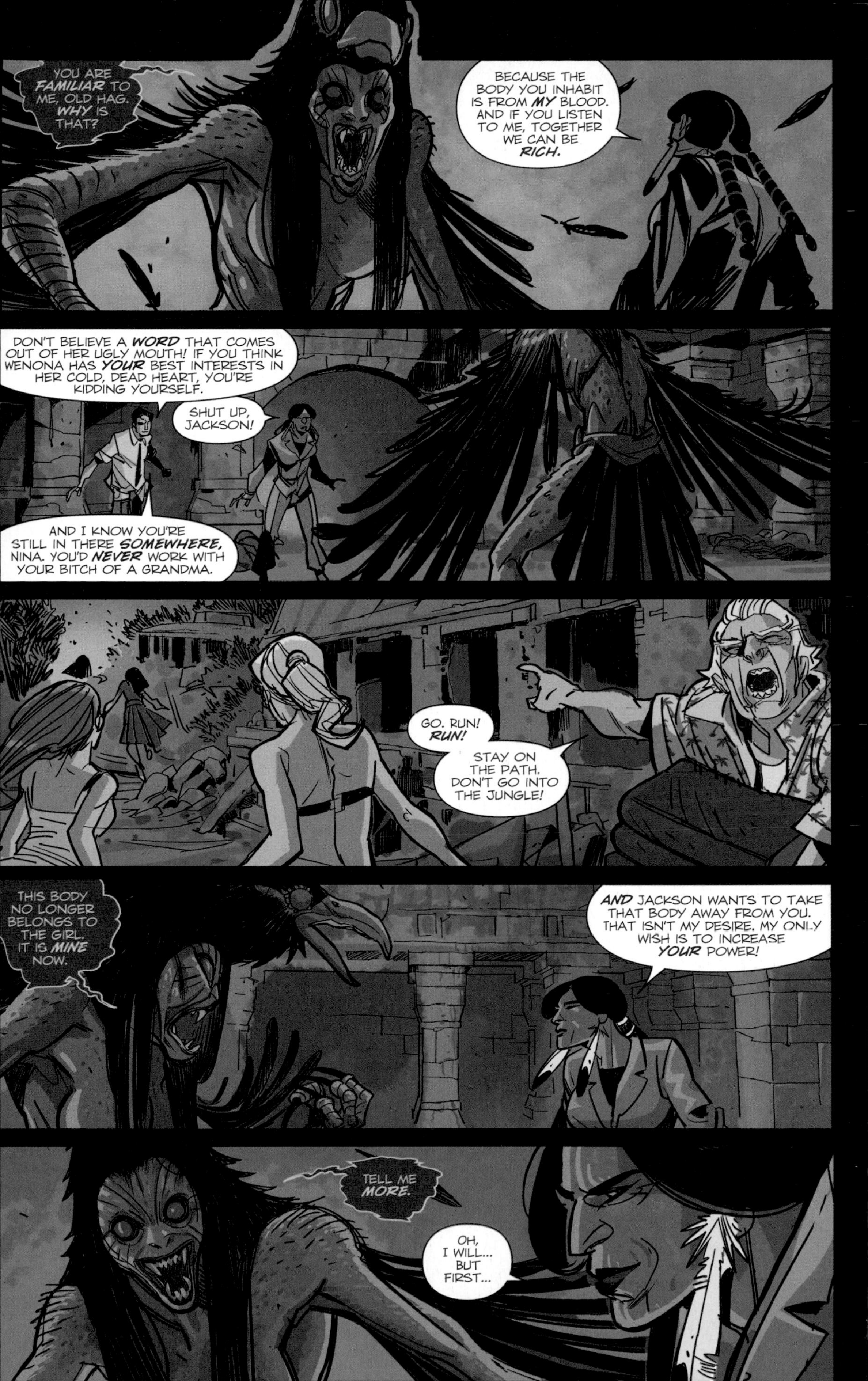
YOU ARE *FAMILIAR* TO ME, OLD HAG. *WHY* IS THAT?
BECAUSE THE BODY YOU INHABIT IS FROM *MY* BLOOD. AND IF YOU LISTEN TO ME, TOGETHER WE CAN BE *RICH.*
DON'T BELIEVE A *WORD* THAT COMES OUT OF HER UGLY MOUTH! IF YOU THINK WENONA HAS *YOUR* BEST INTERESTS IN HER COLD, DEAD HEART, YOU'RE KIDDING YOURSELF.
SHUT UP, JACKSON!
AND I KNOW YOU'RE STILL IN THERE *SOMEWHERE,* NINA. YOU'D *NEVER* WORK WITH YOUR BITCH OF A GRANDMA.
GO. RUN! *RUN!*
STAY ON THE PATH. DON'T GO INTO THE JUNGLE!
THIS BODY NO LONGER BELONGS TO THE GIRL. IT IS *MINE* NOW.
AND JACKSON WANTS TO TAKE THAT BODY AWAY FROM YOU. THAT ISN'T MY DESIRE. MY ONLY WISH IS TO INCREASE *YOUR* POWER!
TELL ME *MORE.*
OH, I WILL... BUT FIRST...

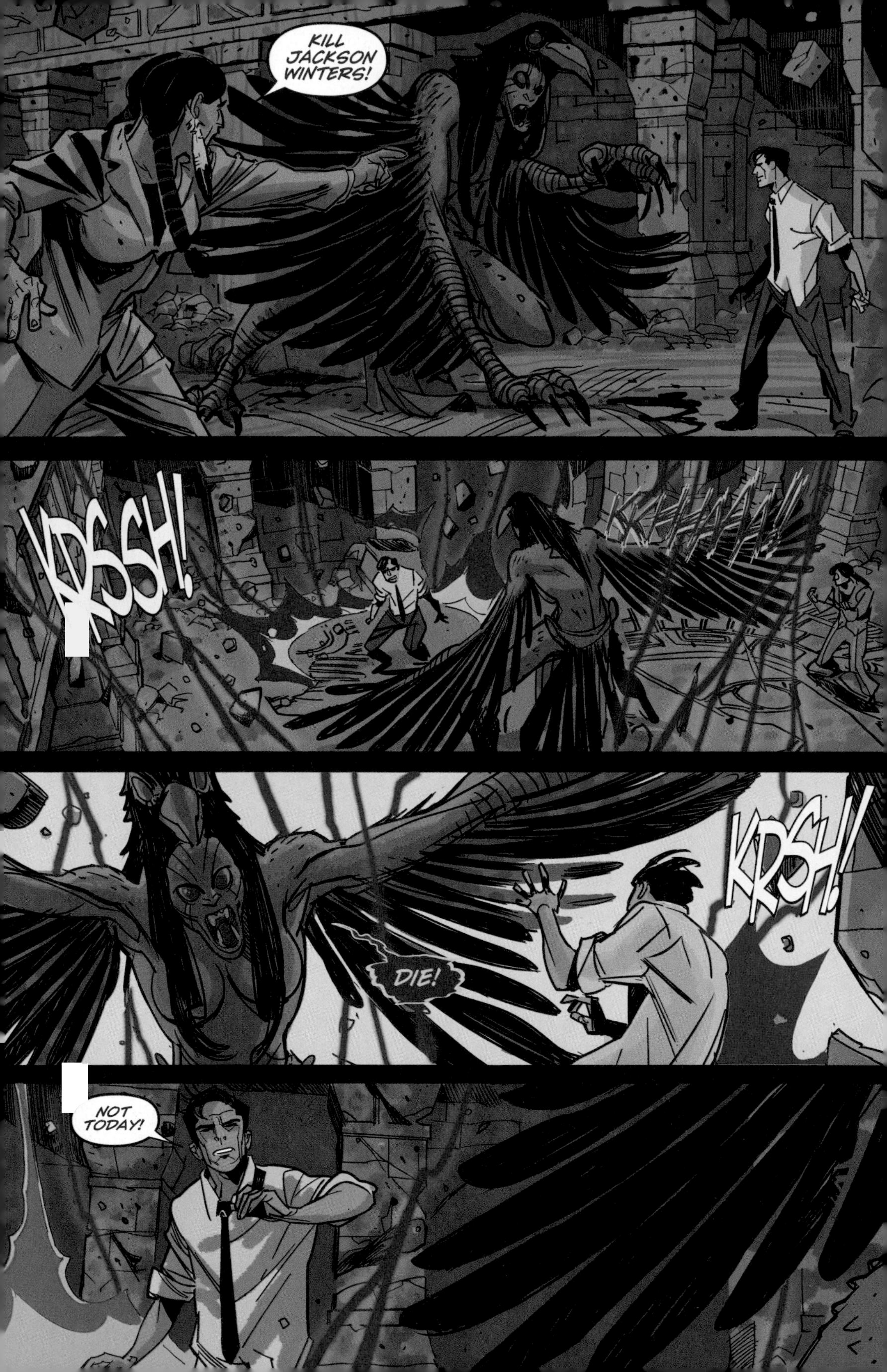
KILL JACKSON WINTERS!
KRSSH!
KHHAAA!!
KRSH!
DIE!
NOT TODAY!

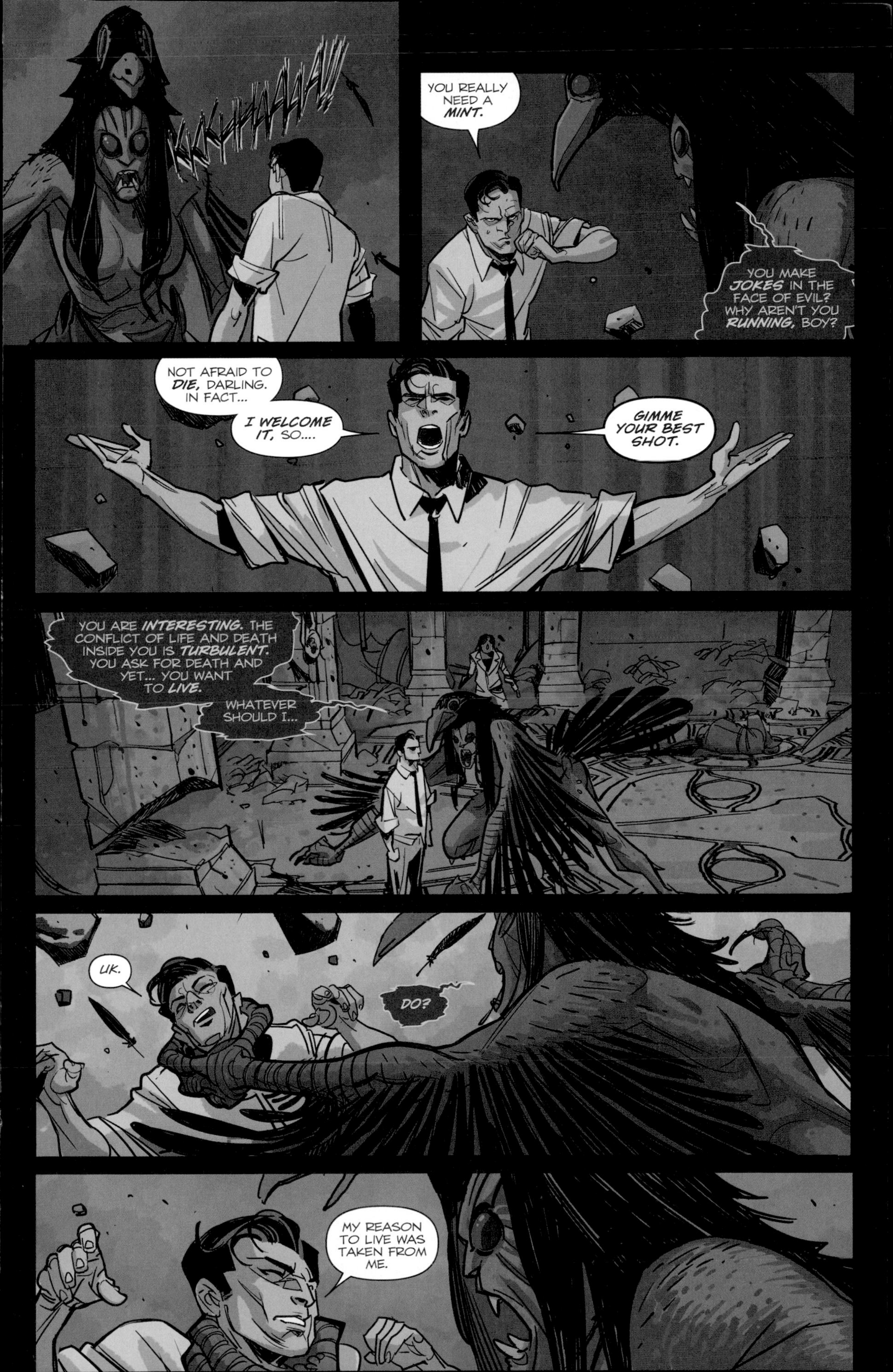
KAKYHAAAA!!
YOU REALLY NEED A MINT.
YOU MAKE JOKES IN THE FACE OF EVIL? WHY AREN'T YOU RUNNING, BOY?
NOT AFRAID TO DIE, DARLING. IN FACT...
I WELCOME IT, SO....
GIMME YOUR BEST SHOT.
YOU ARE INTERESTING. THE CONFLICT OF LIFE AND DEATH INSIDE YOU IS TURBULENT. YOU ASK FOR DEATH AND YET... YOU WANT TO LIVE.
WHATEVER SHOULD I...
UK.
DO?
MY REASON TO LIVE WAS TAKEN FROM ME.

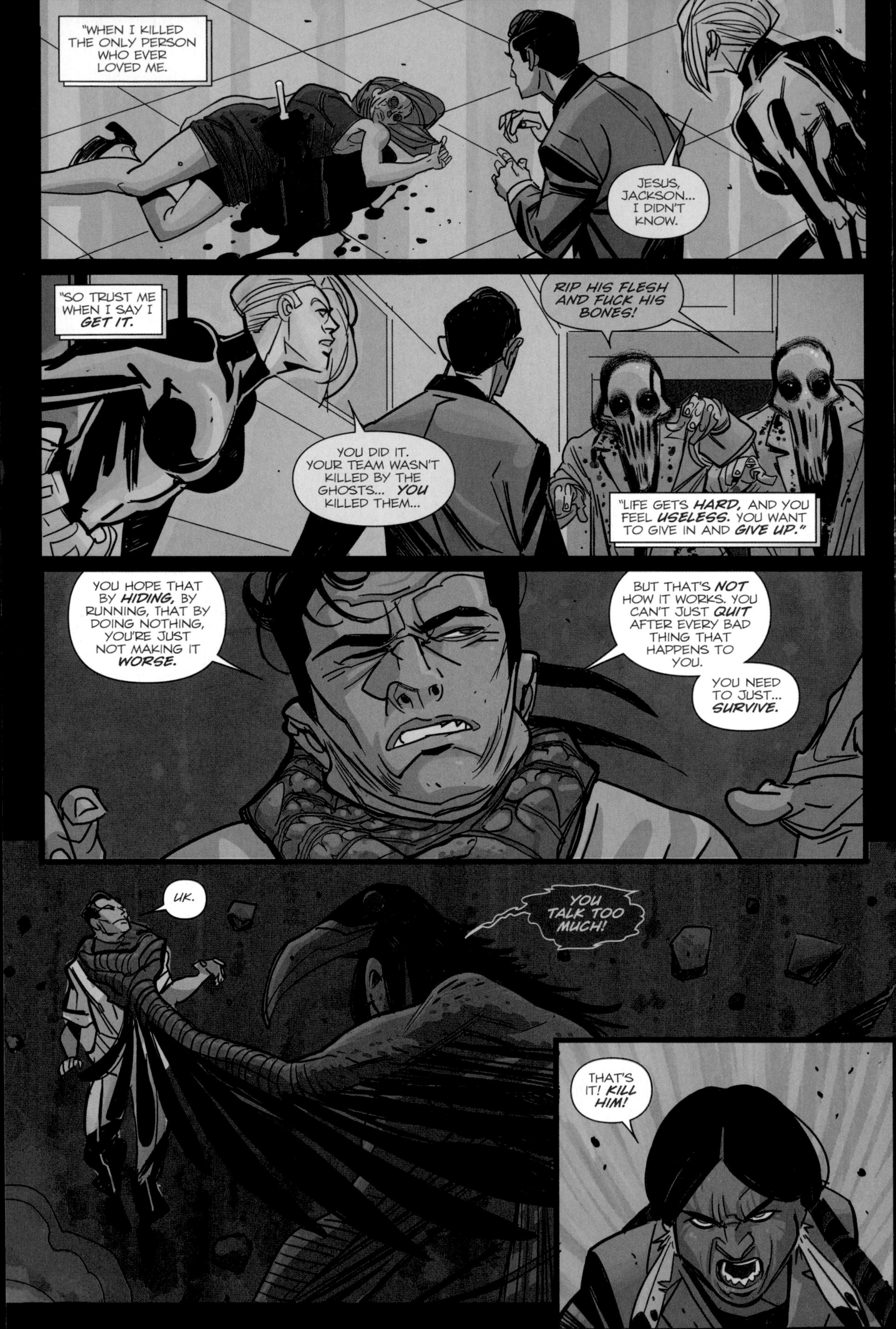
"WHEN I KILLED THE ONLY PERSON WHO EVER LOVED ME.
JESUS, JACKSON... I DIDN'T KNOW.
"SO TRUST ME WHEN I SAY I GET IT.
RIP HIS FLESH AND FUCK HIS BONES!
YOU DID IT. YOUR TEAM WASN'T KILLED BY THE GHOSTS... YOU KILLED THEM...
"LIFE GETS HARD, AND YOU FEEL USELESS. YOU WANT TO GIVE IN AND GIVE UP."
YOU HOPE THAT BY HIDING, BY RUNNING, THAT BY DOING NOTHING, YOU'RE JUST NOT MAKING IT WORSE.
BUT THAT'S NOT HOW IT WORKS. YOU CAN'T JUST QUIT AFTER EVERY BAD THING THAT HAPPENS TO YOU.
YOU NEED TO JUST... SURVIVE.
UK.
YOU TALK TOO MUCH!
THAT'S IT! KILL HIM!

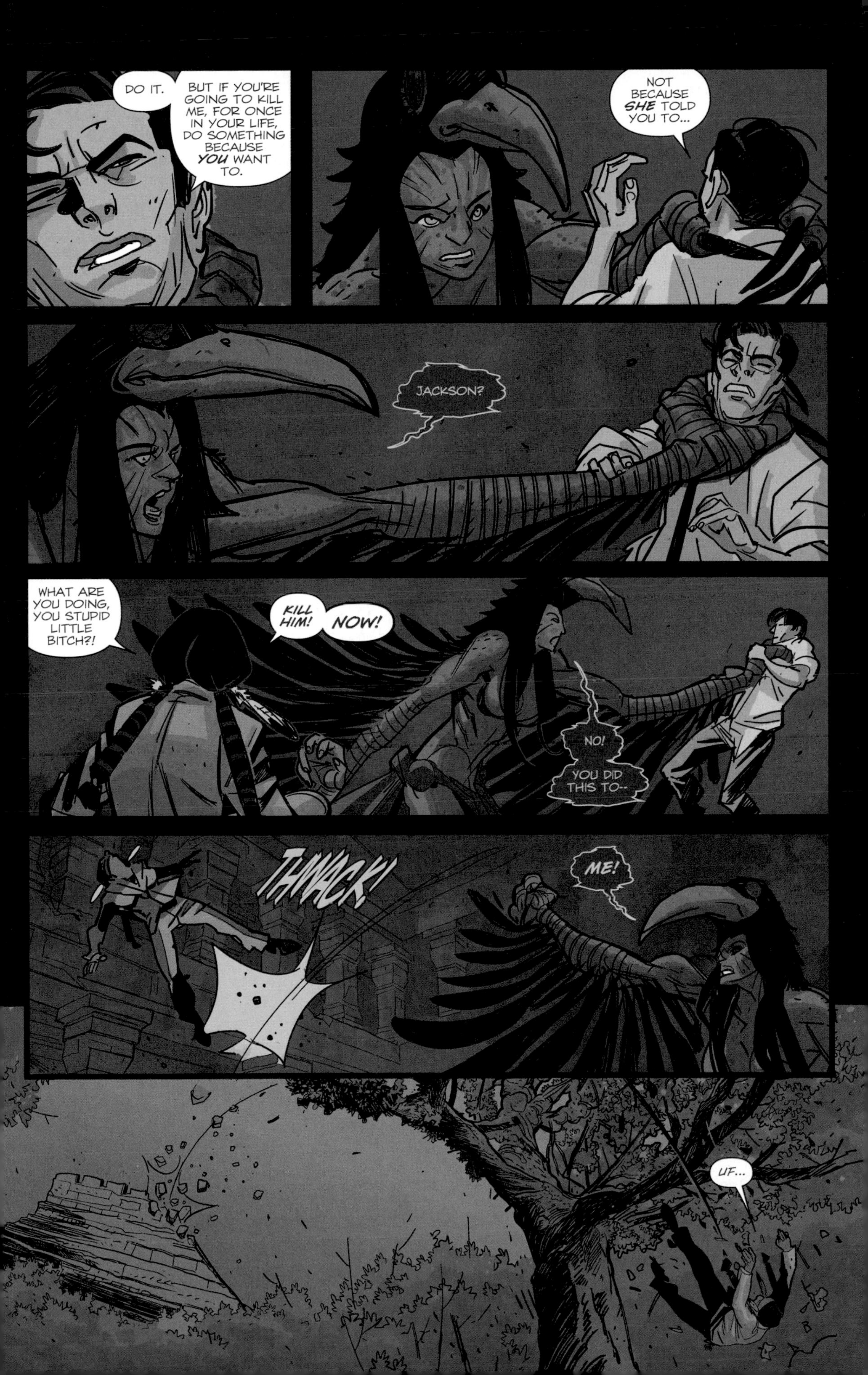
DO IT.
BUT IF YOU'RE GOING TO KILL ME, FOR ONCE IN YOUR LIFE, DO SOMETHING BECAUSE YOU WANT TO.
NOT BECAUSE SHE TOLD YOU TO...
JACKSON?
WHAT ARE YOU DOING, YOU STUPID LITTLE BITCH?!
KILL HIM!
NOW!
NO!
YOU DID THIS TO--
THWACK!
ME!
UF...

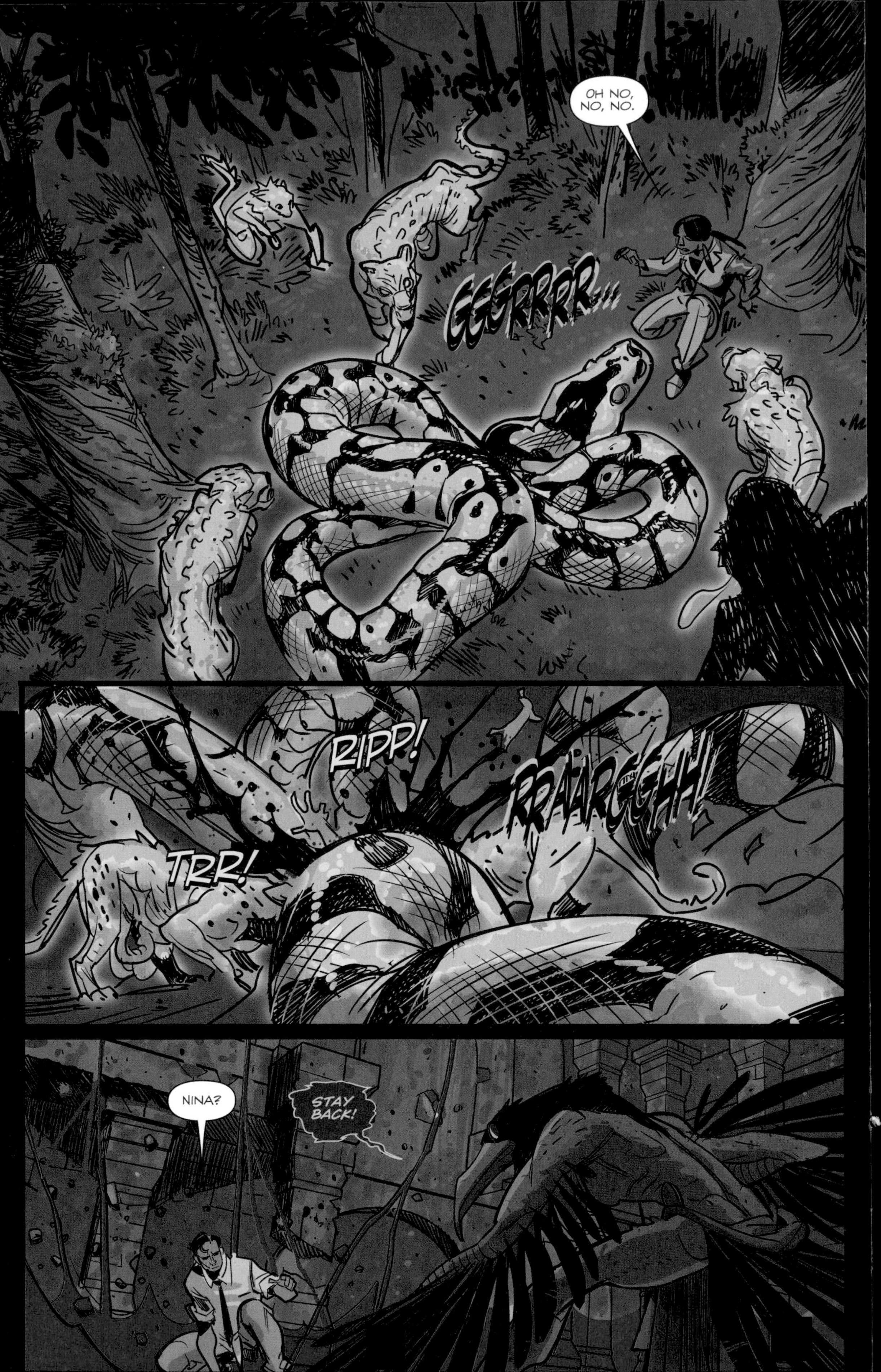
OH NO, NO, NO.
GGGRRRR...
RIPP!
RRAARGGHH!
TRR!
NINA?
STAY BACK!

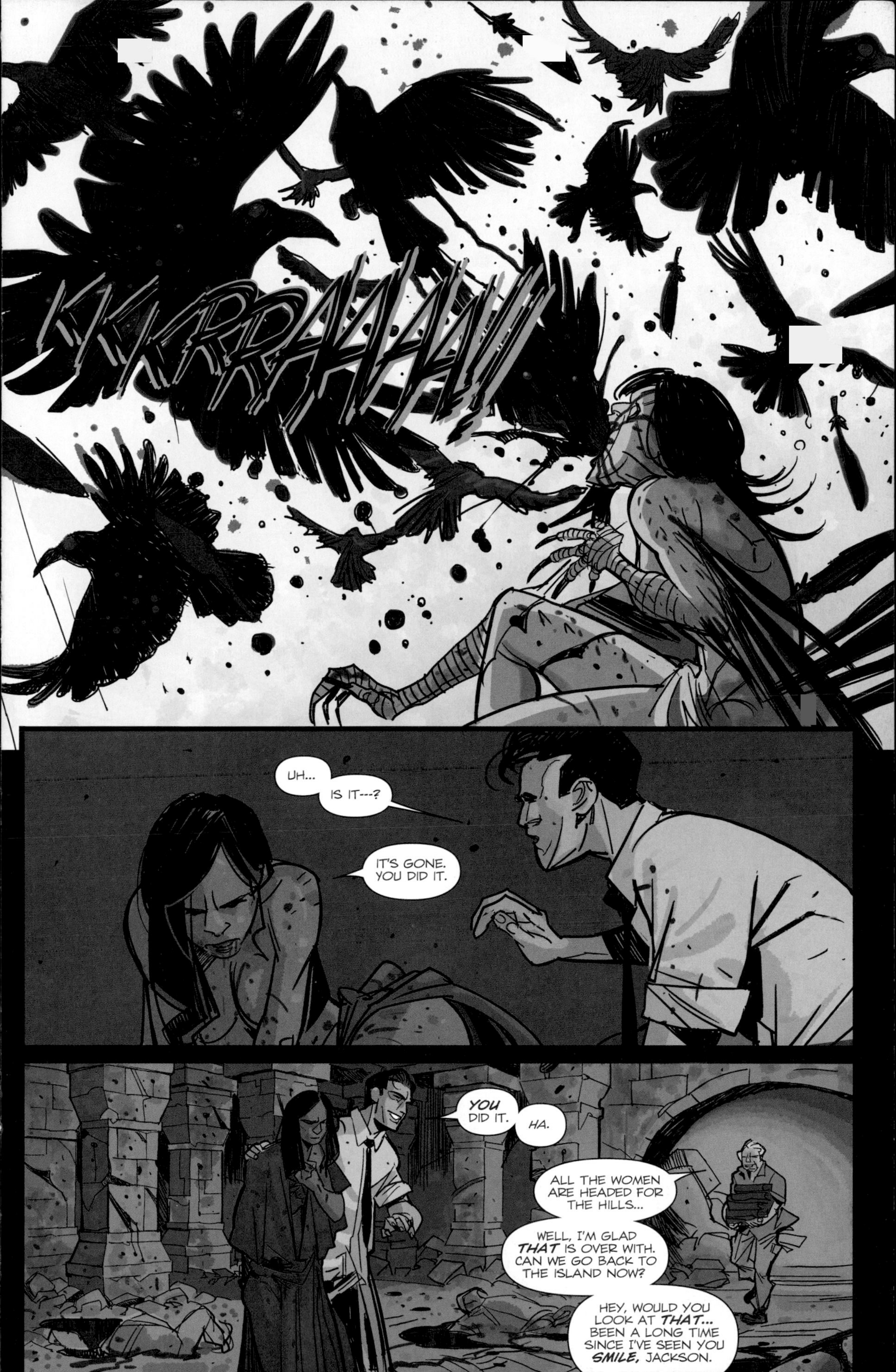
KKKRRAAAAW!!
UH...
IS IT---?
IT'S GONE. YOU DID IT.
YOU DID IT.
HA.
ALL THE WOMEN ARE HEADED FOR THE HILLS...
WELL, I'M GLAD THAT IS OVER WITH. CAN WE GO BACK TO THE ISLAND NOW?
HEY, WOULD YOU LOOK AT THAT... BEEN A LONG TIME SINCE I'VE SEEN YOU SMILE, JACKSON.

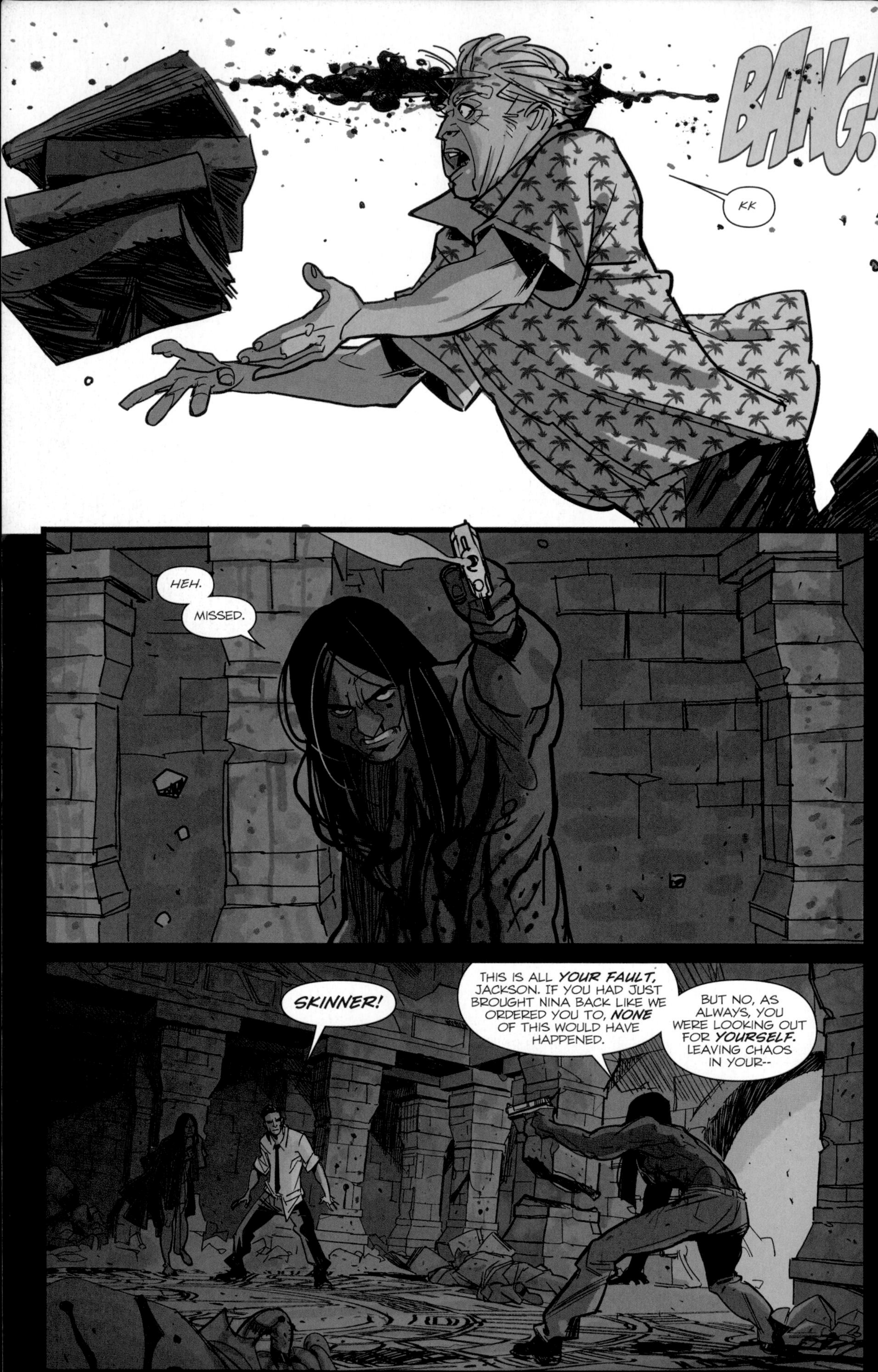
BANG!
KK
HEH.
MISSED.
SKINNER!
THIS IS ALL YOUR FAULT, JACKSON. IF YOU HAD JUST BROUGHT NINA BACK LIKE WE ORDERED YOU TO, NONE OF THIS WOULD HAVE HAPPENED.
BUT NO, AS ALWAYS, YOU WERE LOOKING OUT FOR YOURSELF. LEAVING CHAOS IN YOUR--

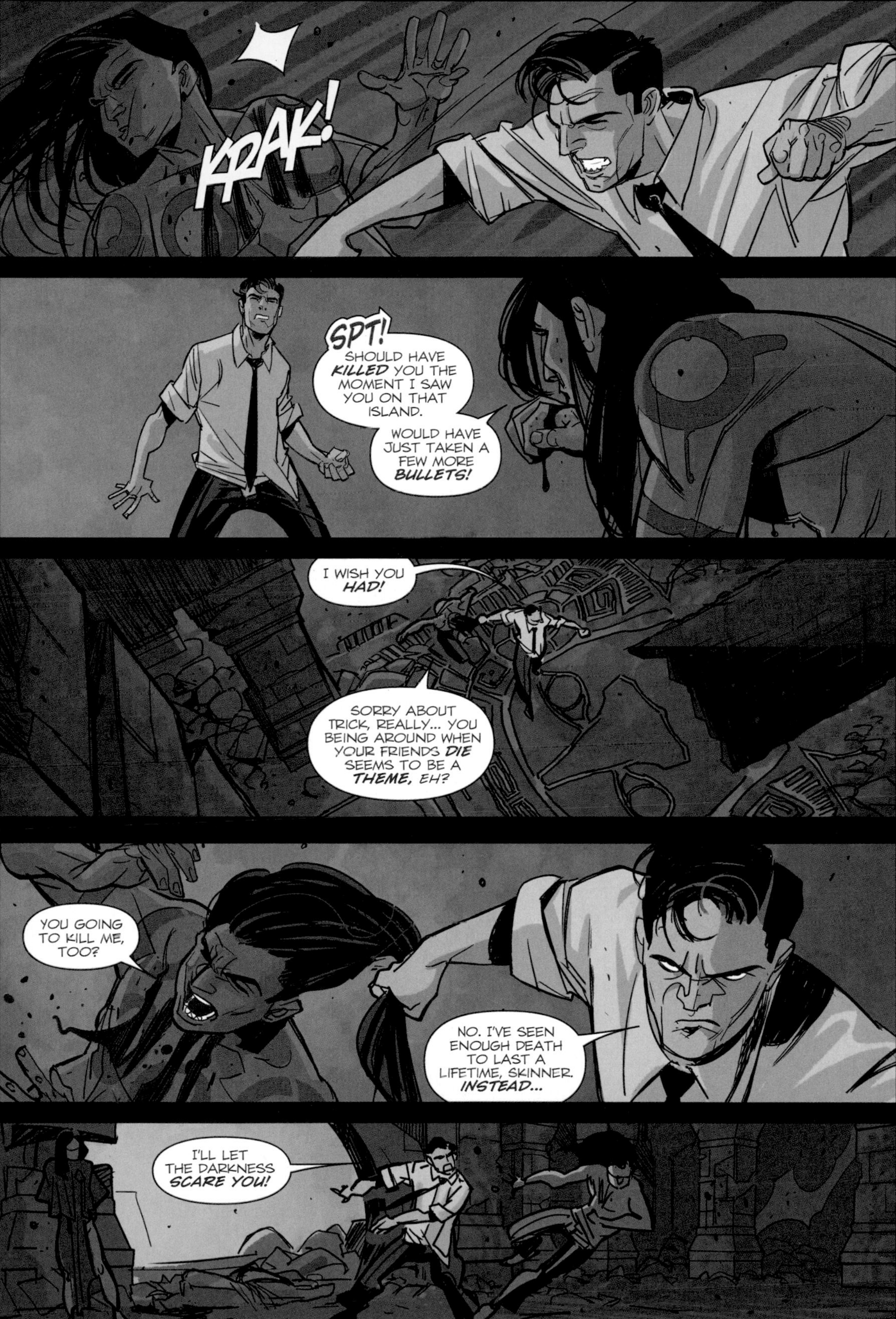
KRAK!
SPT!
SHOULD HAVE KILLED YOU THE MOMENT I SAW YOU ON THAT ISLAND.
WOULD HAVE JUST TAKEN A FEW MORE BULLETS!
I WISH YOU HAD!
SORRY ABOUT TRICK, REALLY... YOU BEING AROUND WHEN YOUR FRIENDS DIE SEEMS TO BE A THEME, EH?
YOU GOING TO KILL ME, TOO?
NO. I'VE SEEN ENOUGH DEATH TO LAST A LIFETIME, SKINNER. INSTEAD...
I'LL LET THE DARKNESS SCARE YOU!

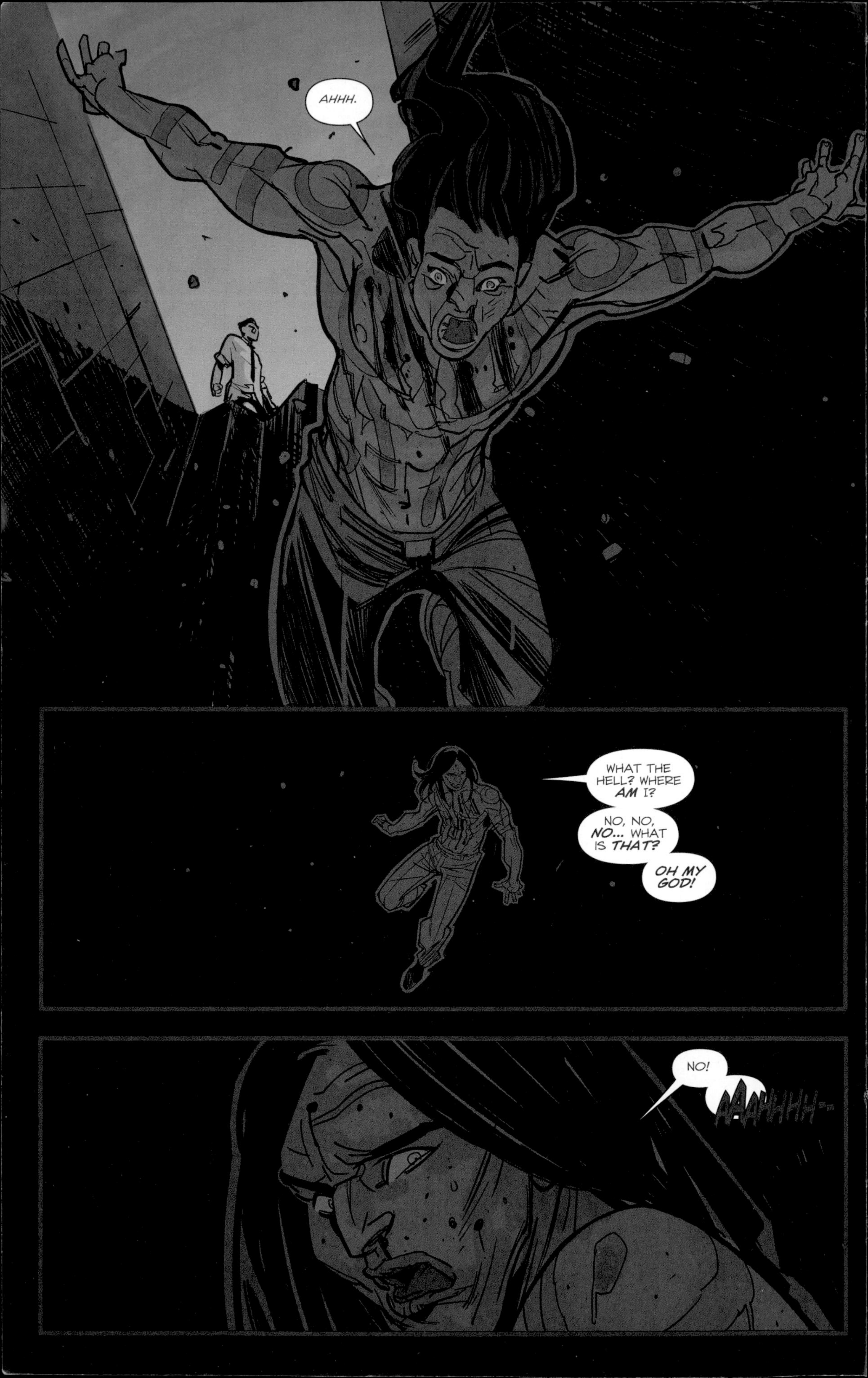
AHHH.
WHAT THE HELL? WHERE AM I?
NO, NO, NO... WHAT IS THAT?
OH MY GOD!
NO!
AAAHHHH--

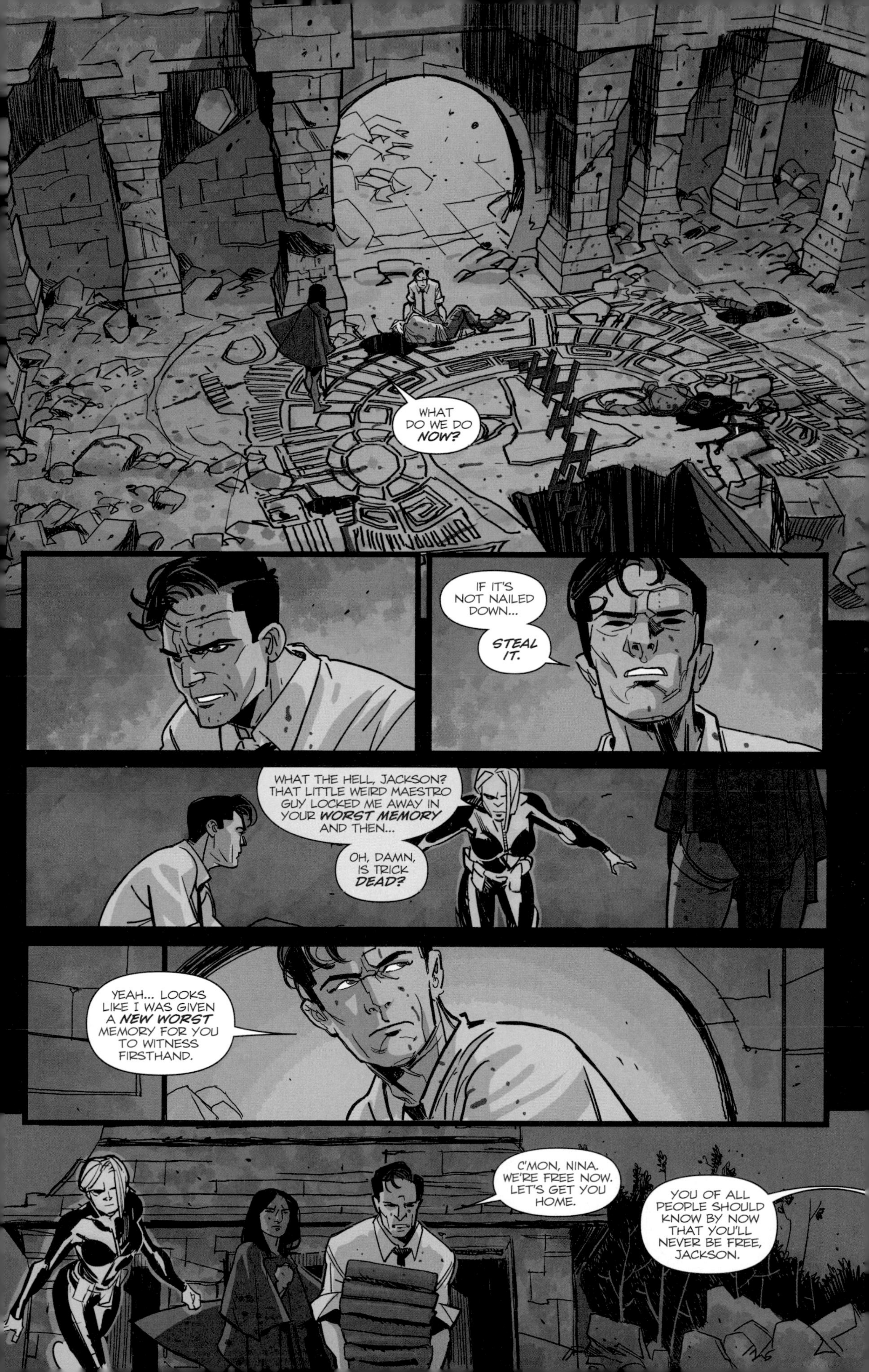

WHAT DO WE DO *NOW?*
IF IT'S NOT NAILED DOWN...
STEAL IT.
WHAT THE HELL, JACKSON? THAT LITTLE WEIRD MAESTRO GUY LOCKED ME AWAY IN YOUR *WORST MEMORY* AND THEN...
OH, DAMN, IS TRICK *DEAD?*
YEAH... LOOKS LIKE I WAS GIVEN A *NEW WORST* MEMORY FOR YOU TO WITNESS FIRSTHAND.
C'MON, NINA. WE'RE FREE NOW. LET'S GET YOU HOME.
YOU OF ALL PEOPLE SHOULD KNOW BY NOW THAT YOU'LL NEVER BE FREE, JACKSON.

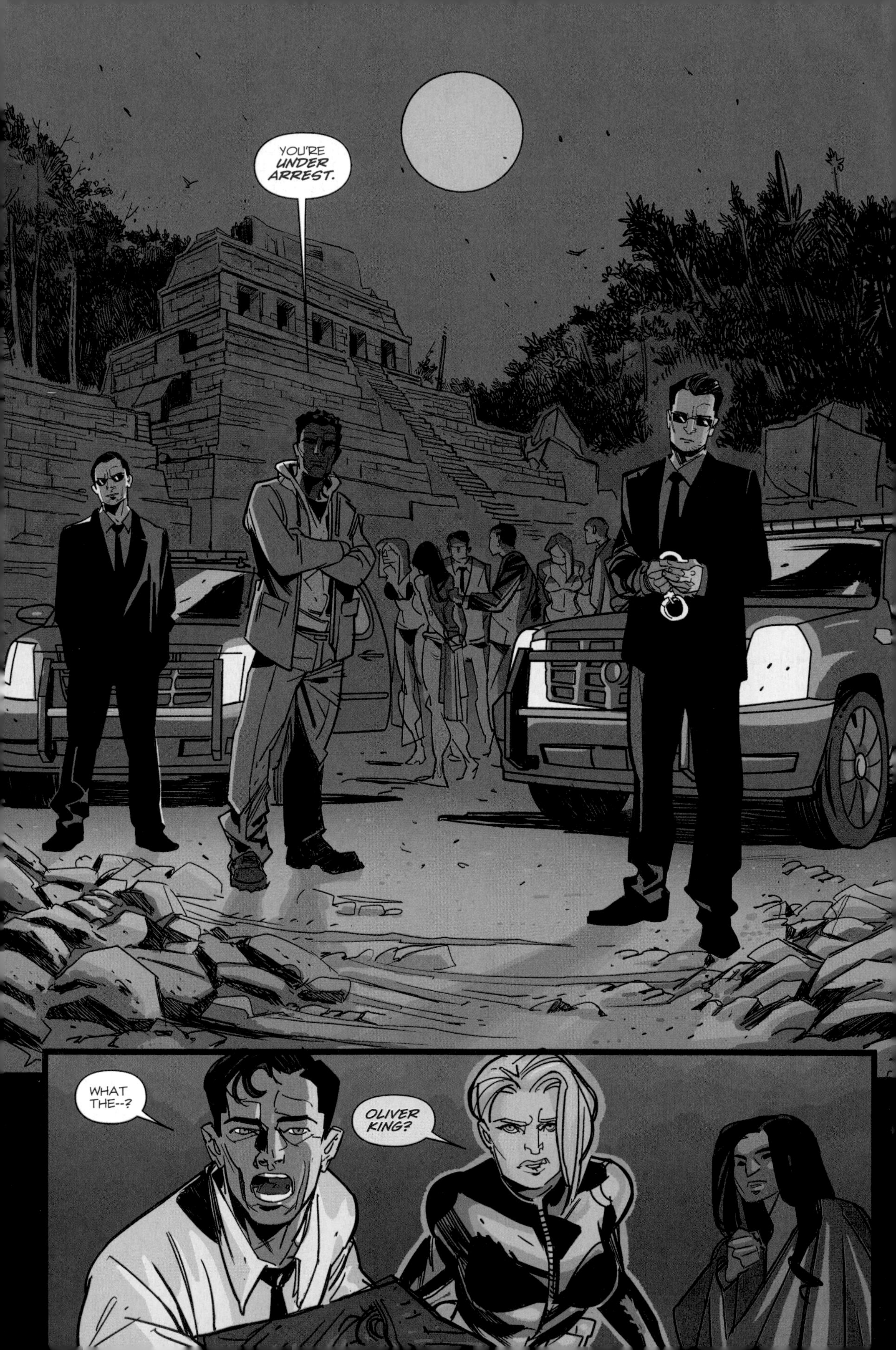
YOU'RE UNDER ARREST.
WHAT THE--?
OLIVER KING?

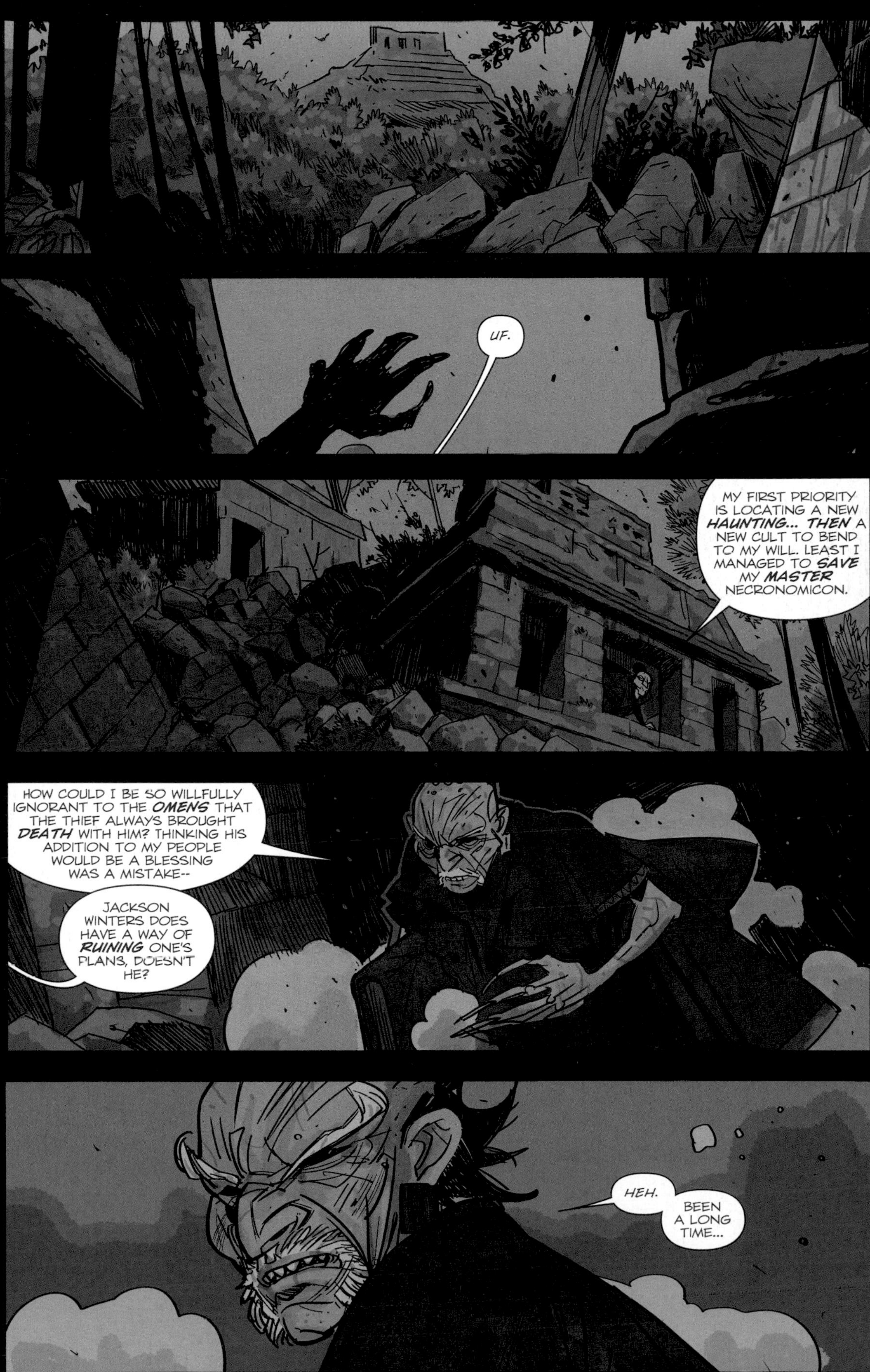
UF.
MY FIRST PRIORITY IS LOCATING A NEW HAUNTING... THEN A NEW CULT TO BEND TO MY WILL. LEAST I MANAGED TO SAVE MY MASTER NECRONOMICON.
HOW COULD I BE SO WILLFULLY IGNORANT TO THE OMENS THAT THE THIEF ALWAYS BROUGHT DEATH WITH HIM? THINKING HIS ADDITION TO MY PEOPLE WOULD BE A BLESSING WAS A MISTAKE--
JACKSON WINTERS DOES HAVE A WAY OF RUINING ONE'S PLANS, DOESN'T HE?
HEH.
BEEN A LONG TIME...

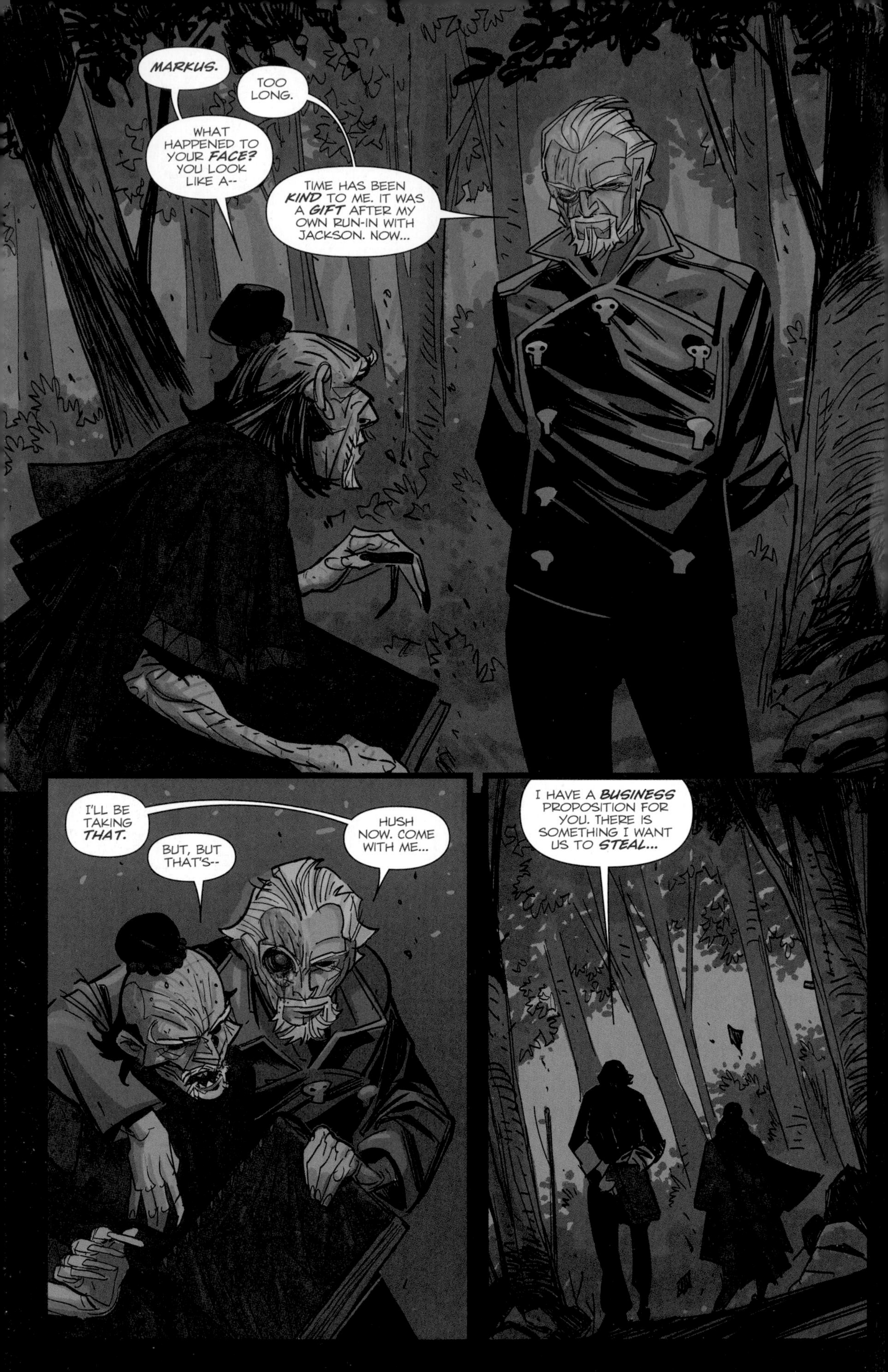
MARKUS.
TOO LONG.
WHAT HAPPENED TO YOUR FACE? YOU LOOK LIKE A--
TIME HAS BEEN KIND TO ME. IT WAS A GIFT AFTER MY OWN RUN-IN WITH JACKSON. NOW...
I'LL BE TAKING THAT.
BUT, BUT THAT'S--
HUSH NOW. COME WITH ME...
I HAVE A BUSINESS PROPOSITION FOR YOU. THERE IS SOMETHING I WANT US TO STEAL...